Notable British Trials

The Stauntons

Notable British Trials Series

General Editor—JAMES H. HODGE

Trial	Date of Trial	Editor
MARY QUEEN OF SCOTS	(1586)	A. Francis Steuart
GUY FAWKES	(1605–6)	Donald Carswell
KING CHARLES I	(1649)	J. G. Muddiman
THE BLOODY ASSIZES	(1685)	J. G. Muddiman
CAPTAIN KIDD	(1701)	Graham Brooks
JACK SHEPPARD	(1724)	Horace Bleackley
CAPTAIN PORTEOUS	(1736)	William Roughead
THE ANNESLEY CASE	(1743)	Andrew Lang
LORD LOVAT	(1747)	David N. Mackay
MARY BLANDY	(1752)	William Roughead
JAMES STEUART	(1752)	David N. Mackay
EUGENE ARAM	(1759)	Eric R. Watson
KATHARINE NAIRN	(1765)	William Roughead
THE DOUGLAS CAUSE	(1761–1769)	A. Francis Steuart
DUCHESS OF KINGSTON	(1776)	Lewis Melville
DEACON BRODIE	(1788)	William Roughead
"BOUNTY" MUTINEERS	(1792)	Owen Rutter
ABRAHAM THORNTON	(1817)	Sir John Hall, Bt.
HENRY FAUNTLEROY	(1824)	Horace Bleackley
THURTELL AND HUNT	(1824)	Eric R. Watson
BURKE AND HARE	(1828)	William Roughead
J. B. RUSH	(1849)	W. Teignmouth Shore
WILLIAM PALMER	(1856)	Eric R. Watson
MADELEINE SMITH	(1858)	F. Tennyson Jesse
DR. SMETHURST	(1859)	L. A. Parry
MRS. M'LACHLAN	(1862)	William Roughead
FRANZ MULLER	(1864)	H. B. Irving
DR. PRITCHARD	(1865)	William Roughead
THE WAINWRIGHTS	(1875)	H. B. Irving
THE STAUNTONS	(1877)	J. B. Atlay
E. M. CHANTRELLE	(1878)	A. Duncan Smith
KATE WEBSTER	(1879)	Elliott O'Donnell
CITY OF GLASGOW BANK	(1879)	William Wallace
CHARLES PEACE	(1879)	W. Teignmouth Shore
DR. LAMSON	(1882)	H. L. Adam
ADELAIDE BARTLETT	(1886)	Sir John Hall, Bt.
MRS. MAYBRICK	(1889)	H. B. Irving
J. W. LAURIE	(1889)	William Roughead
THE BACCARAT CASE	(1891)	W. Teignmouth Shore
NEILL CREAM	(1892)	W. Teignmouth Shore
A. J. MONSON	(1893)	J. W. More
OSCAR WILDE	(1895)	H. Montgomery Hyde
W. GARDINER (PEASENHALL)	(1903)	William Henderson
G. CHAPMAN	(1903)	H. L. Adam
S. H. DOUGAL	(1903)	F. Tennyson Jesse
ADOLF BECK	(1904)	Eric R. Watson
ROBERT WOOD	(1907)	Basil Hogarth
OSCAR SLATER	(1909–1928)	William Roughead
H. H. CRIPPEN	(1910)	Filson Young
J. A. DICKMAN	(1910)	S. O. Rowan-Hamilton
STEINIE MORRISON	(1911)	H. Fletcher Moulton
THE SEDDONS	(1912)	Filson Young
GEORGE JOSEPH SMITH	(1915)	Eric R. Watson
SIR ROGER CASEMENT	(1916)	George H. Knott
HAROLD GREENWOOD	(1920)	Winifred Duke
FIELD AND GRAY	(1920)	Winifred Duke
BYWATERS AND THOMPSON	(1922)	Filson Young
RONALD TRUE	(1922)	Donald Carswell
H. R. ARMSTRONG	(1922)	Filson Young
J. P. VAQUIER	(1924)	R. H. Blundell
J. D. MERRETT	(1927)	William Roughead
BROWNE AND KENNEDY	(1928)	W. Teignmouth Shore
DR. KNOWLES	(1928)	Albert Lieck
SIDNEY H. FOX	(1930)	F. Tennyson Jesse
A. A. ROUSE	(1931)	Helena Normanton
THE ROYAL MAIL CASE	(1931)	Collin Brooks
RATTENBURY AND STONER	(1935)	F. Tennyson Jesse
BUCK RUXTON	(1936)	Prof. H. Wilson
FREDERICK NODDER	(1937)	Winifred Duke
PATRICK CARRAHER	(1938–1946)	George Blake
NEVILLE HEATH	(1946)	Macdonald Critchley
WILLIAM JOYCE	(1945)	J. W. Hall
LEY AND SMITH	(1947)	F. Tennyson Jesse
JAMES CAMB	(1948)	G. Clark
PETER GRIFFITHS	(1948)	George Godwin
JOHN GEORGE HAIGH	(1949)	Lord Dunboyne

Further Volumes in Preparation

Trial of
The Stauntons

EDITED BY

J. B. Atlay, M.A., F.S.A.

Barrister-at-Law

LONDON   EDINBURGH   GLASGOW

WILLIAM HODGE AND COMPANY, LIMITED

First Published in "Notable English Trials", 1911
New Edition, in "Notable British Trials", 1952

PRINTED BY LITHOGRAPHY IN GREAT BRITAIN
BY JARROLD AND SONS LIMITED, NORWICH

TO THE RIGHT HONOURABLE

SIR EDWARD CLARKE, K.C.,

FEARLESS ADVOCATE

AND

STATESMAN WITHOUT REPROACH,

THIS BOOK IS DEDICATED

BY THE EDITOR

AS A TOKEN OF ADMIRATION

AND RESPECT

CONTENTS.

PAGE

Introduction, - - - - - - - - - - - - - 1
Table of Dates, - - - - - - - - - - - - 31

The Trial—

FIRST DAY—WEDNESDAY, 19TH SEPTEMBER, 1877.

The Indictment, - - - - - - - - - - - 35
The Attorney-General's Opening Speech, - - - - - 36

Evidence for the Prosecution.

Harriet Butterfield,	46	James Thomas Hilder,	55
George Cakebread,	53	Charles Hepplethwaite,	55
Henry Watson,	54	Emma Chalklin	56
Robert Marsh,	54		

SECOND DAY—THURSDAY, 20TH SEPTEMBER, 1877.

Evidence for the Prosecution (continued).

Ellen Goodinge,	61, 189	Prof. J. E. Disbrowe Rodgers,	86
Joseph Lee,	64	Dr. Thomas Bond,	87
Mr. Dean Longrigg,	65	Dr. J. G. Creasey,	89
Dr. John Meaburn Bright,	79	Charles Edward Hoar,	90
Dr. Frederick Wilkinson,	83	Thomas Keene,	90
Dr. Alan Pigott,	86		

THIRD DAY—FRIDAY, 21ST SEPTEMBER, 1877.

Evidence for the Prosecution (continued).

Clara Brown,	91, 114, 151	W. Marchant,	111
Thomas Keene,	97, 109	George Dewsbury,	112
Frederick Henry Caiger,	109	John Staples,	112
Frank Quested,	110	Alfred Nicholls,	113
Alfred Hollands,	111	Owen Davey,	113
George Tucker,	111	Henry West,	113

FOURTH DAY—SATURDAY, 22ND SEPTEMBER, 1877.

Evidence for the Prosecution (continued).

Mary Ann Weatherley,	114	Elizabeth Uridge,	131
Mary Ann Longridge,	115	Harriet Day,	132
Frederick C. Coley,	115, 119	Charles Joseph Carttar (Coroner),	132
Dr. William Smyth Russell	116	Deposition of Louis Staunton,	133
Susannah Crockett,	117	Deposition of Alice Rhodes,	137
Robert Hogg,	119	Deposition of Mrs. Patrick	
Frank Charles Joseph,	119	Staunton,	138
George Wells,	120	Deposition of Patrick Staunton,	140
Police-Sergeant Bateman,	122	Depositions of Clara Brown,	144

CONTENTS.

FIFTH DAY—MONDAY, 24TH SEPTEMBER, 1877.

PAGE

Mr. Montagu Williams' Speech on behalf of Louis Staunton, - - - 153
Mr. Straight's Speech on behalf of Mrs. Patrick Staunton, - - - 168

Evidence for the Defence.

Dr. Joseph Frank Payne, - 176 | Dr. John Stern Bristow, - 184

SIXTH DAY—TUESDAY, 25TH SEPTEMBER, 1877.

Evidence for the Defence (concluded).

Dr. Smith Greenfield, - - - - - - - - - - 187

Mr. Clark's Speech on behalf of Patrick Staunton, - - - - - 190
Mr. Gye's Speech on behalf of Alice Rhodes, - - - - - - 224
The Attorney-General's Reply, - - - - - - - - 230

SEVENTH DAY—WEDNESDAY, 26TH SEPTEMBER, 1877.

The Judge's Summing-up, - - - - - - - - - 243
Verdict, - - - - - - - - - - - - 285
Sentence, - - - - - - - - - - - - 286

APPENDICES.

I. Death Certificate of Harriet Staunton, - - - - - - 291

II. Telegram to Mrs. Butterfield, dated 15th April, 1877, - - - 292

III. Sir James Stephen's Charge to the Grand Jury, - - - - 293

IV. Proceedings at postponement of the Trial, - - - - - 298

V. Emma Denton's Evidence, - - - - - - - - 301

VI. Final Statement made by Clara Brown to *Daily Telegraph* Reporter, - - - - - - - - - - - 302

VII. Dr. Harman's Letters to the *Daily Telegraph*, - - - - 306

VIII. Charles Reade's Letters to the *Daily Telegraph*, - - - - 308

IX. Dr. Greenfield's Remarks on the Medical Evidence, - - - 316

X. *The Lancet* on the Verdict and Evidence, - - - - - 323

XI. Chronological Sequence of the Letters, - - - - - - 325

XII. Publications on the Subject of the Staunton Case, - - - 327

LIST OF ILLUSTRATIONS.

Harriet Staunton,	*facing page*	16
Sir John Holker,	,,	32
Sir Hardinge Giffard,	,,	49
Mr. H. B. Poland,	,,	64
Mr. Douglas Straight,	,,	81
Mr. Montagu Williams,	,,	144
Mr. C. W. Mathews,	,,	161
Mr. Edward Clarke,	,,	208
Sir Henry Hawkins,	,,	225

STAUNTON TRIAL.

INTRODUCTION.

ON the evening of Friday, the 13th of April, 1877, a gentleman, bearing the historic but unusual name of Casabianca, was in a small shop in Forbes Road, Penge. Forbes Road happens to be on the boundary line between Kent and Surrey, and while Mr. Casabianca was despatching his business, a stranger came in and asked the shopkeeper, who was also the postmaster, where he ought to register a death which had occurred that morning at No. 34. The deceased, he added, was a lady from Cudham, in Kent. The name of Cudham excited Mr. Casabianca's curiosity; his wife's sister, Mrs. Louis Staunton, had last been heard of in that vicinity, and her family had reasons for fearing that she was the victim of serious maltreatment. Following up the clue, he had an interview next morning with Mr. Longrigg, the medical man who had attended the deceased and had signed the certificate of death. He was shown the dead body, and identified it as that of his sister-in-law, and as a result of what he told the doctor, the certificate was withdrawn, the funeral postponed, and the coroner communicated with. On the following Wednesday an inquest was begun on the body of Mrs. Staunton, in the course of which one of the strangest stories in our criminal annals was disclosed.

Harriet Staunton was by birth Harriet Richardson. Her mother had married a second time, and was now the wife of a country clergyman, the Rev. John Butterfield, of Great Burstead, Essex. By her former marriage there were four children, a son and three daughters, of whom Harriet was the youngest. An elder sister, wife of the Mr. Casabianca already referred to, had been prominently before the public eye a few years earlier in connection with the Wicklow peerage case, when, as the widow of the Hon. William

Staunton Trial.

George Howard, she had striven unsuccessfully to convince
the House of Lords that she was the mother of the infant
claimant to the earldom.[1] Harriet was born in the year 1841,
and from childhood had shown traces of weak intellect. In
many respects she comported herself like other girls of her
age. She was fond of dress, neat and tidy in her person;
but it was impossible to give her the ordinary education, she
could only express herself with great difficulty in a letter, and
she could not spell the simplest words. In 1874 she left her
mother's house and took up her abode in Walworth with her
cousins, the Hincksmans.[2] Mr. Hincksman was a nephew of
Mrs. Butterfield, and he had two step-daughters, Elizabeth and
Alice Rhodes. The elder of these, Elizabeth, was married
to a very juvenile husband, Patrick Staunton, whose
brother, Louis, a year or so older than himself, was a frequent
visitor at the Hincksman's.

Harriet Richardson was entitled in possession and
reversion to something under four thousand pounds;
Louis Staunton was an impecunious youth of three-and-
twenty, an auctioneer's clerk by calling, insignificant
in stature, but of the type, as a critic remarked at
a later stage of his career, which housemaids call
handsome. After a brief courtship they became engaged
to be married. Mrs. Butterfield felt strongly that her
daughter, though robust in health and of normal physique,
was not a fit person to enter into matrimony in any circumstances, and she was more than sceptical as to the disin-
terestedness of this particular suitor. Her opposition, however, was unavailing, and had the effect of making her daughter
passionately angry and violent in her behaviour. She then
attempted to place Harriet under the protection of the Court of
Chancery as a lunatic, but the application was unsuccessful,
and tended, not unnaturally, to increase the estrangement
between parent and child.

The marriage took place at Clapham on the 16th of June,
1875, from the house of the bridegroom's sister, without any
countenance from Mrs. Butterfield, who declined to be
present. As there was no settlement, Louis Staunton

---

[1] See Annual Register, 1870.
[2] See pp. 46, 50.

2

Introduction.

became possessed, under the existing law, of all the property to which his wife was then or might at any future time become entitled. Three weeks later Mrs. Butterfield made a call on the married couple, who were occupying a small house in Loughborough Park Road. She was not altogether satisfied with what she saw, but the meeting passed off without any apparent friction. The next day she received two letters, from her daughter and son-in-law respectively, requesting her not to come to the house again. After that date she never saw her daughter alive. In the spring of the following year she heard that Harriet had given birth to a boy, but no announcement of the fact was made to her by the parents, who shortly afterwards quitted Loughborough Park Road, and left no address behind them. Rumours reached Mrs. Butterfield, however, with regard to the conduct of Louis Staunton towards the girl Alice Rhodes, and she began to make inquiries of the Hincksmans, which brought down upon her, in January, 1877, a furious letter from Louis, denouncing her, in his wife's name and his own, for unnatural conduct. A chance meeting with Alice Rhodes at a London railway station a week or two later only served to increase her anxiety. Alice refused at first to tell her what had become of the Louis Stauntons, but eventually declared that they were living at Brighton, which Mrs. Butterfield subsequently discovered to be untrue; she also added that Harriet had been very ill, and Mrs. Butterfield recognised a brooch she was wearing as being one of the latter's favourite trinkets.

Though still unable to obtain definite information of her daughter's whereabouts, Mrs. Butterfield ascertained that the Patrick Stauntons were living at Cudham, and thither she went on the 5th of March. As she was taking her ticket she came across Patrick Staunton. He denied all knowledge as to where her daughter was living, and was most abusive to her. On alighting at Halstead station, some 5 miles from Cudham, she learnt that Mr. Louis Staunton occupied a farm in the neighbouring village called Little Grays. She drove there at once in a cab, and found Louis and Mrs. Patrick Staunton in the parlour. They would give her no tidings of her daughter, and she was finally hustled

3

out of the house. On her return to London she communicated with the police, and a watch was set on the neighbourhood of Little Grays farm, but no one was seen who corresponded to the description of Harriet Staunton. Suddenly, on Sunday, the 15th of April, Mrs. Butterfield was summoned by telegram to 34 Forbes Road, Penge, where she found her daughter's corpse. Harriet had died on the preceding Friday.

The little that is known of her short and unhappy married life can be given very briefly. Her child, a boy christened Thomas Henry, was born on the 23rd of March, 1876. She got well over her confinement, and was described afterwards by the doctor who attended her as being in good general health and bodily condition. Besides the professional nurse, she was looked after by Alice Rhodes, whose cousin, an orphan girl of fifteen, named Clara Brown, acted as general servant. Alice Rhodes herself was only nineteen, and of attractive appearance; and a guilty intimacy between her and Louis seems to have begun at that period, perhaps even earlier. In June the Louis Stauntons went to live at Gipsy Hill, Norwood, but shortly before their removal the baby had been taken down by them to the Woodlands, near Cudham, which had recently been taken by Patrick Staunton, who made a precarious livelihood as an artist. The Woodlands, also known as Frith Cottage, was a tiny house in a desolate and unfrequented corner of Kent, standing away from the road, and hemmed in at the back by a plantation. Mrs. Patrick had two small children of her own, more or less under the care of Clara Brown, and it was agreed that Harriet should leave her baby with them while she and her husband continued at Norwood. In August an arrangement was made by which Harriet became a regular inmate of the Woodlands, her husband paying his sister-in-law £1 a week for her board. It is clear, from an ill-spelt, affectionate letter to her husband, written in the following month, that Harriet did not look upon the separation as a permanent one. What Louis intended is not so certain, but he had, as his letters to his brother showed, contracted a strong aversion to his wife. If Harriet entertained any suspicions, she had not the strength of character to give expression to them—she was mentally and physically in the power of her husband and his relations.

4

Introduction.

In October she was brought up to London by her husband to meet the Commissioners for taking the acknowledgments of married women. Louis had sold for £1100 the reversionary interest to which she was entitled under the will of her aunt, Lady Rivers,[3] and her formal consent was necessary. The deed of assignment was explained to her by her solicitor, Mr. Keene. He had seen her frequently on business both before and after her marriage, and he did not now notice any change in her condition or appearance.

From the 23rd of October, 1876, to the 12th of April, 1877, Harriet Staunton disappeared from the outer world. She was seen once or twice by chance visitors who came to the house, but the regular tradesmen who called for orders had no idea of her existence. Nor could it be suspected that Mrs. Louis Staunton was an inmate at the Woodlands, in view of the fact that a young woman was living with Mr. Louis Staunton, as his wife, at Little Grays farm, barely half a mile away. That young woman was Alice Rhodes. Louis Staunton had taken and stocked Little Grays in October with the last vestige of his wife's fortune.

The nature of the treatment to which Harriet was subjected during these sad months was strongly disputed at the trial; but it is certain that she was kept in duress, and forbidden to go outside the door of the house. Whether she was starved and actively ill-treated is more questionable; as to the theory of starvation, I say nothing for the present, but Patrick Staunton was a man of violent temper, and there seems no reason to doubt that more than once he struck both his sister-in-law and her little child. This unfortunate infant, confined like its mother to the house, was gradually pining away, and on Sunday, the 8th of April, it was taken, a little wizened being, to Guy's Hospital by Mr. and Mrs. Patrick Staunton. It died the same evening, and the following day Patrick told the hospital authorities that the child's name was Henry Stormton; it was the son of a carpenter, he said, and the mother was a

---

3 Horace Pitt, the sixth (and last) Baron Rivers of Sudley Castle, married, 10th April, 1845, Eleanor Suter, of Brighton, better known to her own generation as " Nellie Holmes "; they parted at the church door. She died 3rd September, 1872; Mrs. Butterfield was her reputed " niece," and Harriet Staunton her " great-niece."

worthy woman, but unable to look after it. On the Tuesday
Louis Staunton, under the name of Harris, gave the undertaker
an order for the funeral.

On Thursday, the 12th, Louis Staunton and Mrs. Patrick
called on a Mrs. Chalklin, who kept lodgings at 34 Forbes
Road, Penge. They wanted apartments for an invalid lady
from Cudham. The local doctor did not understand her case,
and they wanted better advice. The lady was "inclined to be
paralysed," and her head had become affected. Her general
health was good, and she could eat perfectly well, but it was
difficult to get her to take food. A bedroom and sitting-room
on the first floor were taken at 15s. a week, and Mrs. Chalklin
being asked to recommend a doctor, gave the name of Mr.
Dean Longrigg, upon whom her visitors immediately called.
They explained that they wanted him to attend a Mrs. Staunton,
a lady of weak intellect. In answer to his questions, they
averred that she was paralysed on the left side, but cleanly
in her habits, and though hearty, extremely thin. She had
been ill for some time, and she had been attended by Dr.
Creasey, of Brastead, but he lived too far away, and could
not give the requisite attention. Mr. Longrigg promised to
pay the invalid a visit between eleven and twelve the next
morning.

Cudham is about 7 miles from Bromley, and, as the 8.26
up train was signalled at Bromley station that evening, a
wagonette drove up containing the four Stauntons and Alice
Rhodes. Harriet Staunton was with great difficulty got out
of the vehicle, and half-dragged, half-carried to a first-class
carriage, in which the whole party took their seats. They
alighted at Penge, a quick ten minutes' run, and here again
Harriet had to be lifted on to the platform. While a cab
was being fetched she was placed in a chair, on the suggestion
of the stationmaster; she was speechless and barely conscious,
but she was seen to stretch out her arm and heard to groan.
Next she was hoisted into the cab, and on arrival at the
lodgings carried out again by the driver, and put to
bed at once. The landlady saw her in bed moaning
and making a gurgling noise. Mrs. Patrick informed
her that the lady had been very ill on the journey,
and they could not account for it. In the course of

Introduction.

the evening Louis Staunton went twice for the doctor, who, however, was not at home, and the two brothers went back by the last Bromley train, leaving the women behind them. It was explained to the landlady that Louis Staunton was the husband of the invalid, and that Alice Rhodes was a young married woman who had come to help nurse her.

About ten o'clock next morning (the 13th) Mr. Longrigg was fetched by Alice Rhodes. He found the patient perfectly insensible, the arms rigid, the pulse quick and weak, the breathing stertorous and laboured. The body was emaciated, and all of it that was visible disgustingly dirty. The doctor saw at a glance that she was in a dying condition, and told the women he did not think she could recover. He prescribed absolute quiet, and ordered them to try beef tea and milk, and on his departure promised Mrs. Patrick to send in a trained nurse. When the latter, Ellen Gooding, arrived in an hour's time the patient was unconscious and lying as if in a fit. At noon she was appreciably worse, and the doctor was fetched again. The patient was dying rapidly, and Mr. Longrigg only remained a few minutes. At half-past one she died; the only person with her when she passed away was the nurse, though Louis Staunton and Mrs. Patrick were in the adjoining room.

It devolved upon Gooding to lay the body out, but on tearing off the chemise and nightgown she found it in so filthy a condition that the ordinary procedure was impossible. The head was alive with vermin, and the dirt on the trunk "was something like the bark of a tree." The brothers made the necessary arrangements for the funeral, which was fixed to take place at Beckenham on Monday, and the whole party quitted Penge in the course of the afternoon, having entrusted to the nurse the key of the rooms in Forbes Road. The next morning (Saturday, the 14th) she registered the death at Bromley, at the request of Mr. Longrigg, whose certificate gave the cause of death as primarily cerebral disease, and, secondly, apoplexy. This was admittedly based on what Louis Staunton had told him rather than on his own observation. He had only seen the deceased for a few minutes, when she was beyond the possibility of examination, and what he saw showed nothing inconsistent with the information supplied to him.

7

Staunton Trial.

We have heard how the certificate came to be withdrawn; the body was actually in the coffin, for the undertaker had been prompt, and his orders were imperative. On the following Wednesday, the 18th, the coroner empanelled a jury and immediately adjourned it, after evidence of identification, in order that a post-mortem might be held. The task of "getting up" the case was entrusted to Police-Sergeant Bateman, who had been down to Cudham on the Sunday, and had there received statements from the three Stauntons, from Alice Rhodes, and from Clara Brown.

The post-mortem was held at 34 Forbes Road on 19th April. The examination was conducted by Mr. Longrigg, assisted by his partner, Mr. Pigott, and his friend, Mr. Lister. There was also present the police surgeon, Dr. Wilkinson, while Dr. Bright watched the proceedings on behalf of the relatives of the deceased, and Mr. Harman on behalf of the Stauntons. The body was fearfully emaciated and filthily dirty, especially the feet, the skin of which was quite horny; there were lice all over the body; the hands and nails were very dirty; but there were no signs of violence. The corpse weighed barely half of what should have been the weight of a healthy body of the height of the deceased. There was very little food in the stomach, some small pieces of undigested bacon. The chief organs of the body—the heart, the liver, the kidneys—were healthy but small, much smaller than they should have been. There were old adhesions between the external and internal lining membranes of the brain, with a slight deposit of a tubercular substance; the internal and external blood-vessels were highly congested and in an apoplectic condition, but, in the opinion of Mr. Longrigg and his assistants, the substance of the brain was perfectly healthy and free from disease. On opening the chest a tubercular deposit was found at the apex of the left lung, which, however, the doctors were convinced had nothing to do with causing the death. The body was absolutely devoid of fat, not a particle of it being discernible. The lower outlets of the body were badly inflamed, as if by the administration of an irritant poison, and the condition of the eyes suggested that a narcotic might have been taken. The contents of the stomach and the intestines were accordingly sent the next day (20th

8

Introduction.

April) to Mr. Disbrowe Rodgers, professor of toxicology at the London Hospital. No traces of poison could be discovered, but the complete absence of fat and the extreme emaciation of the body drove Professor Rodgers to the conclusion that death was due to starvation and neglect. He found also that the condition of the liver precluded the idea that the deceased had been addicted to intemperance.

The inquest was resumed on the 10th of May, and continued over the 11th, 14th, 15th, 17th, and 19th. Mr. (now Sir Harry) Poland appeared for the Treasury, and Mr. Percy Gye, afterwards reinforced by Mr. (now Sir Douglas) Straight for the three Stauntons and Alice Rhodes, all of whom elected to be sworn and give evidence. Louis, who was called first, said he had separated from his wife by mutual consent in the previous November; they had remained, however, on excellent terms, and saw one another two or three times a week. The separation was due to her intemperate habits; she was a heavy drinker, and they had difficulty in preventing her from getting access to spirits. Up to Monday, the 9th of April, his wife was in perfect health, eating well and having a craving for food, but on the Tuesday and Wednesday in that week she became seriously unwell, with perpetual drowsiness, and her memory appeared to fail her. He had never regarded his wife as being of weak intellect. She refused to see her mother and relatives because they had tried to shut her up in a lunatic asylum. She was always well clothed, and never complained of being neglected. On being pressed he admitted that Alice Rhodes had passed as his wife at Little Grays.

Alice herself was the next witness. She swore that she did not know the deceased was ill until Wednesday, the 11th of April, and even then she did not consider her very ill. The illness had come on quite suddenly and unexpectedly. Though Harriet was carried into the house in Forbes Road she was perfectly capable of walking; she undressed herself and took out her own ear-rings. Alice admitted that she had deceived Mrs. Butterfield by telling her that the deceased was living at Brighton with her husband and child, but she did so at the request of Harriet herself. She had never noticed that the deceased was in a filthy condition, and she had intended to share her bed at the lodgings. She had seen deceased the worse for drink on several occasions.

Staunton Trial.

Mrs. Patrick Staunton said that the deceased had come to them at Cudham of her own free will. She was always nicely dressed and had clean clothes. On their arrival at Forbes Road she appeared perfectly sensible. At the Woodlands she had her meals with the rest of the family, and was constantly out and about. She came down daily to breakfast, and washed and dressed herself regularly.

Patrick Staunton asserted that he had frequently seen the deceased the worse for liquor. She had shown no surprise on hearing of the death of her child; the child suffered from convulsions, and it was at the mother's request that it was taken to Guy's. He knew that Alice Rhodes was passing as his brother's wife, but he was not aware of any criminal intimacy between them. No restraint of any kind was put upon the deceased at the Woodlands; he had noticed no change in her health until Monday, the 9th of April, and he saw no symptoms which could render the drive to Bromley inadvisable or dangerous. It was put to him by the coroner whether the removal, first of the child and then of the mother, was not to evade inquiry,[4] and he answered indignantly in the negative.

Clara Brown was the only other adult—if a girl of sixteen may be so designated—who could throw light on the establishment at the Woodlands. She corroborated in fullest detail the evidence of the Stauntons. According to her, Harriet was out morning, noon, and night; she shared the family meals; she showed no signs of ill-health until the Monday before her departure for Penge, and during her last days at the Woodlands she ate heartily of cold roast beef, fowl, and steak. Witness declared that she had seen the deceased the worse for liquor, which she used to obtain from the village. At a later date, as will be seen, Clara Brown told a totally different story, and said that her original evidence was put in her mouth by the Stauntons.

Mrs. Butterfield was then called, and the other witnesses included—besides the flymen, the railway officials, the nurse, the undertaker, the lodging-house keeper, and the medical men —a couple of constables who had gone down to the Woodlands

---

4 Had No. 34 Forbes Road been situated a few yards further westward, it would have been within the boundary line of the county of Surrey, and the death would have been registered at Croydon.

Introduction.

on the 10th of May, almost exactly a month after the removal of Harriet Staunton. There was no one at home, for the occupants were all at the inquest, and they made their entry through a back window. Going upstairs they found the front bedroom properly furnished, but the back bedroom, which had been Harriet's, was bare and dirty. There was no carpet; a piece of board was laid across three tressels, and this formed the bedstead. The mattress was very dirty, and the pillow was without a case; there was no washstand.

An important piece of evidence relating to the early stage of the story was given by Emma Denton, the nurse who had attended Harriet Staunton in her confinement. She said that Alice Rhodes acted as complete mistress of the house in Loughborough Park Road, and that Harriet frequently cried and was in deep distress over her husband's behaviour towards his sister-in-law. This witness was examined before the magistrate, but for some unexplained reason she was not called at the trial.[5]

On Saturday, the 19th of May, the jury returned a verdict of wilful murder against the three Stauntons and Alice Rhodes. The contradictions between their evidently concerted narrative and the cumulative testimony of a cloud of independent witnesses were overwhelming. None of the four were in Court when the finding of the jury was announced, and they surrendered by appointment to the police officers in the course of the afternoon. In staying away they had followed the advice of their counsel. Sir Douglas Straight can still recall the ferocity with which his clients were greeted as they emerged from the room in the Park Tavern where the inquiry was held. That was at a comparatively early stage in the proceedings, and the demeanour of the mob had become more threatening day by day. The sufferings of a helpless child and a half imbecile woman, the revolting revelations of the nurse, the conviction of the doctor that death was due to deliberate starvation, the adultery committed in circumstances which doubly aggravated the original guilt of both parties— all had combined to excite the crowd to frenzy.

The prisoners were taken to Maidstone Gaol, and on Monday,

---

5 See Appendix v., p. 301.

the 21st of May, were brought before the bench at Bromley. Here the demonstrations were no less hostile than at Penge, and the progress from the station to the Court and the Court to the station was a terrible ordeal. The hearing of the case was continued on the 23rd and 30th of May, and on the 1st, 3rd, 10th, 11th, and 13th of June. On the latter day they were all four committed to the ensuing Kent assizes on the charge of murder. The evidence put forward by the prosecution was substantially the same as that which we shall find given at the trial, with the important exception, however, that Clara Brown was not called. The police were convinced that when she was sworn before the coroner she was completely under the control of the prisoners and their relations, with one of whom she had taken up her residence after the home at the Woodlands had been broken up. She was now removed from this " sphere of influence," and placed under supervision with a family at Penge.

The Kent assizes are held at Maidstone, but on the 24th of June, a fortnight before Commission Day, application was made in the Queen's Bench Division of the High Court before Justices Lush and Mellor that the case might be removed under Palmer's Act[6] to the Central Criminal Court. Affidavits were tendered to prove the impossibility of obtaining a fair trial from a Kentish jury in the existing state of public opinion. Neither of the judges gave a very encouraging reception to the argument of Mr. Straight; but on the ready acquiescence of the Attorney-General, Sir John Holker, the rule was granted, On the 28th of June Alice Rhodes was delivered in Maidstone Gaol of a child whose father was registered as Louis Staunton.[7]

The commitment having been to the Kent assizes, the indictment came before the Grand Jury of that county on the

---

6 When it became obvious that the poisoner Palmer could not get a fair trial in Staffordshire, the Attorney-General (Sir Alexander Cockburn) got a bill rapidly through Parliament so as to enable the trial to take place at the Central Criminal Court. The Act (19 Vict. c. 19) applies generally to all cases in which " it is expedient to the ends of justice " that the indictment should be tried there. If Palmer could know what is going on in this world, it must give him melancholy satisfaction to find that this most useful measure of law reform is, and will be, for all time known as " Palmer's Act."

7 A few weeks later Mrs. Patrick Staunton was brought to bed in what Mr. Edward Clarke styled " the same shameful birthplace."

Introduction.

10th of July; until a true bill was found the order of the Court of Queen's Bench was inoperative. Sir James Fitzjames Stephen, not yet a judge but sitting as Commissioner, was in the Crown Court at Maidstone, and his charge suggested that to the mind of one great criminal lawyer, at any rate, the case was by no means free from difficulty. Whilst leaving the matter in the hands of the jurors he indicated not obscurely that in his judgment the evidence would not support a heavier verdict than that of manslaughter, and that against Alice Rhodes there was no evidence of any offence of which the criminal law takes cognisance. The general feeling of horror and resentment, however, was too strong to be denied, and a bill for wilful murder was found against all the prisoners, together with a supplementary bill for manslaughter.

The next session of the Central Criminal Court was at the end of July, and on the 9th of August the Lord Chief-Justice of the Queen's Bench, Sir Alexander Cockburn, came down in full State to the Old Bailey to try what had become known as the Penge mystery. The Attorney-General, Sir John Holker, the Solicitor-General, Sir Hardinge Giffard (now Lord Halsbury), and Mr. (now Sir Harry) Poland conducted the prosecution.[8] For the defence Mr. (now Sir George) Lewis, then midway in his remarkable professional career, had retained a strong bar. The prisoners were separately represented, Louis Staunton by Mr. Montagu Williams and Mr. (now Sir Charles) Mathews; Patrick Staunton by Mr. (now Sir Edward) Clarke; Mrs. Patrick by Mr. (now Sir Douglas) Straight and Mr. Purcell; Alice Rhodes by Mr. Percy Gye. All was apparently in readiness, but a surprise was in store; Mr. Montagu Williams applied, on behalf of his client, for an adjournment to the next sessions on the ground that he had not had time to master the medical details of the case, on which fresh light had been thrown during the last few days. The Chief-Justice, who was extremely unwilling to be baulked of a sensational trial, gave him no encouragement. He had read the depositions, he said, and he could not imagine, considering the number of medical men who figured therein, that any additional evidence of that

---

8 Mr. Charles (afterwards Lord) Bowen, the Treasury "devil," was also briefed, but he did not appear in the trial itself.

description would elucidate the cause of death. It was not, in his opinion, a case of scientific hypothesis, but of what had been seen by the doctors who had attended the deceased, conducted the post-mortem, and made the analysis. The other counsel, however, supported the application, and the Attorney-General, with that tenderness for the interests of the prisoners which was characteristic of Sir John Holker, declared that the Crown raised no opposition. The Lord Chief-Justice yielded, though with evident reluctance, and the case was adjourned to the September sessions. It should be added that on the 9th of August the Grand Jury had found a true bill for the manslaughter of Harriet Staunton's child against Louis and Mr. and Mrs. Patrick.

On the 19th of September the long-deferred trial began. The interval had brought about no change in the counsel either for the prosecution or the defence, but the Chief-Justice's place on the Bench was now occupied by Sir Henry Hawkins, the junior judge, who had received his well-merited promotion in the November of the previous year, and who had not hitherto tried a murder case.[9]

The issue before the jury was explained to them by Sir John Holker in terms as simple as the facts permitted. They had got to try whether Harriet Staunton had met her death through the culpable misconduct of the prisoners or any of them, and, if so, whether that culpable misconduct amounted to murder or manslaughter. And it was open to them to find that, while some only of the prisoners were guilty of actual murder, the others were accessories after the fact. If the deceased was kept without food and otherwise neglected with the design of causing her death, or with the knowledge that the consequence would be her death, those who kept food from her or abetted the guilty design would be guilty of murder. But suppose it to have been merely a case of cruel negligence, then those whose duty it was to supply Harriet Staunton with the necessaries of life would be guilty of manslaughter only. It would be a question of some nicety as to which of the prisoners it was upon whom that duty rested, and the Attorney-

---

9 So Lord Brampton says (Reminiscences, p. 219, one volume edition); I have not verified the statement, and the dates render it improbable.

Introduction.

General made the significant observation that, though Alice Rhodes was living in adultery with Louis Staunton, he could not see that she was responsible for the maintenance of Louis Staunton's wife.

The examination and cross-examination of the witnesses occupied five days. Mrs. Butterfield was the first to enter the box; then came the porters and railway officials from Bromley and Penge, the flyman who had driven the deceased to Forbes Road; Emma Chalklin, the landlady, and Ellen Gooding, the nurse. Mrs. Chalklin swore positively that Louis Staunton told her that his wife had been under a doctor at Cudham, and she described her intense surprise at the condition in which Harriet Staunton reached her house. Lee, the undertaker, completed this part of the case, and the medical witnesses were now called.

First of all came Mr. Longrigg, who related his interview with Louis and Mrs. Patrick Staunton, his visits to the dying woman, and the reasons which influenced him in giving the death certificate. He described the post-mortem, the state of the internal organs, and the gorged condition of the vessels of the brain, which, he suggested, might have been produced by suddenly giving a meal to some one who had been for a long time without food. It was the failure to discover any traces of poison which convinced him that it was a case of starvation. The state of emaciation to which the body had been reduced might have been brought about in three months. For a considerable time before Harriet Staunton's death it must have been apparent to those about her that she was wasting away.

When Mr. Clarke got up to cross-examine Mr. Longrigg, the crux of the case had been reached. The publication of the evidence taken before the coroner and the magistrates had convinced Dr. Bristowe and other leading authorities on diseases of the brain that, entirely apart from the treatment Harriet Staunton had received from her husband and his relatives, the cause of her death was tubercular meningitis (inflammation of the membranes of the brain), as demonstrated by the presence therein of tuberculous matter. Meningitis is now a well-recognised disease, especially common in children, difficult to diagnose and impossible to cure. In

Staunton Trial.

1877 it was unfamiliar to those outside the ring of brain specialists, and was the last thing which would occur to a general practitioner in a small London suburb as a rival hypothesis to·what seemed a clear case of starvation.

By agreement with the counsel for the other prisoners, the entire conduct of the medical questions involved in the case was left to Mr. Clarke. His object was to show that the post-mortem had not been carried out with thoroughness; that the doctors had been predisposed from the outset to the theories, first of poison, then of starvation, and that they had entirely neglected the clue which was furnished them by the presence of tubercle both in the lung and the meshes of the brain. He sought to establish that the two most conspicuous features of death by starvation—thinness of the coats of the stomach and paleness of the brain—were absent, and that the emaciation of the body was directly caused by the brain trouble. In addition, he urged upon them whether the symptoms attending the dying hours of the deceased, as well as the appearance of the body, were not consistent with the existence of diabetes or of Addison's disease. To none of these suggestions could Mr. Clarke obtain any assent, but he pressed the doctors hard, and obtained a number of admissions which laid the foundations of his address to the jury a day or two later.

Among the medical men who were called by the prosecution was Mr. Creasey, the parish doctor from Brastead, who denied that there was any truth in the statement made to Mr. Longrigg by Louis Staunton that the deceased had been under his care. He had attended one of Mrs. Patrick's children for a trifling ailment, but, though his work took him past the Woodlands twice every week, he was unaware of the existence of Harriet Staunton or of her baby.

Next came Clara Brown. She was, as the Attorney-General had pointed out, the only available witness who could give the jury a perfect and correct account of the treatment of the deceased. But he had warned them not to accept her evidence any further than it was corroborated by other testimony; the story she had told before the coroner was in flat contradiction with the statements she had subsequently made to the police and to the Treasury authorities. She now declared that after returning from her visit to the London

Harriet Staunton

Introduction.

solicitor's in October, Patrick Staunton had forbidden Harriet to leave the house, and that he had ordered witness to prevent her from doing so, and not to allow any one to see her. She (Clara Brown) had heard Louis request Mrs. Patrick to lock up his wife's hat and jacket, so that she should not come after him. Up to Christmas Harriet had taken her meals with the family, but about that date she was banished upstairs, and practically kept there as a prisoner. She used to complain bitterly to witness of not having enough to eat, and sometimes for a whole day nothing was sent up to her. On more than one occasion witness had seen Patrick Staunton strike her. During the whole time she was at the Woodlands Harriet possessed only one pair of boots. She had become ill gradually; there was no fit or sudden change for the worse. She was very weak, and quite impassive, both when her child was taken away to the hospital and when she was told of its death. On the days immediately preceding her own removal, she was unable to take any nourishment, though she was tried with boiled fowl and bread and milk. On the Thursday she had to be carried downstairs in Patrick Staunton's arms. She was very drowsy and her brother-in-law remarked that if she were to go to sleep she very likely would not wake again. Louis Staunton frequently came over from Little Grays to the Woodlands. Sometimes he saw his wife, but not always. Harriet had no idea that he was living in the vicinity, or that Alice Rhodes was passing as his wife. Shortly before Harriet came to reside at the Woodlands, witness had picked up a letter in one of the bedrooms. It was from Louis Staunton to Alice Rhodes. She had burnt it, but she could remember part of the contents. It began, " my own darling," and continued—" I was very sorry to see you crying so much when I left you. It seems as though it never would be, but there will be a time when Harriet will be out of the way, and we shall be happy together. Dear Alice, you must know how much I love you by this time. We have been together two years now."

Much of Clara Brown's cross-examination was naturally devoted to the contradictions and evolutions which her evidence had gone through in its various stages, and, under the handling of Mr. Clarke, she gave a much fuller and more vivid picture

c

of the ménage at the Woodlands than had yet been laid before the Court. Though Patrick Staunton was an artist, he had no studio; there were only two sitting rooms, and he used to work in the larger. On the same floor was the kitchen, with wash-house and pantry. Upstairs were two bedrooms, front and back, and that was all. Mr. and Mrs. Patrick Staunton, with one of their children, occupied the front bedroom; the other child slept in the back bedroom with witness, and the deceased and her own child shared it with them. There was no washing accommodation in the back bedroom; they used the wash-house and the kitchen.

In re-examination the Attorney-General elicited some fresh and rather important facts. When Harriet Staunton paid her week-end visits to the Woodlands, before taking up her abode there, she was nicely dressed and tidy, and seemed to be proud of her personal appearance. From Christmas onwards she used constantly to complain of suffering in her hands and feet, and elsewhere. When Patrick Staunton and his wife were both away at the same time witness had orders not to let any one see Harriet. Occasionally, when people came to the door, she would want to come down, and witness would threaten " to tell the master," at which she always retreated. When Patrick was annoyed by the crying of her child he would beat it cruelly.

Clara Brown was followed by a group of witnesses from the neighbourhood of Cudham. The tradesmen who used to call regularly for orders at the Woodlands had never seen Harriet Staunton or heard of her existence, but a gamekeeper named Marchant had frequently noticed her in the early autumn of the previous year wandering about the woods. The last time he saw her was in November; he was talking to Patrick Staunton in the stable when she appeared at the door without her bonnet. Patrick said to her, " I've a policeman here, and if you ain't away he'll run you in." The deceased seemed to be in good health, and was properly dressed. Lastly, two girls, friends of Clara Brown, related how they had gone to spend the evening of Christmas Day with her under the impression that she was alone at the Woodlands, as the Patrick Stauntons and their children were away. While they were sitting together in the parlour they suddenly heard footsteps

Introduction.

crossing the kitchen, whereupon Clara went to the door, and exclaiming, " Go back, ma'am," turned the key in the lock.

The flyman who had driven Mrs. Butterfield to Little Grays on the 5th of March confirmed her account of the interview which took place there, so far as he had been a witness of it. And Sergeant Bateman described the various conversations which he had held with the prisoners before their arrest. He was severely cross-examined as to his dealings with Clara Brown, but his declaration that he had never endeavoured to exercise any undue influence over her bore the stamp of truth. The depositions of the four prisoners taken before the coroner were then read and put in, and the case for the prosecution closed.

Mr. Straight submitted that there was no case against Mrs. Patrick Staunton on the ground that she must be presumed to have been acting under the coercion of her husband, and, further, that she was under no liability to supply the deceased with food. The judge decided against him without hesitation, and gave a similar ruling with regard to Alice Rhodes. Clara Brown was then recalled, at the request of Mr. Straight, and was asked whether she had ever seen Patrick Staunton strike his own wife. She replied, yes, she had. Before she was allowed finally to leave the box she was subjected to a searching re-examination by Mr. Justice Hawkins.

Counsel for the defence then entered upon their uphill task, the difficulties of which had increased as day by day the evidence accumulated. Their addresses are given in the body of this volume, but I ought to say that, with the exception of Sir Edward Clarke, who has included this in the published collection of his speeches, I have had to rely on the rather meagre reports contained in the newspapers of the day.

Mr. Montagu Williams, on behalf of Louis Staunton, made no endeavour to extenuate the sordid intrigue which his client had been carrying on with Alice Rhodes; he could only urge upon the jury that the offence they had to try was murder, not adultery. He trimmed down in the customary forensic manner the evidence of the hostile witnesses. Harriet Staunton, he contended, was completely estranged from her mother, and had no desire to see her. The removal to Penge was due to a genuine desire for good medical advice, and the prisoners had no suspicion of the dangerous condition of the deceased on the 12th of April. The state of her body was due to her own neglect and the growing enfeeblement of a mind that was always weak. The whole story of her ill-treatment at the Woodlands rested on the more than equivocal evidence of Clara Brown, who, if she spoke the truth, had been herself an accomplice, and he urged that the damning sentences in the so-called "lost letter" were an effort of that girl's imagination.

Mr. Straight renewed his former plea that Mrs. Patrick Staunton had acted throughout under the coercion of her husband. She had a strong motive, indeed, for keeping the identity and even the existence of Harriet from the villagers at Cudham; she wished to screen the shame of her sister, who was passing as the wife of Louis within half a mile of the Woodlands, and she was equally desirous that the truth should be kept from Harriet. But what evidence was there of a conspiracy to effect the death of the latter? Could anything have been more clumsy than the behaviour of the prisoners if they were guilty? And for the life led by Harriet Staunton while under his client's roof, as well as for her condition when she was taken away to Penge, he asked the jury to rely upon the statement made by Clara Brown to the coroner rather than upon the "fostered and manured" version which she had given them in the witness-box.

Then came the turn of Mr. Clarke. Hitherto it had only been clever sparring, or, to vary the metaphor, a creditable attempt to make bricks with no straw and only a modicum of clay. If Harriet Staunton's end had been caused by starvation there was no possibility of acquittal for, at any rate, her husband, her brother-in-law, and his wife. But if it could be shown that death was attributable to organic disease, then the case for the prosecution collapsed, however callous and censurable the conduct of the prisoners might have been. Mr. Clarke had indicated his defence in cross-examination; he now called strong affirmative testimony.

Dr. Payne, an anatomist and pathologist of the highest reputation, expressed his positive conviction, based on the reports of the inquest and on the medical evidence which he had heard during the present trial, that Harriet Staunton died

Introduction.

from tubercular meningitis, and that the theory of starvation failed to explain sufficiently either the symptoms before death or the post-mortem appearances. Emaciation was a frequent and early concomitant of meningitis, part, in fact, of the disease, and often the only premonitory symptom. Meningitis in adults was rare, but absolutely fatal; the acute stage might last any period from a few days to months. Dr. Payne was entirely confirmed by Dr. Bristowe, one of the greatest authorities on all questions of morbid anatomy; and he added that vermin would spread rapidly after death from the head to other parts of the body, and that their presence did not necessarily indicate any great amount of filth before death. Dr. Bristowe, it should be said, had not heard the evidence for the prosecution as given in Court, and his knowledge of the case was entirely derived from the newspapers. It was a letter from him to Mr. Clarke, with whom he was personally acquainted, which had brought about his presence in the witness-box. Both witnesses were agreed that the congestion of the stomach and the inflammation of the peritoneum were inconsistent with starvation. They were closely cross-examined by the Attorney-General with the object, *inter alia*, of showing that tuberculosis might be produced by starvation. To this they would not assent, and no admissions important enough to qualify their evidence were extracted from them.

Mr. Clarke's speech was one of the most forcible and persuasive which have been delivered in a Court of justice within living memory, and it had, so he tells us, a very marked effect upon his progress in the profession.[10] Patrick Staunton, for whom he appeared, was, in the view of the prosecution and of the public, an even more abandoned criminal than Louis. He was the gaoler of the unhappy woman and the executioner, and the blows he had inflicted on her and her equally wretched child were as dark a feature of the case as the aggravated adultery of his brother. But they rested, urged Mr. Clarke, on the testimony of Clara Brown, damaged already beyond recall by

---

[10] " The result of this case and the detective case, which was tried in the following month, was that my income, which had steadily increased to £3000 a year, suddenly rose to £5000."—*Clarke's Speeches*, p. 311.

the speeches of his learned brethren. He dealt effectively with her contradictions, with her utter untrustworthiness, and with the influences to which she had been exposed; and he drove home the point that, up to the very day of Harriet Staunton's departure from the Woodlands, her bedroom in the tiny cottage was shared by Clara Brown and by one of Patrick Staunton's own children. He pieced together the various statements which his client had made both to witnesses in the case and before the coroner, and he contended that they were entitled to at least as much credit as those of Clara Brown. In Patrick's case, unlike that of his brother, there was no motive of money, or of guilty love, which could have induced him to become the daily witness of the slow agonies of starvation, or to have run the appalling risk which had eventually involved him and his family in utter ruin. Mr. Clarke contended that on more than one important point Mr. Longrigg's memory had failed him, and he urged that the doctors who conducted the post-mortem had been thrown off the real scent by the suspicion that death was due to poisoning; hence its perfunctory character, and the very grave omission to use the microscope either on the lungs or the brain. The jury had heard the evidence of two eminent specialists for the defence; their description of the development of tubercular meningitis from a slow wasting complaint to sudden collapse was in exact conformity with the account which the prisoners had given of Harriet Staunton's condition during the latter part of her stay at the Woodlands, and on her removal to Penge. But if Harriet Staunton had died from tubercular disease no crime had been committed, at least no crime of which that Court could take cognisance, and his client was no more guilty of manslaughter than of murder. In a very moving peroration Mr. Clarke asked for an acquittal.

On behalf of Alice Rhodes, Mr. Gye pointed out that she had no control over the Stauntons; she could not have prevented them from moving Harriet to Penge; there was no liability imposed upon her to provide the deceased with food or necessaries. If there was any felonious design on the part of the other prisoners she, at any rate, had no participation in it, and her conduct at Penge towards the dying woman was consistent, to put it no higher, with the greatest care and solicitude. At the time of her seduction his client was a girl of nineteen, carried away by affection, and her whole subsequent conduct was dictated by the wish to hide her weakness and its consequence.

The Attorney-General, in reply, reminded the jury that they had heard the condition of the deceased at the time of her death. Did she come into this state through disease alone, or through ill-treatment and disease combined? If from the former no one could be held culpable, if from the latter some one was clearly responsible. Even if tubercular meningitis was the actual cause of the wasting away, which he did not admit, yet the ill-treatment and neglect to which she had been subjected at the Woodlands must have expedited the operation of any fatal disease that was upon her. While Clara Brown was technically an accomplice, there was sufficient corroboration on the most material points of her evidence to justify the jury in accepting her evidence. The defence asked them to believe that Harriet Staunton was merely secluded in order that the adultery of her husband might be hidden, but such seclusion could not last for ever. Louis had got all her money, and was resolved upon making Alice Rhodes his wife. Surely the facts of the case pointed to a design to reduce Harriet to such a state that she would not be likely to live, and then to let her die in some place where the history of her life would not be investigated. Patrick Staunton had not the same overwhelming motive as his brother, but he was devotedly attached to him, and his wife had every reason, on the admission of her own counsel, for concealing her sister's disgrace. The nature of Louis had been shown sufficiently by the way in which he had allowed his own infant child to die of neglect; and on him rested the primary duty for the proper maintenance of his wife. It was Patrick who, by contract, was bound to provide the necessaries of life, and it was he who gave the order for confining Harriet Staunton to the house. Mrs. Patrick, if they believed Clara Brown, had carried out his instruction, and she had constant opportunities of aiding the dead woman had she so desired, and of seeing she was properly fed. Alice Rhodes could not have been ignorant of the design against Harriet's life, if design there existed. She had taken part, admittedly, in concealing

23

her whereabouts from Mrs. Butterfield, and she had assisted in the journey to Penge. The jury would have to consider whether the removal of the deceased in the circumstances detailed to them was not likely, to the knowledge of the prisoners, to accelerate death. On this point it was immaterial by what means she had been reduced to the lamentable plight of which they had heard. Was the deceased in a fit state for such a journey? From their own language the prisoners must have known the terrible responsibility they were incurring,[11] and they must be held answerable to the law for the consequences.

Sir Henry Hawkins began his summing up at half-past ten o'clock on the morning of Wednesday, the 26th of September, and he did not conclude till twenty minutes to ten that evening, when the jury were sent out to consider their verdict. It was one of those *tours de force* too familiar in English Courts of justice, which place an impossible strain on the faculties and endurance of the twelve men cooped together in a comfortless box, and sodden with the foul, overheated atmosphere. Baron Brampton, in those unfortunate " Reminiscences " which have done so little to enhance their author's reputation either on the Bench or off it, has declared of his charge on this occasion that no duty more arduous was ever subsequently imposed upon him : " I performed it in my honest conscience without swerving from what I believed, and believe still, to be my strict line of duty." As to the extraordinary forensic ability displayed in it there can be no possible dispute, or as to the dramatic skill with which the facts were marshalled so that every point was made to tell and every fact to fall into its proper place. But it was the speech of an advocate and not of a judge ; of a man who had convinced himself that a peculiarly cold-blooded and cruel murder had been committed, and that it would be a crime against Heaven and against Justice if a single one of the prisoners escaped. Certainly he left the jury no loophole. And in a charge by Sir Henry Hawkins the beautifully phrased, clean-cut English was reinforced by the emphasis and gestures which a consummate elocutionist and advocate alone can impart, and which render the most faithful report a pale and ineffectual reproduction.

---

11 See p. 95.

Introduction.

Out of doors the summing up created a sensation second only to the case itself, and procured for its author the title of "Hanging Hawkins," which, in his lordship's later years at any rate, grew to be a mere memory of the past. By the legal profession generally it was viewed with stern disapproval, and Sir Edward Clarke tells a story with reference to it which certainly does not increase our respect for the judge.

"When the summing up was interrupted by the luncheon adjournment Montagu Williams came to me and said, ' Hawkins wants to know if you wish him to deal with the medical evidence, and says, if he does, he will have to make some serious observations which will not help you.' I said, ' That is not a question for me to answer ; I have done my duty, the responsibility for the summing up is with the judge, not with me.' Mr. Justice Hawkins scarcely dealt with that evidence at all, and in his direction practically ignored it."[12]

The report contained in a later page will show that Sir Henry brushed away the testimony of Dr. Payne and Dr. Bristowe as being of no account against the witnesses who had actually seen the body. Expert evidence in a Court of law, when it clashes with a " common sense " explanation, does not usually meet with a very cordial reception. I do not propose to say more with regard to the summing up than to indicate the ruling as to the law which was laid down by the judge for the guidance of the jury. Every person, he told them, who was under a legal duty, whether by law or contract, to take charge of another person, was bound to provide that person with the necessaries of life. Every person who has that duty imposed upon him or her, and neglects it so that death ensues, is guilty of murder if the neglect has been intentional, of manslaughter if the neglect has merely been due to carelessness without such intention. In applying this doctrine to the female prisoners he indicated that the guilt of Mrs. Patrick Staunton would depend upon whether she had been supplied by her husband with the means of providing necessaries for the deceased. To Alice Rhodes he did the doubtful service of pointing out that in her case the verdict of manslaughter was inapplicable, as she was under no obligation to provide

---

12 *Clarke's Speeches*, p. 311.

Staunton Trial.

necessaries. Her fate must rest upon the view taken by the jury of her complicity in a design to murder Harriet Staunton.

As the jury withdrew they asked for a copy of the indictment; this request the judge refused on the ground that, being in legal phraseology, it could be of no assistance to them. After an absence of nearly an hour and a half they returned at five minutes past eleven with a verdict of guilty of murder against all four persons; they recommended both the female prisoners to mercy, Alice Rhodes strongly. The judge passed sentence of death in words which must have fallen like whipcord upon the miserable creatures in the dock. Such fortitude as they possessed had been exhausted by the seven days' ordeal. Louis Staunton and his paramour were stupefied and livid with terror; Patrick's voice was heard for a moment imploring his wife to be firm, but before the words of doom were finished he, too, was in a state of abject collapse. Yet, as they left the dock for the cells Patrick, whose affection for his brother had been the one gleam of light in the wretched story, was seen to exchange with Louis a passionate clasp of the hand.

The scene while a man, and, worse still, a woman, receives sentence of death is solemn and " eerie " enough in any circumstances. But when morning has slowly worn away to evening to the accompaniment of a single steady, unfaltering voice, until flickering candle or flaming gaslight add their quota to the tainted air, the strain on the least responsive spectator becomes almost unendurable.[13] Yet the benches of the Old Bailey were filled even at this dread hour with the bevy of smartly dressed, overjewelled women who had drunk champagne in the luncheon interval and skimmed the pages of *Punch* when the interest flagged. Without the walls, and blocking up the neighbouring thoroughfares, a dense crowd was awaiting the verdict. It was drawn from the same elements which ten years earlier had made an execution outside Newgate the most degrading sight in Christendom. While the judge was delivering sentence the yells of execration and shouts of triumph were heard distinctly by all in Court.

---

13 I can never forget the occasion at Worcester Assizes, shortly after my call to the Bar, when at one o'clock in the morning three Evesham poachers, who had brutally kicked to death one of the Duc d'Aumale's gamekeepers, received their death sentence from Sir Henry Hawkins.

26

Leading Dates in the Staunton Case.

1874. Engagement between Louis Staunton and Harriet Richardson.

December. Mrs. Butterfield takes unsuccessful proceedings in Chancery to have Harriet declared a lunatic.

1875.
June 16. Harriet marries Louis Staunton.

July 7. Mrs. Butterfield visits her daughter at Loughborough Park Road ; they never meet again.

November. The Patrick Stauntons take "The Woodlands," Cudham.

1876.
March 23. Harriet Staunton gives birth to a boy. Alice Rhodes stays in the house during her confinement.

May. The Louis Stauntons remove to Gipsy Hill, Norwood; their child is sent to "The Woodlands."

*August. Harriet Staunton goes to reside at "The Woodlands."

†August 16. Date of "the lost letter" from Louis Staunton to Alice Rhodes.

October. Louis Staunton and Alice Rhodes passing as man and wife come to live at Little Grays farm, near "The Woodlands."

October 23. Harriet Staunton signs the deed disposing of her reversionary interests at Mr. Keene's office in London.

1877.
February. Mrs. Butterfield meets Alice Rhodes at London Bridge Station.

March 5. Mrs. Butterfield goes down to Cudham, but is denied access to her daughter. She communicates with the police.

April 8. Harriet Staunton's child is taken to Guy's Hospital and dies the same evening.

---

* The precise date is uncertain, but it was early in the month. See p. 152.

† Approximately ; see pp. 96, 253.

Staunton Trial.

1877.

April 12.	Harriet Staunton is removed to Penge.
,, 13.	Death of Harriet Staunton.
,, 14.	Dr. Longrigg withdraws the death certificate.
,, 18.	Inquest opened.
,, 19.	Post-mortem examination.
May 10.	Inquest resumed.
,, 19.	Coroner's jury find a verdict of wilful murder against the three Stauntons and Alice Rhodes.
,, 21.	The four prisoners are brought before the magistrates at Bromley.
June 13.	They are committed for trial.
,, 24.	The case removed to the Central Criminal Court.
,, 28.	Alice Rhodes gives birth to a child.
July 10.	True bill found at Maidstone.
Sept. 19.	Trial begins before Sir Henry Hawkins.
,, 26.	The four prisoners are convicted and sentenced to death.
Oct. 16.	The death penalty remitted.

Sir John Holker

THE TRIAL

On the Queen's Commission of Oyer and Terminer and Gaol Delivery for the City of London and Gaol Delivery for the County of Middlesex and the parts of the Counties of Essex, Kent, and Surrey within the jurisdiction of the Central Criminal Court.

WEDNESDAY, 19TH SEPTEMBER, 1877.
The Court met at Ten o'clock.

Judge—

SIR HENRY HAWKINS, KNIGHT, one of the Justices of the Exchequer Division of the High Court of Justice.

Present on the Bench—

The Right Hon. Sir THOMAS WHITE, Knt., Lord Mayor of the City of London; THOMAS QUESTED FINNIS, Esq., Alderman; SIMEON CHARLES HADLEY, Esq., Alderman; and WILLIAM QUARTERMAINE EAST, Sheriff.

Counsel for the Crown—

THE ATTORNEY-GENERAL (*Sir John Holker, Q.C.*).
THE SOLICITOR-GENERAL (*Sir Hardinge Giffard, Q.C.*).
HARRY BODKIN POLAND, Esq.

Instructed by A. W. POLLARD, Esq., on behalf of the Treasury.

Counsel for the Prisoners—

For Louis Staunton—MONTAGU WILLIAMS, Esq., and CHARLES WILLIE MATHEWS, Esq.

For Patrick Staunton—EDWARD CLARKE, Esq.

For Elizabeth Ann Staunton—DOUGLAS STRAIGHT, Esq., and H. F. PURCELL, Esq.

For Alice Rhodes—PERCY GYE, Esq.

All instructed by Messrs. LEWIS & LEWIS.

D

The Indictment.

The four prisoners were charged with having on the 13th day of April, 1877, wilfully murdered Harriet Staunton at Penge, in the county of Kent, to which charge they severally pleaded not guilty,[1] certain of the prisoners were also charged as principals and others as accessories after the fact.[2]

---

[1] The pleas had been taken at the August Sessions.

[2] KENT} The Jurors for our Lady the Queen, upon their oaths, present to wit }that LOUIS ADOLPHUS EDMUND STAUNTON, PATRICK LLEWELLYN STAUNTON, ELIZABETH ANN STAUNTON, and ALICE RHODES, on the 13th day of April, A.D. 1877, at the parish of Beckenham, in the said county of Kent, feloniously, wilfully, and of their malice aforethought, did kill and murder one Harriet Staunton, against the peace of our Lady the Queen, her crown, and dignity.

2. That the said Patrick Llewellyn Staunton, Elizabeth Ann Staunton, and Alice Rhodes, well knowing the said Louis Adolphus Edmund Staunton to have feloniously, wilfully, and of his malice aforethought, killed and murdered one Harriet Staunton on the day and year in the first count mentioned, against the peace of our Lady the Queen, afterwards, to wit, on the day and year aforesaid, and at the parish aforesaid, and in the county aforesaid, him, the said Louis Adolphus Edmund Staunton did feloniously receive, harbour, maintain, comfort, and assist against the peace of our Lady the Queen, her crown, and dignity.

3. That the said Louis Adolphus Edmund Staunton, Elizabeth Ann Staunton, and Alice Rhodes, well knowing the said Patrick Llewellyn Staunton feloniously, wilfully, and of his malice aforethought to have killed and murdered the said Harriet Staunton, on the day and year in the first count mentioned, against the peace of our Lady the Queen, afterwards, to wit, on the day and year aforesaid, and at the parish aforesaid, and in the county aforesaid, him, the said Patrick Llewellyn Staunton, did feloniously receive, harbour, maintain, comfort and assist against the peace of our Lady the Queen, her crown, and dignity.

4. That the said Louis Adolphus Edmund Staunton, Patrick Llewellyn Staunton, and Alice Rhodes, well knowing the said Elizabeth Ann Staunton feloniously, wilfully, and of her malice aforethought to have killed and murdered the said Harriet Staunton on the day and year in the first count mentioned, against the peace of our Lady the Queen, afterwards, to wit, on the day and year aforesaid, and at the parish aforesaid, in the county aforesaid, her, the said Elizabeth Ann Staunton, did feloniously receive, harbour, maintain, comfort, and assist, against the peace of our Lady the Queen, her crown, and dignity.

The indictment for manslaughter, to which the prisoners were not called upon to plead, ran as follows:—

KENT} The Jurors for our Lady the Queen, upon their oath, present to wit }that LOUIS ADOLPHUS EDMUND STAUNTON, PATRICK LLEWELLYN STAUNTON, ELIZABETH ANN STAUNTON, and ALICE RHODES, on the 13th day of April, A.D. 1877, at the parish of Beckenham, in the county of Kent, feloniously did kill and slay one Harriet Staunton, against the peace of our Lady the Queen, her crown, and dignity.

2. That the said Patrick Llewellyn Staunton, Elizabeth Ann Staunton, and Alice Rhodes, well knowing the said Louis Adolphus Edmund Staunton to have feloniously killed and slain one Harriet Staunton on the day and year in the first count mentioned, and

35

Staunton Trial.

The jury having been duly empanelled and sworn, the Attorney-General proceeded to open the case for the Crown.

Attorney-General My lord and gentlemen of the jury—The male prisoners, Louis Staunton and Patrick Staunton, are brothers; Elizabeth Ann Staunton is the wife of Patrick, and Alice Rhodes is her sister. Although there are several counts in this indictment, practically the charge against the prisoners is that they did wilfully murder Harriet Staunton, who was in her lifetime the wife of Louis Staunton, and who died on 13th April in this year. That charge of murder involves the minor charge of manslaughter, and you will have to consider, in the first place, whether Harriet Staunton met her death through the culpable misconduct of the prisoners, or any of them, and, if you come to that conclusion, whether that culpable misconduct amounted to the crime of murder or manslaughter. Of course, it may be necessary for you also to direct your attention to the question whether, if some of the prisoners are guilty of murder, others of the prisoners are guilty as being accessories after the fact. Your main duty will be to consider whether the death was caused by the culpable misconduct of the prisoners, and, if so, whether that misconduct amounted to murder or manslaughter. But before I trouble you with any explanation of the law with reference to this case, and before I make any comments upon the bearing of the evidence, I will give you a succinct, a brief, and, I hope, clear statement of the history of this very sad case. The deceased Mrs. Harriet Staunton was the daughter of Mrs. Richardson, who married for her second husband a clergyman named Mr. Butterfield.

---

against the peace of our Lady the Queen, afterwards, to wit, on the day and year aforesaid, and at the parish aforesaid, and in the county aforesaid, him, the said Louis Adolphus Edmund Staunton, did feloniously receive, harbour, maintain, comfort, and assist, against the peace of our Lady the Queen, her crown, and dignity.

3. That the said Louis Adolphus Edmund Staunton, Elizabeth Ann Staunton, and Alice Rhodes, well knowing the said Patrick Llewellyn Staunton to have feloniously killed and slain one Harriet Staunton on the day and year in the first count mentioned, and against the peace of our Lady the Queen, afterwards, to wit, on the day and year aforesaid, and in the parish aforesaid, and at the county aforesaid, him, the said Patrick Llewellyn Staunton did feloniously receive, harbour, maintain, comfort, and assist, against the peace of our Lady the Queen, her crown, and dignity.

4. That the said Louis Adolphus Edmund Staunton, Patrick Llewellyn Staunton, and Alice Rhodes, well knowing the said Elizabeth Ann Staunton to have feloniously killed and slain the said Harriet Staunton on the day and year in the first count mentioned, and against the peace of our Lady the Queen, afterwards, to wit, on the day and year aforesaid, and at the parish aforesaid, and in the county aforesaid, her, the said Elizabeth Ann Staunton, did feloniously receive, harbour, maintain, comfort, and assist against the peace of our Lady the Queen, her crown, and dignity.

The Attorney-General's Opening.

She will be called before you, and a good deal of this case will depend upon her testimony. In 1874 Harriet Richardson left her mother's house and went to live with her aunt, Mrs. Ellis, at 53 Heygate Street, Walworth. There she became acquainted with Mr. and Mrs. Hincksman, and Mrs. Hincksman had been a Mrs. Rhodes, and is the mother of Mrs. Patrick Staunton and Alice Rhodes. Now, Louis Staunton visited the Ellises' house, and there became acquainted with Harriet Richardson, and paid his addresses to her, and he ultimately married her. In Mrs. Butterfield's opinion, Harriet Richardson, her daughter, was a woman of weak intellect. She had the same educational advantages as the other children of Mrs. Butterfield, who has several, but she never progressed. She could not spell the simplest words, or express herself in a letter like ordinary people. The mother did not approve of the marriage, and she made some application to the Court of Chancery to have her daughter declared a lunatic. Evidence was offered to sustain it, and evidence offered on the other side, but the Court of Chancery did not entertain the application. Although that was so, I think you will come to the conclusion that, without being absolutely an imbecile, still she was a person whom you would regard as of weak intellect. Indeed, I think there is no doubt of that, because Louis Staunton and Patrick Staunton, in a conversation with a medical man just before Harriet Staunton's death, described her as a woman of weak intellect. Her daughter was possessed prior to her marriage of some fortune—£1500 or £2000 or thereabouts—and she would have had, on the death of relatives, some additional sums of money. Louis Staunton was the clerk of an auctioneer. I believe he had not himself a fortune. Whether that was the ground of Mrs. Butterfield's objection or not I cannot tell, or whether the reason was that she thought her daughter was not in a fit condition to contract marriage. However, she did object, but her objections were of no avail, and on 16th June, 1875, the marriage took place. At the time Louis Staunton was twenty-four or thereabouts, and his wife was considerably older—about ten years older; that is, she was thirty-four.

They were married, but there was no settlement made at the marriage, and the consequence was that Louis Staunton came into possession of such money as his wife was entitled to, and subsequently came into possession of further sums from relatives of his wife on their deaths. I think, altogether, he came into possession of about £3000. After the marriage, which took place at Clapham, Mr. and Mrs. Louis Staunton went to live at 8 Loughborough Park, Brixton. I believe Mr. and Mrs. Patrick Staunton lived in the same street, on the other side of the road. After a little time, in July, 1875, Mrs. Butterfield went to see her daughter. The deceased was physically a strong

Staunton Trial.

and robust woman. A day or two after Mrs. Butterfield received a letter of an offensive character from Mr. Louis Staunton, forbidding her to enter the house again, in consequence of her conduct towards her daughter—that was the effect of the letter, which is lost. In the letter was enclosed one from her daughter, asking her not to come to the house again, and I believe she never again saw her daughter alive.

It appears that Louis Staunton and his wife lived there till May, 1876, and then they removed to Gipsy Hill, Norwood. On 23rd March, 1876, Mrs. Harriet Staunton was delivered of a son, Thomas Henry Staunton. Prior to the birth of the child Alice Rhodes, a sister of Mrs. Patrick Staunton, came to live in the house with Mr. and Mrs. Louis Staunton. It seems that about the time the child was born Mrs. Harriet Staunton became aware that undue familiarities were going on between her husband and Alice Rhodes. This seems to have caused her great distress. She was frequently seen in tears, and she complained of the conduct of her husband as to Alice Rhodes. It would seem that her suspicions were well founded, for soon afterwards Louis Staunton and Alice Rhodes were living together as man and wife. Indeed, Alice Rhodes has been delivered of a child, which there can be no question is the child of Louis Staunton. At Gipsy Hill they lived until the latter part of 1876. In November, 1875, Mr. and Mrs. Patrick Staunton went to live at Frith Cottage, Cudham, in Kent. It is sometimes called the Woodlands, and is in a lone part of the country, and they lived there until the death of Harriet Staunton. I suppose they are in occupation of that place still. Some time about August, 1876, Mrs. Harriet Staunton appears to have gone to Frith Cottage to see Mr. and Mrs. Patrick, and she had her child with her. An arrangement was made between Louis and his brother Patrick and his wife that they should have charge of Mrs. Harriet Staunton, and they were to be paid £1 a week by Louis for taking care of her. This must have been about November, 1876, because about that time Louis Staunton took a place called Little Grays farm, at Cudham, about twenty minutes' walk from the Woodlands, and he lived there. Alice Rhodes also came to live there, and she did live there with Louis Staunton as his wife, and she passed as Mrs. Louis Staunton. Before this some letters passed between the two male prisoners, which I may as well read at this part of the case, not because there is anything very particular about them, but because they show there complaints made by Louis against his wife of intemperate habits, which was the excuse he afterwards alleged for separating from her. The first letter was one from Louis Staunton to Patrick, dated 28th June, 1876, from Gipsy Hill. It began—" My dear Bay "—the name

38

The Attorney-General's Opening.

Patrick was known by was at first " Baby," then it became
" Bab," and, finally, " Bay "—" Many thanks for your kind
letter." He goes on to describe his wife's temper as " something frightful." " From the time she gets up and goes to bed
she does nothing but try to aggravate and make me miserable.
I am truly unhappy; but, oh, dear Bay, I cannot enough thank
you and dear Lizzie for all your kindness; but, rest assured,
I shall not forget it." Although there are complaints in this
letter about his wife, there is no complaint that she indulged
in excessive drink or in drinking at all. On 28th August, 1876,
there is a further letter. It begins—" Dear Bay," and he
" grieves that the two children are still so ill, but trusts they
may soon get better. It makes me quite miserable to think
that you and dear Lizzie are in such trouble and I cannot help
you. I want you to send Harriet up to-morrow, because I am
sure you cannot be bothered with her." On 31st August, 1876,
there is another letter, in which he says—" I am very sorry
Harriet should have give you so much trouble.[3] What to do
with her I do not know." On 1st September, 1876, there is
one more letter—" My dear Bay,—I have received your letter,
and I am sorry I have said anything, but the fact is, I was
very annoyed at the time to think Harriet had been giving
you any trouble, for I know you have enough already with the
two children ill, but I trust you will not say or think anything
more about it."

In all these letters Louis seems to have expressed his
annoyance and sorrow that his wife should have given
his brother and sister-in-law so much trouble; but, nevertheless, shortly after an arrangement was entered into
by which Louis Staunton's wife was to stay at Woodlands
under the charge and care of Mr. and Mrs. Patrick Staunton,
who were to receive as remuneration £1 a week. Louis
Staunton and Alice Rhodes lived at Little Grays farm as man
and wife. All the neighbours thought that Alice Rhodes was
his wife, while his real wife, Harriet, was living at the Woodlands, and living there, I think I shall show you, practically
in confinement. The prisoners say that after Harriet Staunton
came to the Woodlands she was treated as part of the family,
and was perfectly well up to 9th or 10th April, 1877. That
is their account, but I think I shall show you that that cannot
have been the truth. There were living at the Woodlands Mr.
and Mrs. Patrick Staunton, Harriet Staunton, and a girl named
Clara Brown. After the close of 1876 we know very little of
what went on there except from Clara Brown, about whose
evidence I will make some remarks presently. Although

---

3 This is apparently the allusion to intemperate habits on the part
of Harriet Staunton to which the Attorney-General referred. I may
say here that his speech is very imperfectly reported.

Staunton Trial.

Attorney-
General people passed by the house frequently, yet from December, 1876, to the middle of April only on two occasions is Mrs. Harriet Staunton seen or heard of. On one occasion Harriet was in the yard, and Patrick Staunton was heard to drive her back into the house in a harsh tone; and on the other occasion Clara Brown was heard to slam the door and drive her back with the expression, " Go back, ma'am." We have some idea of what was going on from a letter written by Harriet Staunton to her husband about a month after her going to the Woodlands—" Friday—My own darling, I write these few lines hoping this will find you well. Will you be down on Sunday? If not, I shall be disappointed. Hope to see you on Monday. If not, will let me know which day will be down. It has been raining all day. Will you bring me down peace ribon and frilling for my colour and slelves "—that is, collar and sleeves—" I hope to return with you soon. Percy[4] is coming back to-morrow night, so I believe. Tom "—that is her child—" is quite well, so good-night. God bless you. Will you let me know? I have not had clean flanal for a month. I have been here for a month on Saturday." Then she says—" My boots is worn out. From your affectionate wife, Harriet." Almost every word in this letter is misspelt. She spells " collar" " colour," and " sleeves" " slelves." But the important part of the letter is that it shows that she had been there a month and had had no clean flannel all that time. It is quite clear, from his statement made before the coroner, that Louis Staunton was in the habit of going to his brother's house repeatedly, several times a week. He went there with Alice Rhodes. I do not know whether Harriet Staunton knew that Alice Rhodes was living as the wife of Louis Staunton, but both Louis Staunton and Alice Rhodes must have known the condition in which this woman was. After Louis Staunton's child was born in March, 1876, there were some rumours afloat that familiarities were going on between Louis Staunton and Alice Rhodes, and no doubt when they went to Little Grays farm they were regarded as man and wife.

Rumours of this kind came to the ears of Mrs. Butterfield, who made inquiries. It seems that she made inquiries from relatives of the Stauntons at Brixton. She received a letter from Louis Staunton on 20th January, 1877, from which it appears that Louis Staunton heard that Mrs. Butterfield was making inquiries about her daughter, and that he was particularly anxious that she should not see her. The letter was dated from Brighton. Louis Staunton

---

4 Percy appears to have been the family name for Patrick. See Appendix vi., p. 304, and for the full text of the letter see p. 50.

40

The Attorney-General's Opening.

was not there, but at the Woodlands. The letter to Mrs. Butterfield was dated 20th January, and informed her that after her "unnatural and brutal conduct" her daughter "never wishes to see you again," and that it was his intention "to visit Brentwood, when he would let every one know your true character." Mrs. Butterfield, however, met Alice Rhodes at London Bridge station, and the latter told her that she did not know where her daughter was. At that time Alice Rhodes was wearing the favourite brooch of Mrs. Butterfield's daughter. The importance of this conversation was that Alice Rhodes assured Mrs. Butterfield that she did not know where her daughter was, while afterwards she said she had been ill, but was better. Mrs. Butterfield subsequently met Patrick Staunton at London Bridge station, and asked where her daughter was. He got very angry, and ultimately said, "Damn your daughter." She told him that she was going to Cudham, and to his house. He said, "There is no use you going to my house, and I warn you not. I have a gun there." On 5th March Mrs. Butterfield does go to Cudham. At Little Grays farm she saw Mrs. Patrick Staunton and Louis Staunton. She asked to see her daughter, but was told that she should not be allowed to see her, and a number of foul names were applied to her. She asked at least to have some assurance that her daughter was alive, and then she would go away. The answer she received was that her daughter was alive and well, but that she should not see her. Louis Staunton took up a knife and threatened to strike her, but the woman interfered, and Mrs. Butterfield was pushed out of the house. This was 5th March in the present year, and Mrs. Butterfield, prosecuting her inquiries, went to the Marlborough Street police magistrate, who communicated for her with the police at Sevenoaks, who gave her some assistance. On 4th April there is a letter written by Louis Staunton to Mr. Butterfield, the husband of Mrs. Butterfield—"I have received a communication from Mr. Hincksman to the effect that you have written to him as to the whereabouts of my wife, which is no business of his." The letter goes on to say that Mr. Butterfield had shown "an amount of impudence in an allusion to Mr. Hincksman's step-daughter. I am surprised that you, a clergyman of the Church of England, should assert any such thing without foundation, and you must remember that an assertion of that sort is actionable." He then spoke of the "disgraceful manner" in which Mrs. Butterfield had acted, "particularly the last time she came to my house," and remarked that he would "spare no expense to stop her, as, this continued, I am quite prepared to tolerate no longer." It is perfectly obvious that the object of the letter was to prevent Mr. Butterfield and his wife from prosecuting inquiries.

41

Staunton Trial.

Attorney-General On 8th April "Tommy," the child, was taken to Guy's Hospital by Mr. and Mrs. Patrick Staunton, Louis Staunton waiting outside.   You will hear how the child was clothed.

Mr. STRAIGHT—I ask your lordship whether this matter should be opened to the jury?

Mr. JUSTICE HAWKINS—I must leave it to the discretion of the Attorney-General.   I am quite satisfied he would not open anything which he did not think was evidence.

The ATTORNEY-GENERAL—Perhaps it was an indiscretion on my part to say anything about the condition of the child beyond this—that it was ill.   On the following day Patrick came to inquire about the child, and he was informed that it had died.   Louis Staunton came himself on 10th April and made arrangements for the burial.   The child had been entered in the books as Henry *Stormton*, and Louis Staunton described himself as Mr. Harris, saying the child belonged to a workman who was in the employ of a firm with whom he was connected.   He paid the undertaker 25s., and took a receipt for that sum in the name of Harris.   This showed, of course, that Louis Staunton was anxious at that time that no one should know it was his child.   On the 10th there is a letter from Louis Staunton to Mr. Butterfield, saying that unless the latter apologised for the " base accusations," he (Louis Staunton) would complain to the bishop and take legal proceedings against Mr. Butterfield.   That was written on 10th April, and on the same day Mrs. Harriet Staunton's feet began to swell ; but according to their story up to that time Harriet Staunton was perfectly well.

On 12th April Louis Staunton, Patrick and Mrs. Patrick Staunton went to Penge to look for lodgings, and engaged rooms at Mrs. Chalklin's house, Forbes Road, Penge.   They said the lodging was for a lady who could eat, but who would not, and they wished to get medical advice for her.   They conveyed to Mrs. Chalklin's mind that the lady was the mother, and not the wife, of Louis Staunton.   She recommended them to Dr. Longrigg, and they saw him.   They told the doctor that the lady had lost the use of one side, that she was very thin, but hearty, and that she had been ailing for some considerable time.   Dr. Longrigg asked whether they had medical attendance for the lady at Cudham, and they told him that the lady had been attended by Dr. Creasey.   After seeing Dr. Longrigg, the Stauntons seem to have gone back to Little Grays, and about six o'clock that same evening Louis Staunton brought his wagonette to take Harriet Staunton to Penge.   It is clear that Mrs. Harriet could not walk without assistance.   On the journey she sat between her husband and Alice Rhodes.   They drove to Bromley, and took train to Penge, where she had to

Evidence for Prosecution.

staying at 53 Heygate Street, Walworth Road, with Mr. H. Butterfield Thomas Hincksman, a nephew of mine, the son of my sister, Mrs. Ellis. Mrs. Thomas Hincksman had been married before to a Mr. Rhodes, and by her first marriage was the mother of the two female prisoners. The two male prisoners are brothers. Some time in 1875 I learnt that Louis Staunton was paying his addresses to my daughter.

Was your daughter entitled to any money?—Yes.

How much?—About £3000 or £4000; it might be a little over.

At the time of her marriage?—Then about £1600.

You were under the impression that your daughter was not in a fit state to be married?—Yes; and I made an effort to get her declared a ward in Chancery. Those proceedings were unsuccessful. My daughter was married to Louis Staunton, at Clapham, on 16th June, 1875. I was not present at the marriage. About three weeks after the marriage I paid her a visit at 8 Loughborough Park. I went to the door, and my daughter opened it.

What happened?—My daughter asked me in, and I asked if her husband was at home, and she said " Yes," and she called, " Louis, mamma is here."

Did he come?—Yes. I went into the dining-room. He was present. I asked my daughter if she was happy, and she answered, " Pretty well, mamma—middling." He said he was sorry he could not drink my health, as he had only spirits in the house. I asked him why he did not keep a servant, and he said he had advertised for one. He said to Harriet, " Go upstairs, my dear, and show mamma the house."

Well?—I made some remarks about the place not being all furnished. I then said I must be going, and he told his wife to see me to the station.

Did he go with you?—Yes. I was only a few minutes in the house—about ten minutes. At the station I shook hands with both of them and said " Good-bye." During that interval there was no quarrel from first to last or words between us.

Did you ever see her alone again?—No. The next day or the day after I received a letter from Louis Staunton enclosing a letter from my daughter.

Have you looked for those letters?—Yes, and I have not been able to find them.

What was in your letter?——

Mr. M. WILLIAMS—When did you see these letters last?— Before I left New Kent Road.

When was that?—I have lived in the country about two years.

Have you looked for the letters?—Yes, everywhere.

SOLICITOR-GENERAL, continuing examination—What was in the

47

Staunton Trial.

H. Butterfield letters?—In her letter she told me her husband objected to my calling upon her, and she thought I had better not come, to prevent any disturbance between them. The letter from him was very rude and insulting, and in it he said he would not have me in the house again.

You did not visit again?—I did not; but in the following year I heard that my daughter had had a boy. Some time in the following year I heard a statement about Alice Rhodes, and began to make inquiries about my daughter. In February this year I met Alice Rhodes myself.

Where?—At the London Bridge railway station. I asked her where Harriet was, and at first she said she did not know. I said, " You must know where she is; you do know." She then said, " Upon my word, I don't know." Afterwards she said, " She is at Brighton with her husband and child." I asked her to give me her address. I noticed she was wearing a brooch given to my daughter twenty years ago, and she was very fond of it. I said, " You have got my daughter's brooch, Alice." She replied that I might have it if I liked, and she gave it me; but I said, " Oh, no, if my daughter has given it to you; but I cannot understand her giving it to you, as it was her favourite brooch." I asked her if my daughter was well, and she said, " No; she has been very ill, but she is better." I asked for the address of her medical man, but she said she did not remember it, but that she would send it to me. I gave her my address.

Did you ever hear from her?—No.

Or of the name of the medical man?—No. I continued to make inquiries about my daughter, and went down to Cudham, near Knockholt, in consequence of some information given to me by a charwoman in the Walworth Road. On my way to Cudham I happened to meet Mr. Patrick Staunton at London Bridge station, near the South-Eastern booking-office. He appeared to be coming from the train. I told him I was going down to Cudham, and I asked where my daughter was. He said, " I know nothing about your daughter," and he then asked me what I was going to Cudham for. I said, " I shall go and see the clergyman." He said, " If you come to my house I'll blow your brains out." He also said, " Damn your daughter; I know nothing about her." He then went away. I proceeded to Halstead station. When I got there I made inquiries, and found Louis Staunton was living in the neighbourhood. I had not known this previously, though I had known Patrick Staunton did so.

What did you do then?—I took a cab and drove to his house, which was called Little Grays farm. This was about four o'clock in the afternoon, the date being 5th March this year.

What next happened?—When I got to the house I knocked at the door, and Mrs. Patrick Staunton answered it.

The Solicitor-General (Sir Hardinge Giffard)

Evidence for Prosecution.

Mr. JUSTICE HAWKINS—What was the distance of the farm from the railway station?

WITNESS—About 5 miles. I asked Mrs. Patrick Staunton to see my daughter. Then Mr. Louis Staunton came forward in a great passion and swore at me and said, "You shall not see her." I said, "If you will only let me hear her voice or see her hand on the bannister I shall then go away content, knowing that she is in her proper place with her husband." He was then going to strike me with a knife, when Mrs. Patrick Staunton said, "Don't hit her—don't hit her." This took place in a little room where they appeared to have been dining.

Did he say anything further?—He called me a dirty old bitch and other names, and said I did not live with my husband I appealed to Mrs. Patrick Staunton to let me see my daughter, and I said to her, "You may have children of your own whom you may want to see some day." She replied, "Your daughter is well cared for, and that's enough for you to know." They then bustled me out.

Explain what you mean by that?—I mean that one or other, or both, I cannot exactly say which, pushed me out of the door. The cabman was standing outside when the door was closed. When I got into the cab the driver pointed out a Dr. Creasey to me who happened to be coming by, and I made some inquiry of him. I then returned home, and shortly afterwards made an application to the magistrate at the Marlborough Street Police Court. I also went down to Sevenoaks on 9th April. I went to the magistrates at Bromley, but I was unable to get any information respecting my daughter. On Sunday, the 15th, I received a telegram from a Mrs. Urridge.[7] Mrs. Urridge was the landlady of Little Grays farm. I had been several times to see her. I then went to 34 Forbes Road, Penge. I there saw my daughter lying dead. When I had last seen her, at the end of June, 1875, she was in very good health. She enjoyed very good general health.

What had been her habits in respect to dress?—She was fond of dress, and knew how to dress, and she was a very clean girl indeed, very particular about her person. She was always very temperate; I won't say she did not take a glass of ale with her dinner.

Was she in the habit of drinking to excess?—Oh, dear, no.

This photograph, which was taken about nine months before her death, fairly represents her at that time?—We always treated her more like a child, because she was so simple.

When you saw her on this Sunday, was she in her coffin?—Yes; and I noticed how greatly she was changed—apart from the difference caused between life and death

---

7 See Appendix i., p. 291.

Staunton Trial.

H. Butterfield *The witness here became much affected.*

Will you tell us in what the change consisted?—She was looking very old, very much older than she really was. She looked very dirty and miserable, and I scarcely knew her.

The SOLICITOR-GENERAL then put in evidence the following letter, which the witness identified as being in the handwriting of her daughter:—

Friday.

My own darling,—I write these few lines hoping this will find you well. Will you be down on Sunday? If not, I shall be disappointed. If not, will let me know which day you will be down by Percy?[8] It has been raining all day. Will you bring me down peace ribon and frilling for my colour and slelves. I hope to return to town with you soon. Percy is going back to-morrow night, so I believe. Tommy is quite well. So good-night, my dear. and God bless you. Will you let me know. I have not had clean flanal for a month. I have been here a month on Saturday. It is time I should be at home. My boots has wore out. From your ever affectionate wife.
HARRIET.

The SOLICITOR-GENERAL—Was that her ordinary way of spelling and writing a letter?—It was. She had never been able to avail herself of much education.

Cross-examined by Mr. MONTAGU WILLIAMS—I was very much averse to the marriage from the first. The proceedings in lunacy with regard to my late daughter were taken, I believe, at the end of 1874. I thought it was my petition, but I understand that it was my son's; I was not aware of it at the time. I have since ascertained that it was my son's petition in his name for me; I remember that I made an abstract of the proceedings.

I did not know that my daughter Harriet had made a voluntary settlement on my son of her money till Mr. Straight read it in Court.[9] I knew nothing of it before, and I have not heard of it since. Mr. Straight read it and spoke to me about it. [*Mr. Straight here stated that he did not read it.*] I never heard from my daughter before her marriage that she wished to register that settlement: she never spoke to me on the subject of any settlement at all.

She had been living with me prior to her marriage, but the last six months prior to her marriage she was living first in Heygate Street with her aunt Ellis, with whom she stayed till her aunt Ellis died, and then she went to live with Mrs. Hincksman. The house belonged to my sister, Mrs. Ellis. Mrs. Hincksman is not my sister; she stayed with Mrs. Ellis

---

8 The version of the letter given in the judge's summing up is much more illiterate than the one in the text, which I have taken from the Sessions Papers, and should think is the more accurate transcript; see *infra*, p. 258.

9 *I.e.* before the magistrates.

Evidence for Prosecution.

four or five months; she ceased to live with me seven or eight months before her marriage. I am speaking to the best of my recollection; I do not think it could have been more.

I remember that I made an affidavit in the lunacy petition. I do not remember what it stated; I do not remember stating that my daughter had occasional fits of violence. I have never stated to my knowledge that my daughter Harriet had always been of weak intellect and had a running of saliva from her mouth. I objected to that when the lawyer put it to me when the affidavit was read. I never remember her having saliva running from her mouth. I was not aware until you told me that I had sworn it, or I would not have done so if I had known it. She was quick-tempered, but quiet and harmless. I said in the affidavit, "Believing her to be of unsound mind and unable to enter into any contract, I advised her not to marry; but when I endeavoured to reason with her on the subject she became very violent, and has always been excited when I have spoken to her on the subject, and has even threatened to kill me." That is true; she did once threaten me. I verily believe she was of unsound mind and incapable of managing her property.

I know that my son Archibald has also made an affidavit, but I have never seen it. He is in Australia, at least he was some months ago. I don't know where he is at the present moment. She showed signs of violent temper to me when I spoke to her of marriage; I persuaded her not to marry. Drs. Tuke and Williams saw her; they reported her to be of sound mind. I say that she was hysterical. I did not say that on one occasion of an altercation I had with her she took out a knife to me, I said a chair—that was a mistake of somebody's. If I said a knife before the magistrate I must have confused it; I meant a chair. She took it up in a threatening way.

The last communication I had with her after her marriage, after I last saw her, was the letter that has been produced.[9] I only saw her on that one occasion after her marriage; the interview lasted about ten minutes. I had come from Essex. The meeting was quite a pleasant and harmonious one. When I saw her previously was before her marriage. I saw her once afterwards, about three weeks. It must have been twelve months since I saw her previously.

Mr. Staunton was present all the time of my last visit; my daughter answered the door. It was Mr. Staunton who spoke to me about a servant; we went into the dining-room, but Mr. Staunton was in a little conservatory close by. I considered it was not right to have no servant. I did not speak angrily. I was only doing my duty as a mother; she had

---

10 This is a mistake; the letter could not be found. See p. 47, *supra.*

Staunton Trial.

H. Butterfield scalded her hand. When he told me he had advertised for a servant I said no more. I then went upstairs. I said the bedroom wanted a bedstead, as there did not appear to be a room for the servant to sleep in. I said so to both; my daughter accompanied me over the house. It is a small house.

I do not know that Alice Rhodes was with my daughter at her confinement. The brooch referred to is of very little value, but my daughter prized it.

Cross-examined by Mr. STRAIGHT—I made Mrs. Patrick Staunton's acquaintance before she was married, some years ago, before I knew of the attachment of Louis Staunton to my daughter. I do not know how many children Mrs. Patrick had. I knew at the time she had been lodging at Loughborough Road she had children; I do not know how many.

I do not say I had not seen my daughter for nearly twelve months prior to her marriage. I saw her in Chancery Lane in 1874. The marriage was on 16th June, 1875; before that she went to Mrs. Ellis and remained till her death, and then she went to Mrs. Hincksman; the period of those visits extended over six months, perhaps more. She never wrote to me while staying with her aunt Ellis and Mrs. Hincksman; she could not write. She seldom or never wrote. She was not a good hand at letter-writing; she was a bad speller.

She was always violent to me if I spoke of marriage. I did not want her to be married; she was not fit. I know nothing of her threatening my son Archibald or of the pecuniary relationship between him and her at the time I took the proceedings in lunacy. She had not communicated with me about his being possessed of her money. I do not believe he knew anything about it; he was not trustee. I do not know that he had the administration of her £1500 or £1600 at the time of her marriage. I have never heard about it till I was cross-examined before. I never wrote a letter to my daughter after I paid the visit to her in the Loughborough Road. I received a letter from her requesting me not to call, also one from Louis Staunton complaining of my conduct.

I took active steps to discover her whereabouts after I heard of her confinement; that would be in March, 1876.

Little Grays farm lies back from the road. There is only a small lawn in front, and then the roadway. I noticed part of a shoulder of mutton on the table. It appeared as if some persons had partaken of a meal. It was a small house. I do not remember saying when in the house that I believed my daughter was in a lunatic asylum. I do not remember Mrs. Patrick Staunton saying that that was a wicked thing of me to say, and that she had had dinner with my daughter that day (5th March), and that she was quite well. I will swear that I did not say to Mrs. Patrick Staunton " That is a lie." or "You

52

Evidence for Prosecution.

are a liar." I was in considerable anxiety and distress about my daughter. I cannot remember saying before the magistrate at Bromley that I begged Mrs. Patrick Staunton to let me see my daughter, or that I said anything about "One day you may want to see one of your children." I recollect it was said, but not before the magistrate. When Patrick Staunton exhibited some anger towards me Mrs. Patrick said, "Don't strike her."

Cross-examined by Mr. GYE—At the meeting at London Bridge with Alice Rhodes I asked about my daughter, where she was. I never mentioned about her confinement. She said, "You should see Harriet with little Tommy; it is great fun." I understood that to be Mrs. Harriet Staunton's child. I did not make any reply to the observation, because I knew what she meant. I knew my girl was a very simple-minded girl, and I knew it would be fun to see her with a baby. I said nothing about little Tommy not being my daughter's child. I asked his name, and she told me it was Thomas Henry. Nothing was said about my daughter's health subsequent to her confinement. I simply asked how my daughter's health was. She said she had been very ill and had got better. That did not refer to the state of her health consequent upon her confinement. I wanted to know how she was at the present moment. She said she would write to me as to whether she had medical attention, and who the medical attendant was. She did not say that that illness was consequent upon her confinement. I cannot swear that when I told Alice Rhodes I wanted to see my daughter very much she said, "It is time you did see her"; if I said so before the magistrate it is correct.

Re-examined by the SOLICITOR-GENERAL—My son Archibald is twenty-five; he has been in Australia a year last January. I did not stay longer than ten minutes on my visit because I thought there might be words. They were kind and civil, and I thought I had better get away while they were civil. I was quite pleased to make friends because I knew Mr. Staunton was very much against me. Mr. Staunton did not in the least resent my remark about the room or the servant.

GEORGE CAKEBREAD, examined by the ATTORNEY-GENERAL—I am a porter at the Bromley railway station. I was there on the night of Thursday, 12th April. I remember seeing all the prisoners there that night. It was just as the train from Bickley was coming in, due at 8.26. It might have been two minutes late, but I cannot say.

One of the male prisoners spoke to me, I cannot say which. He asked me to ask the guard to keep the train, as he had got an invalid lady to go by the train. I was in the booking-office. I told him I could not do that. I then went outside the station.

Staunton Trial.

G. Cakebread I saw the two male prisoners lifting a female out of a wagonette. I saw the female prisoners come through the booking-office. The lady was got into the booking-office by one man getting hold of each side of her, and they lifted her down, when one of her slippers came off, and I picked it up and gave it to one of the male prisoners. I do not know what he did with it.

The lady was carried on to the platform. I took hold of one side of the lady, while one man got into the carriage, a first-class one; when in the carriage he took her arm from me; the other male prisoner had hold of the other arm in lifting her into the carriage. During that time I believe the slipper was dropped again. I did not see it.

All the prisoners got into the same carriage. I heard one of the female prisoners ask for five first-class tickets to Penge. I saw the lady; she looked very bad, and seemed to roll her eyes about very much. I never heard her speak. She did not seem as if she was able to stand on her legs.

Before the train started one of the prisoners asked me to put the trap up for him. I asked him where, and he said, " Over at Beaumont's "; that is a livery stable by the Two Brewers, opposite the station. I said yes, and they said they would see me when they came back. The train started towards Penge and London. No one else was in the carriage except the four prisoners and the lady.

I believe Cudham is about 7 or 8 miles from Bromley. The journey by train from Bromley to Penge would be about a quarter of an hour. I saw the two male prisoners again the same night at Bromley station. They arrived either by the 10.56 or 11.56 train, I cannot say which. One of them spoke to me about the trap before leaving the station. I did not see them in the carriage; I saw them leave the carriage.

I did not see a slipper at the station next morning. It was picked up by a porter named Watson. I saw it in the afternoon. It was a list slipper, similar to this one (*produced*) I picked up when the lady was getting out of the carriage.

H. Watson HENRY WATSON—I am a porter at Bromley station. I remember seeing a lady helped into a first-class carriage at 8.26 on 12th April; she was not able to walk; her feet dragged. I picked up a list slipper lying between the rail and platform the next morning.

R. Marsh ROBERT MARSH, examined by the SOLICITOR-GENERAL—I am a ticket collector at the Penge railway station. I remember the 8.36 p.m. train coming in on 12th April. The prisoners were in the train, and they had an invalid lady with them. Mr. Patrick Staunton lifted her out of the carriage. I noticed her condition and fetched a chair, and they put her on to it. She was unable to stand by herself. I cannot say whether she

54

Evidence for Prosecution.

was conscious. She was carried to a cab by the two male prisoners, and the driver was ordered to go to 34 Forbes Road. When Louis Staunton went to give up the tickets the female put out her arm; Mrs. Patrick Staunton put the shawl over her arm and said, " All right, you shall have your supper directly." The cab then drove away.

Cross-examined by Mr. EDWARD CLARKE—The prisoners were at the station about ten minutes altogether, and they stood round the chair while the lady was sitting in it. I did not hear the lady speak; she merely groaned. I heard her groan when she put her arm out. Louis Staunton was supporting her in the chair. The two female prisoners went away before the cab arrived; they went two or three minutes before the men did.

JAMES THOMAS HILDER, examined by the ATTORNEY-GENERAL— I was stationmaster at Penge in April last. I remember the 8.36 p.m. train coming in on the 12th. I saw the prisoners supporting a female on the platform, and I ordered the last witness to get a chair, which he did. The female was shaking very violently. I did not hear her speak. A cab was sent for. We had to send up into the village for one, and I advised the prisoners to carry her to it in the chair. This they did. The chair was put as close to the opening of the door as it was possible to get it, and in this way she was got into the cab.

CHARLES HEPPLETHWAITE, examined by Mr. POLAND—I am a cab driver. On the night of Thursday, 12th April, I was sent for to the Penge railway station. I got there about nine o'clock or a little after. I saw a lady brought out of the station in a chair, and she was put into the cab by the ticket collector and stationmaster. I think one of the gentlemen got inside the cab first. I saw nothing of any women there, only the two gentlemen.

I did not take any notice of the state of the lady. She did not speak; I did not notice her move. I was told to drive to 34 Forbes Road. The two gentlemen got into the cab with the lady. I could not get to 34 Forbes Road because the road was bad. I drove in at the other end of the road, to No. 26 or 27, as near as I could to No. 34. The lady was taken out by the two gentlemen, who carried her as far as the gate of No. 34, and I assisted one of the gentlemen with her up the steps and through the passage to the back room, which was level with the street door.

When we got to the house the street door was already open. I suppose the back room was a bedroom. We sat her down in a chair just inside the door. We got her up the steps by taking hold of her arms. She was not able to stand at all.

55

Staunton Trial.

She did not speak at that time. I did not take particular notice of her, only I thought she was rather light.

When we got into the back room I saw all four prisoners there. It took about five minutes to get from Penge railway station to the house. There was no luggage, only some parcels which they had inside with them.

Cross-examined by Mr. M. WILLIAMS—One of the men paid me my fare, and I went about my business in the ordinary way. It was about 20 yards from where the road was up to No. 34 Forbes Road, where we carried the lady. I helped to put her into the chair inside the room, but not when they brought her out of the station. I heard nothing more of it till Sergeant Bateman called me as a witness. I took no further notice about it.

E. Chalklin

EMMA CHALKLIN, examined by the SOLICITOR-GENERAL—I am the wife of David Chalklin. In April last I let apartments at 34 Forbes Road, Penge. On Thursday, the 12th of that month, about one o'clock, Louis Staunton and Mrs. Patrick Staunton came to inquire about the lodgings. They said they wanted them for an invalid lady for three weeks or a month. I let them the apartments—a sitting room and bedroom on the first floor—at 15s. per week. Louis Staunton gave me a card, on which was written, "Mrs. Staunton, Frith Cottage, Cudham." He said the invalid lady had had a doctor at Cudham, but he did not understand her case. Mrs. Patrick Staunton said their object in bringing her to Penge was to be nearer London for advice. Louis Staunton said he understood there were very good doctors in Penge, and asked if I could recommend one; I recommended him to go to Dr. Longrigg, who had attended my little girl.

Was anything said as to what the lady was suffering from? —Louis Staunton said she was inclined to be paralysed; her feet had begun to swell, and I think they considered that her head would become affected. They said that it would be better to bring her that night, and the doctor could see her in the morning. They said she was in good bodily health, and could eat, but she would not. Mrs. Staunton said it was only after a deal of persuasion they had that morning got her to take a little tea and some bread and butter and an egg. I was told to light a fire in the bedroom, and that the female would arrive about half-past nine o'clock that night. Louis Staunton said when they left my house they would go to Dr. Longrigg. In the evening the two female prisoners came to my house. One of them said the invalid lady had been very ill on the journey, and they could not account at all for her being taken so ill. I subsequently saw the invalid lady in bed. She had been brought in without my seeing her. She did not speak, but

Evidence for Prosecution.

made a kind of gurgling noise. She also moaned a great deal. **E. Chalklin**
I told the prisoners I was surprised to find the lady was so
ill that she had had to be put to bed. I said I expected to
have seen an elderly lady. Mrs. Patrick Staunton said the
invalid was thirty-six years of age, and was the wife of the
gentleman who had been there in the morning. She also said
that Miss Rhodes was married, but her husband was away,
and she had come to nurse the invalid lady. Miss Rhodes had
a wedding ring and keeper.

Was anything said of what had become of the two male
prisoners during this time?—Mrs. Patrick Staunton said they
had gone to the doctor. I asked if anything was wanted,
when Mrs. Staunton said they had brought all their provisions
with them except bread. Some time afterwards I was called
into the room, when I saw Louis Staunton. I do not know
how he had got into the house. I had not opened the door
to him. He said he had been to Dr. Longrigg's, but he was
out, and would not be home till one in the morning. He said
there was no one to take a message. I recommended
another medical gentleman, Dr. Turner, but Louis Staunton
said he did not think the case was so pressing—that
they could wait until the morning; he did not like to behave
like that to Mr. Longrigg without speaking to him. Shortly
after that Alice Rhodes came to the top of the stairs and asked
me to boil some eggs. She said the lady had woke up, and
fancied she would eat some supper, and she said, " I am sure
she must require some supper after her long journey." I
boiled the eggs and brought them to Alice Rhodes in the
sitting room. Mrs. Patrick Staunton then gave me another
egg to boil, which I did. Alice Rhodes was alone in the
sitting room putting on the cloth for supper.

Had the prisoners any luggage when they arrived at your
house?—Nothing but a large basket. They brought their own
table and bed linen. The next morning, about a quarter-past
eight o'clock, the bell was rung, and I went into the sitting
room. I there saw the two female prisoners sitting near the
window. They said they had been sitting up all night waiting for the doctor. Then they gave me another egg to boil.
Mrs. Patrick Staunton asked me to light the fire, as the doctor
would soon be there. I lit the fire; they had the folding doors
open, and were watching me all the time. The invalid lady
was in the next room, lying perfectly still in the bed. I
thought she was asleep. On the dressing table I noticed an
egg spread on some bread and butter. Subsequently Mrs.
Patrick Staunton asked me to send for the doctor. I said,
" When? " and she replied, " Presently will do." Shortly
after this Alice Rhodes called out from the sitting room, "Can't
you let the little girl go and fetch the doctor at once? " I said,
" Yes; the little girl shall go." Alice Rhodes said the lady

Staunton Trial.

E. Chalklin was very ill indeed, and I said, " Had not one of you better go and fetch the doctor ? " Alice Rhodes then got her jacket. She seemed to be very anxious, and I showed her the way to get to Dr. Longrigg's house. While Alice Rhodes was away Mrs. Patrick Staunton said the invalid lady came to her house on Saturday to see her, and they dined together. She said she was then apparently in good health; they had steak, potatoes, and turnip tops for dinner, and she said what a nice steak it was. She stayed during the remainder of the afternoon, and in the evening Mrs. Patrick Staunton said she went home with her. They had supper at the invalid lady's house, and it was after that she was taken poorly. Mrs. Patrick Staunton said she called upon the lady on Monday morning to see how she was, and she found her very ill. She said to her, " How ill you look, dear," to which the lady replied, " I am very ill." On Tuesday she seemed better, but on Wednesday and Thursday she was very poorly again. Mrs. Patrick Staunton said the invalid lady lived close to her.

About half-past ten o'clock the doctor arrived. He remained about ten minutes. After he had left I asked Mrs. Staunton what the doctor had said. She replied that the doctor said the lady had had an epileptic fit, and she must be kept very quiet, and have plenty of nourishment. It was likely her illness might last three weeks. She said the doctor was coming back in half an hour. I asked her when she thought the lady had had the fit, to which she replied, " Goodness gracious, I don't know." The doctor came a second time, between twelve and one o'clock. After he had gone, Mrs. Patrick Staunton rang the bell and called for a jug of hot water in a great hurry. About half-past two the baker came, and I was talking to him at the door when Mr. Lee, an undertaker, arrived. At that time I was not aware the lady was dead, and I sent the undertaker away, thinking he had made a mistake. About ten minutes afterwards I saw Mrs. Patrick Staunton standing at the sitting room door, and I asked how the lady was. She said, " She's gone." Later in the day there was a rap at the front door, and when I opened it I was surprised to see Mrs. Patrick Staunton, for I did not know she had gone out. She said, " Will you be kind enough to send my husband on to Bromley after me. He will understand what I mean." I asked whether Louis Staunton was in time to see his wife before she died. Mrs. Patrick Staunton said, " Yes, he was in the bedroom when she died." She added that herself and Alice Rhodes were away at the station at the time the death occurred. I had not seen Alice Rhodes since she went to fetch the doctor in the morning. I asked Mrs. Patrick Staunton whether I was to tell her husband about the death, and she said I was to please myself about that. I asked if there was anybody else in the house. She said, " No." I

58

Evidence for Prosecution.

said, " What! am I alone in the house, then? " She replied, E. Chalklin
" Yes, my sister has been gone some time, and the nurse will
come during the evening, and I will see you again." She
then went away. About a quarter to six Mr. Patrick Staunton
came, and I told him of the death. He said, " I knew she
was very ill when I was here this morning." He went away,
and after he had gone I found the door in which the deceased
lady was lying was locked, as well as the sitting room door.
On Saturday night the undertaker came, accompanied by the
nurse, who had got the keys of the doors. On Sunday Mrs.
Butterfield came, and she was allowed to see her dead daughter.
On the Sunday night the police came to the house with the
doctor.

Cross-examined by Mr. M. WILLIAMS—On Thursday morning
when Louis Staunton came to my place he wrote down on an
envelope, " Mrs. Staunton, Frith Cottage, Cudham, Kent,"
as being the address of the invalid lady. I have not got the
envelope. That was her proper address.

Before the magistrates I said that Louis Staunton said
he had had a doctor, but he did not understand the
work. I said to the Solicitor-General that he said he
had had a doctor at Cudham, but he did not understand
the case. I was asked the question where she had
a doctor; I said so before the magistrates at Bromley.
I did not say that he said a doctor had not seen her
at Cudham because he thought he would not understand
the case. I had been downstairs to get the envelope, and when
I came back he made that remark. He said he thought of
taking her to London at first, but that it would not suit her
head; it would be too noisy, and that he understood there
were very good doctors at Penge.

It was arranged they should bring their own linen. They
seemed surprised at her being taken so ill. When Mrs. Patrick
Staunton told me that the invalid lady was the wife of Louis
Staunton she volunteered that information to me, as also that
Alice Rhodes was Mrs. Patrick Staunton's sister. She brought
a high basket with her, somewhat higher than a hamper. I
think I said before the magistrates, " I got the breakfast, and
they wanted me to send for bacon, but Miss Rhodes went
because I could not send. I boiled an egg for the deceased
lady; I understood it was for the invalid lady." The egg was
lying on the plate, and I asked whether I should boil it, and
Mrs. Staunton said, " Yes, you may as well."

Cross-examined by Mr. STRAIGHT—The expression that Mrs.
Patrick made use of to me was that the doctors said Mrs.
Harriet had had an epileptic fit, not an apoplectic fit. Before
the magistrate I said that he said she must be under the

E. Chalklin   doctor's care three weeks. At the inquest I said, " She did not say whether the doctor said she would recover, but that he thought he could bring her round in three weeks." I noticed on the Friday morning when I saw Mrs. Patrick Staunton that she seemed tired and worn out. I think I used the expression that she seemed as if she had been sitting up all night. During the time she was at my house she seemed to be making every effort she could to assist the unfortunate lady. They both did.

Cross-examined by Mr. GYE—When Alice Rhodes said that the invalid had woke up and wanted some supper, she seemed anxious for her to have it.

By the ATTORNEY-GENERAL—Several times Alice Rhodes made the remark that she could not understand her being taken so ill.

By Mr. GYE—In the morning, about nine o'clock, when Mrs. Staunton asked me to send for the doctor, Alice Rhodes was present. Afterwards Alice Rhodes asked me the same question; they were in the sitting room the first time they asked. I went downstairs, and when I came up again they were in the bedroom, and then Alice Rhodes asked me if I could send for the doctor directly. It was a few minutes before Mrs. Staunton asked me that Alice asked me. They had just had time to go into the bedroom. When Alice Rhodes asked me she said, " Can she go at once? " She came into the sitting room with her jacket in her hand, put it on, and Mrs. Patrick Staunton said, " You go, my dear; you can go quickest," and Alice Rhodes went immediately. I went down to the gate with her, and I made the remark to her, " I would not return without the doctor," and she said, " No, that I won't." I showed her the quickest, the straightest way. She appeared to go off in a great hurry for him.

I assumed that Louis Staunton and Mrs. Patrick Staunton had engaged the rooms of me, and I thought the patient was living with them. Mrs. Patrick Staunton, I thought, had charge of the woman Harriet Staunton. She did not say so, but I thought so. I was not asked the question before the magistrate whether Mrs. Patrick Staunton had the charge of her that I can remember. I thought Mr. Louis Staunton and Mrs. Patrick Staunton were man and wife. I considered Mrs. Patrick Staunton had charge of the woman who was ill when they were in the house on the Thursday morning. I did not see anything in the conduct of Alice Rhodes inconsistent with anxiety for the invalid. She seemed very anxious.

Re-examined by the SOLICITOR-GENERAL—I have told you all I saw with regard to the treatment of the invalid lady.

It now being twenty minutes past five o'clock, the further hearing of the case was adjourned.

Second Day—Thursday, 20th September, 1877.

ELLEN GOODINGE, examined by the SOLICITOR-GENERAL—I was E. Goodinge engaged by Dr. Longrigg as nurse to Harriet Staunton. That was about eleven on the morning of Friday, 13th April, this year. I went at once. Alice Rhodes showed me into the room where the patient was. Alice Rhodes gave me a blister. I went downstairs to make beef tea, and then went direct into the room. The patient was lying as if in a fit. She never moved at all until she died.

Did you try to ascertain if she was conscious?—Yes, I spoke to her. Then I went for Mr. Louis Staunton to see if she would speak to him. He came into the room with his brother. They both stood some minutes in the room. I pointed them out to her, but she took no notice of them. They did not speak to her. About twelve o'clock I told them to send for the doctor, as the lady was much worse. That was in the front room. Louis at once went. I tried to give her food and some medicine, but she could not swallow anything. I noticed, about half-past one, that she was dying, and I asked Louis Staunton, who was in the sitting room, if he would like to see the last of his lady, as I did not think she would be here very long. Mrs. Patrick Staunton, who was also in the sitting room, said, " Don't ask him, nurse; you worry him so."

What happened next?—She died.

How soon after?—Not many minutes.

The JUDGE—Did either of them go into the room before she died?—No, my lord.

By the SOLICITOR-GENERAL—The rooms were on the same floor, communicating by folding doors. From the time I saw her until she died, she had neither moved nor spoken. I told them the lady was dead. I wanted sheets to lay her out, and asked if I should ask the landlady. Mrs. Patrick Staunton said that I had better not ask the landlady, as she might not have any, for the room was poorly furnished and there was no blind to the window. I asked if I should borrow sheets, and she said she would be very much obliged if I would.

Yes?—I went to where I had been nursing before and borrowed a pair. I got a little water to wash her.

What was the condition of the body?—I went to wash her, but the body was in so filthy a state I could not. The head was alive with lice, but the body was not—at least, I did not

61

E. Goodinge see any on it. The dirt on the body was of such a kind that I could not wash it off with a flannel. I never saw anything like it before. I did not examine the legs or feet.

What kind of dirt was it?—Something like the bark of a tree, as if it had been on the body for a long time and not washed at all.

What had she on?—A nightgown and chemise.

Did you take them off?—Yes.

How?—I tore them off.

Did you put a clean nightdress on?—Yes. Before her death Dr. Longrigg came in and said to me she was dying. He then went into the front room to the Stauntons. I did not hear what passed.

Did you hear anything about the undertaker?—I mentioned to Mr. Louis Staunton about Mr. Lee, an undertaker, and he told me to give him an order for a black coffin, a hearse and coach, and to say that the funeral was to take place on Monday. When I went for the sheets I left word at the Park Tavern for the undertaker to come. When I had laid out the body Louis Staunton and Mrs. Patrick Staunton spoke to me about going home, as they lived so far away. The two rooms were locked up, and I had the key of the front room, Mrs. Staunton saying I should keep it; they expected friends to see her, and it would be handier for me to keep the key.

Did you register the death?—Yes; in consequence of a conversation with Dr. Longrigg. That was on the Saturday morning.

On the Saturday night the police came to you for the key?—Yes. The police and Dr. Longrigg came up with another gentleman and called for the body. From the Friday till the Saturday night the body was left alone.

Mr. JUSTICE HAWKINS—Quite alone?—Yes; the door was locked, and I had a key at the Park Tavern.

Cross-examined by Mr. WILLIAMS—Louis Staunton told me when I took the key that I was to show the body to anybody that came. I do not remember that on the Friday morning I had a conversation with Mr. Patrick Staunton about a patient that died in a fit, and lay for some time without taking any notice; but I told him that Harriet Staunton lay as I had seen other people lie in fits before. I do not think she could understand what was going on, but I tried to make her understand. I do not think she was conscious any time after I first saw her.

Did you at any time on the Friday morning say to Louis Staunton, " If you come into the room, sir, I think she will know you "?—Yes.

Did you say you had seen a great many people suffering from the same kind of fits?—Yes.

Evidence for Prosecution.

Did he say, " How she has changed "?—I don't remember ; **E. Goodinge**
but I cannot say that he did not. It was about eleven o'clock
when I asked him to go for the doctor, and he at once did so.

After the death did you ask Mr. Staunton to " leave everything to me "?—I did not. I did not say, " Don't bother
yourself, it will do no good ; leave everything to me, I
will see to everything." He told me to look after everything, and show the body to anybody who came. The key
was to be left at the Park Tavern, but the barman was not to
show the body to strangers. If strangers came I was to go
over and show the body to them. The conversation took place
after I had laid the body out.

Did you say anything to him about the dirty state of the
body ?—No.

Or about the state you say her head was in ?—No.

Had you discovered that before the women left ?—I had not
seen the dirt on the body or the state of the hair before Mrs.
Patrick Staunton left. I did not mention it to any of the
prisoners.

Cross-examined by Mr. STRAIGHT—I did not notice whether
the deceased's arm was rigid for the last half-hour of her life.
She never moved her eyes ; they were fixed.

Did Mrs. Patrick Staunton appear to be exhausted and
distressed ?—She appeared very nervous when I spoke to her.

She did not look to you as if she had been sitting up all
night ?—No ; neither of them did.

When did the police come ?—Between nine and ten on the
Saturday night.

Cross-examined by Mr. GYE—Alice Rhodes gave me the
blister and the beef tea ; it was by the doctor's orders. I
endeavoured to get the patient to swallow the beef tea.

And Alice Rhodes assisted you ?—She held the cup. The
hands and face of the patient were cleaner than the other
parts of the body. There was dirt from illness on the nightdress, and it looked as if it had been worn for a week or
rather more. Before the magistrate I said there was no
particular dirt on the nightdress. I do not remember using
the words, " I did not observe any dirt on the nightdress or
on the face neither during life or when I laid her out."

There was a great deal of hair ?—Yes.

Mr. JUSTICE HAWKINS—Do you mean real or false hair ?—
False, I believe it was, but I did not remove it.

The SOLICITOR-GENERAL—Had the hair been attended to ?—I
did not examine it when I saw the state in which the head was ;
her hair was alive with lice.

By Mr. JUSTICE HAWKINS—During the night she had suffered
much from diarrhœa. In the morning, when I first went,
I saw Alice Rhodes. I don't remember that she told me any-

63

Staunton Trial.

thing about the diarrhœa. No one said a word about it until I discovered it myself.

Did you mention it?—No.

Do you think the hair had been combed or brushed for any time?—It had not been combed or brushed for a very long time.

JOSEPH LEE, examined by Mr. POLAND—I am an undertaker at Penge. On Friday, 13th April, Dr. Longrigg's assistant came to me about two o'clock. I went to 34 Forbes Road at Mrs. Chalklin's. In the front parlour I saw two of the prisoners, Louis Staunton and Mr. Patrick Staunton. I got instructions to bury the body at Beckenham on the Monday. I said forty-eight hours' notice would have to be given to open the ground. It was arranged that the funeral should take place on the Monday at two o'clock. Louis Staunton gave me the name, Harriet Staunton, aged thirty-four, to put on the coffin.

Did he give you his address?—Yes.

What address?—Mr. L. Staunton, Little Grays farm, Cudham.

What for?—In case I should want to write to him in order to let him know what time the funeral would take place.

Was anything said about the cost of the funeral?—He said he would want it respectable, but not too expensive. I was not told what relation the lady was.

Was anything said about the number of followers?—I understood they were to be him and a lady—the mother, I thought, of the deceased. On the Saturday I took the coffin, and put the body in it, but the coffin was not screwed down. The nurse opened the room for me.

Is Penge in two counties?—Yes ; Kent and Surrey. Part of Forbes Road is in one county and part in the other ; No. 34 is in the county of Kent and the parish of Beckenham. The place of registration would be Bromley ; but for the Surrey part of Forbes Road the registration would have to take place at Croydon. The funeral did not take place on the Monday. There was an inquiry, and it was postponed for some time. Mr. Staunton paid me £9 6s.

Cross-examined by Mr. M. WILLIAMS—When there was any suggestion of an inquest did Louis Staunton stop the funeral?— He said he would rather wait than that there should be anything wrong. He said that to me at Cudham when I had gone down on the Sunday when everything was ready.

Re-examined by the ATTORNEY-GENERAL—On the Saturday night Sergeant Bateman told me not to carry out the funeral. On Sunday I went to Cudham to know what I was to do. I knew then that inquiries had been made.

Mr. H. B. Poland

Evidence for Prosecution.

to refer to the whole of the book, and two and a half pages of them were my notes made at the post-mortem examination; they were the only notes I made. The book is lost and cannot be found.

I have some notes with me. I made the first set of notes, which I have still in my possession, half an hour or an hour after the post-mortem examination. I had not seen Dr. Bright's notes; I have my notes here; my dispenser has them in the bag. They are not an exact copy of the notes in the book that I lost; there is a great addition to them. The set of notes I made half an hour after the examination are on the blue paper. They were made before I had seen Dr. Bright at all; the other set of notes, Dr. Bright's, were made on the Sunday. The post-mortem examination was on the Thursday, I think.

I read Dr. Bright's notes all over; he gave them to me. The notes endorsed " Dr. Longrigg's notes of the post-mortem examination," were sent to Professor Rodgers. The second set of notes I made contain a narrative of the conversation that took place; I put it down, and then an account of the post-mortem appearances in cases of death from starvation; they are for my own observation; it was not written when the notes were written; it was a day afterwards. The two sets of notes are the only papers or notes I have of the post-mortem examination.

The chief part of the post-mortem examination—the dirty part of it—was done by my partner, Mr. Piggott. I dissected all the viscera and the brain. I think the height of the woman was 5 feet 5 inches; you will see it in the notes. When I speak of the average weight as between 9 and 10 stones I compare it to a woman of that height; the lightest weight I have known for a woman of that height in average health is about 9 stones or 9 stones 4 lbs.; it depends upon the build.

I was not informed by Harriet Staunton's mother that her daughter's weight at her healthiest did not exceed 8 stones; Dr. Bright told me that. The weight depends upon the build; it depends upon the framework; if the framework is slight it might not be 9 stones   It is within my experience that a person of the height of 5 feet 4½ inches might be considerably less than 9 stones in weight, and yet a healthy person.

The weights of the particular organs were calculated in reference to the weight of the whole body. The heart would be one two hundred and fortieth part of the weight of the whole body calculated in that way. Taking the actual weight of the body, the weight of the different organs of the body corresponded with the natural proportions. Whatever the weight of the body might be, the heart would be one two hundred and fortieth of it.

By the COURT—In this case the heart, for instance, corresponded with the actual weight of the body as I found it; if the

D. Longrigg body had been 9 stones the heart would have been so much larger. Taking the weight of the body, the organs were considerably under the size I expected to find them. Nine or 10 stones should be the average weight of a woman 5 feet 5½ inches; if the weight had been from 9 to 10 stones then the internal organs, the liver and so on, would have been much larger than the organs as I found them in the body that was before me; the organs of the body as I found them were of the same size as I should expect to find them in a body that was only 5 feet 5 inches; the internal organs were proportionate to the weight.

By Mr. CLARKE—The spleen weighed 4½ ounces, and should have weighed 7 ounces. I gave a lower weight than 7 ounces before the magistrate as a natural weight; I said 5½ ounces to 7 ounces; 5½ ounces would represent a healthy state, but it is a mistake that it averages 5½ to 7 ounces. What I said before the magistrate was, "Weighing 4½ ounces against 5½ ounces to 7"; 5½ ounces is correct. The proportionate weight of the liver to the whole body in ordinary cases would be about one thirty-fifth. I did not weigh the brain.

My observations during life showed me nothing inconsistent with the account given by the prisoners. I believed what was told me. When I gave my certificate I had no reason to suspect anything; I gave it in good faith, and, so far as I was able, the cause of death stated in my certificate was the cause. I had no idea at the time that there was any starvation. Her symptoms did not indicate either poison or starvation.

The chief of the head symptoms before death was the dilatation of the pupils and stertorous breathing; the pupils were unequally dilated, and that is evidence of brain mischief, an unmistakable sign. If I had felt any doubt on the matter as to the cause of death I should have asked who the doctor was that had been attending her, and probably have put myself in communication with him before I gave my certificate; there was a special hurry about the certificate; there is not in an ordinary case, but there was in this.

I saw Mr. Casabianca the following day; he called on me; he was a perfect stranger to me. Mrs. Casabianca did not come with him. It was the day after the death that Mr. Casabianca came, the same day that the certificate was given.

I did not know anything about the Stauntons having gone back to Cudham when I gave my certificate. I had not heard that either of them was going back. I had seen the nurse I recommended in attendance myself. I wrote this letter to the coroner, after seeing Mr. Casabianca, on the strength of what he said.

16th April, 1877,
Penge, S.E.

My dear Sir,—On Friday last I was called to a case of a some-

72

Evidence for Prosecution.

what peculiar character, and, from information afforded me, considered the symptoms sufficient to justify my giving a certificate of death; but from what I have since been told me I am of opinion that the circumstances necessitate an inquisition into the cause. The sergeant who delivers this to you will be able to give you all needful information. With kind regards, your faithfully,

DEAN LONGRIGG.

P.S.—The name of the deceased is Mrs. Staunton, a niece of Lord Rivers.

Mr. Casabianca gave me the information contained in the postscript. He gave me a history of the lady and the family. He said there had been foul play. In consequence of that I put myself in communication with the police and the coroner. Then the post-mortem examination took place.

I was suspicious of poisoning at one time of the post-mortem examination; I did not come to that conclusion; there were symptoms resembling poison; the idea was not suggested to me, it was my own observation. We had a conversation about it. We came to the conclusion that death was from starvation. It was after we had finished the examination that I and the other medical gentlemen came to the opinion there had been poisoning, and determined to send the intestines to Dr. Rodgers. We could not find enough disease to account for death.

The congested state of the upper part of the stomach was the first symptom that gave me the idea of poisoning; that was discovered in the early part of the post-mortem examination. The brain was opened first and the chest afterwards. I will undertake to say the word starvation was mentioned during the examination; I dare say I mentioned it; I mentioned it as one of the causes of death; we all mentioned starvation.

I have seen several cases of persons who died in a state of great emaciation. I have seen post-mortem examinations of cases called starvation, and have seen similar appearances; cases not exactly from disease, but from want of food, exposure to the cold, and want of proper nourishment. I have attended such persons before their death; there is no difficulty in inducing them to take food; it depends upon the state of their sensibility. I did not find anything in this case that looked like a refusal to take food. The egg remained on the tongue from insensibility and from inability to swallow it.

Indications of intemperate habits would easily be discovered; there would always be a trace of those habits if they had ceased some months before death, though not of a very serious kind— I am of that opinion. I do not think there would be any difficulty in discovering it. In the case of a woman who had contracted a habit of intemperance which had been indulged in for, say, twelve months, and who was deprived of the opportunity, and who died six months afterwards, traces of that

D. Longrigg would be discovered; you would find an enlargement of the liver and of the heart and a dilated condition of the blood-vessels of the brain—that would always be present if the person had been a drunkard or a person of strong intemperate habits. In the case of a woman who, living at her own house, takes too much wine or too much spirit, you would have symptoms of it then, but not so well marked as in a strictly intemperate person. I think that would necessarily be visible if a person is given to indulging, although it had been abandoned six or seven months.

The heart and the liver were not enlarged, but the blood-vessels of the brain were distended. I attribute that to other causes. Congestion of the coats of the stomach led me early in the post-mortem examination to a suspicion of poison. The principal matters discovered in the post-mortem examination which led me to the conclusion of poison were the congestion of the stomach, congestion about the rectum, the congestion of the vagina and uterus, and the congested condition of the brain externally and internally. I did not form so strong an opinion that poison had been administered as I did of starvation.

I do not recollect whether I said before the magistrate that the symptoms conveyed to my mind that it was a suspicious case of poisoning, or that I agreed that there were strong signs of poisoning. We thought that it was poison or starvation, and I thought that Professor Rodgers' analysis would find it out. My memory will not carry me so far back as to recollect positively what I said—it is three or four months since I was examined, and you cannot expect me to recollect. If I said I thought Professor Rodgers' analysis would find that there had been sufficient poison to cause death it is true, of course. What I said before the magistrate was taken down, but I do not recollect using the expression. The symptoms I have mentioned to you as indicating the presence of poison would also be referable to starvation. All the symptoms I did observe were fairly traceable to starvation. I do not think I said the inflammation of the peritoneum was, for instance; but the peritoneum was slightly inflamed.

I have never heard of a case where the simple absence of nourishment has produced inflammation of the peritoneum, not what I call peritonitis. That is a symptom of starvation. I know it from what I have heard other medical men say and from what I have read. I cannot say that I have ever seen it.

I cut the stomach open and examined it carefully. I have given you all that I observed as far as I am aware. The stomach was not of its ordinary size, substance, and thickness. It was rather thinner than in nature; the mucous membrane

Evidence for Prosecution.

of the stomach was thin.   I had my notes with me before **D. Longrigg**
the magistrate, but they were taken from me.   I have had
them back since from the Treasury.   I have been examined
two or three times.   I have never mentioned the thinning of
the coats of the stomach until you put the question.[1]

Before the magistrates, did you say that all the organs of the
deceased were healthy except the left lung?—I said the left
lung was diseased.

Did you say all the organs were healthy except the left lung?
—I might have done so.

Did you say so?—If I said so, it was an answer given in
confusion.

But you are not confused now?—No; but you are trying to
make me so.

Do you remember what you said before the magistrates?—I
do not remember all I said.

Mr. JUSTICE HAWKINS—The evidence of the witness before the
magistrates extends over thirty pages, and you cannot expect
a man to remember every word he said in such an examination.

Mr. CLARKE—I do not ask him to remember every word he
said before the magistrates, but to remember a matter of the
utmost importance.

Mr. JUSTICE HAWKINS—Well, he says he does not recollect
that he said so.

Mr. CLARKE—Did you say anything in the notes you made of

---

[1] At this point the Court adjourned for luncheon, and on his
return Mr. Justice Hawkins said that he proposed to sit until six
o'clock to-day; but he understood the jury would like to have a
little fresh air if the Court could rise earlier.

The FOREMAN OF THE JURY—I did not know at the time I asked that
we might adjourn earlier that it was such a wet day, and that there
was, therefore, little chance of our going out.

Mr. JUSTICE HAWKINS—There appears to be little chance of the
weather clearing up to-day, so I think it may be settled that we
sit till six o'clock, as I am anxious we should make the best of our
time in order that the case may finish on Saturday night.

Mr. M. WILLIAMS—I may say that I do not think there is any
chance of the case finishing on Saturday night.

Mr. JUSTICE HAWKINS—If I had known that yesterday I certainly
should not have taken this case until Friday morning. We commenced this case on the understanding that it was to finish on
Saturday night, and if it does not, it has misled everybody.

.Mr. M. WILLIAMS—I have not misled anybody.   I could only
express a hope that it might be finished on Saturday; but I could
not possibly tell how long the examination of some witnesses might
last.

Mr. JUSTICE HAWKINS—Well, we will see what can be done by
sitting late to-morrow and on Saturday.

The FOREMAN OF THE JURY—If the case is not to finish on Saturday, I hope it may not be necessary to keep us sitting in the box
so many hours each day.

Mr. JUSTICE HAWKINS—I am not at all certain that we may not
finish the case by Saturday.

The FOREMAN OF THE JURY—Thank you, my lord.

Staunton Trial.

D. Longrigg the post-mortem examination about the coats of the stomach being thin?—No, I do not think I did.

But you have been examined from your notes, and ought to know?—No, I have not been examined from my notes.

Mr. JUSTICE HAWKINS—The witness has not been examined from his notes to-day.

Mr. CLARKE—He had the notes when he was examined before the magistrates?—No, the notes were taken from me then, the same as they have been to-day.

Have you not had your notes since you were before the magistrates?—Yes, I got them from the Treasury.

Mr. JUSTICE HAWKINS—You have got the notes to-day, Mr. Clarke, and can surely see what is in them, and if they are put in you can cross-examine upon the point.

WITNESS—I think it is very unfair Mr. Clarke should have my notes at all. They are my private property.

The thinning of the coats of the stomach would be a strong indication of starvation; one of the most natural and obvious signs. That is a matter which I have considered as important,

The condition of the brain was firm; that is a condition indicative of the healthy condition of the brain, that it should be firm several days after death. It was a very healthy conditioned brain. The brain was not wasted and pale. In a case of starvation of the brain, I will not say would be wasted, but it would be pale; I should expect to find it pale. The brain was healthy. I will not be positive, but I believe in cases of starvation the brain is very little affected, or the nervous system at all. I should expect to find it pale, but not wasted. There was a very general congestion of the external and internal blood-vessels.

I do not consider the inequality of the pupils of the eyes a condition of starvation; it is a marked symptom of brain disease.

Phthisis will produce emaciation. There was a small patch of it in the present case, but not enough of it to account for death.

The taking of certain poisons, I believe, would cause emaciation and a bronzing of the skin. Diabetes produces emaciation and a dark or bronzed condition of the skin. There is a dark appearance in the skin caused by diabetes, but I never saw a case where the skin was so bronzed as in this case.

I have not had much experience of Addison's disease; it is an obscure disease, and I am not sufficiently acquainted with it to give an explanation of it. There are frequent head symptoms in diabetes and in Addison's disease, and in the former you have coma sometimes and stertorous breathing, and they would be similar to the symptoms observed in this case.

Evidence for Prosecution.

In diabetes there is sugar in the urine. I did not test the urine in this case. There were 3 ounces of urine in the body. Addison's disease would leave its trace in the super-renal capsules. I examined the kidneys, but not separately. In diabetes, as death approached you would find occasionally coma and stertorous breathing and dilatation of the eyes. That appearance is not at all uncommon. I have read that tubercles on the lungs are often found in connection with Addison's disease.

I did not examine the tubercles on the brain with a microscope. I did not attach importance to it, as they were so plain to be seen. I did not consider it necessary to go further. The finding of tubercles in the brain was important, but not more so than the finding of tubercles in the lungs, but I did not follow up that discovery by any microscopic examination.

I know a disease called granular or miliary tubercle. It takes its name from grains like millet seeds in the brain, and is the same sort of thing that I found in this case. The presence of tubercles in the meshes of the brain constitutes tubercular meningitis.

It is a fatal disease. I have never seen a case recover. I had five cases in one house after fever. It was in children; the eldest was eighteen. It did not produce great emaciation in those cases. They got much thinner, but I could not call it true emaciation. Its effects are very rapid. It is seven or ten days, and sometimes only forty-eight hours, before death ensues.

Local disease may exist without tubercular disease, but if in combination with tubercle in other parts of the body it would create a serious complication. It would produce the disease called acute general tuberculosis. Of that disease I have had considerable experience. It produces great emaciation, and there are head symptoms in some cases.

Tubercular meningitis or acute general tuberculosis would not account for the symptoms in this case. In this case an acute tubercular disease was not sufficiently established to produce the symptoms I saw; there was not enough of it.

If there had been a stronger condition of the disease itself it would have produced all the symptoms which appeared in this case, except the rigidity of the muscles of the upper extremities. I have not seen any rigidity in death from tuberculosis. I will not say positively that it might not exist, but I have never seen it; and that is the only symptom I can point out that might not have been caused by those diseases. In this case the disease was not sufficiently advanced. I express that opinion positively. The amount of tubercle was very slight, both in the lungs and the brain.

I did not examine the brain with a microscope. The

Staunton Trial.

D. Longrigg microscope is a great advantage to diagnosis, but it would not have told me more than I knew, namely, that there was tubercle. You could see with the naked eye the amount of tubercle that was there. I cannot speak so positively as if I had resorted to the use of the microscope. I speak positively that what I saw was tubercle. I did not see what the microscope would show me. I have no hesitation in my mind; I still adhere to the opinion which I have expressed all through. We all found the appearance of cerebral disease in the shape of these tubercles which have been spoken of.

My original certificate does not fairly represent my views. I consider it correct to a certain extent, with modifications. I arrived at the conclusion that there was poison, and was surprised to find Professor Rodgers did not discover any. I thought he might have done so. I formed my opinion before the analyst's report. I said I believed Professor Rodgers might find poison.

Re-examined by the ATTORNEY-GENERAL—They came to my house for the certificate several times when I was away on a visit. It was filled in, but there was no signature. Louis Staunton came himself and saw my wife. He pressed for the certificate. He saw it in the surgery. I did not have any conversation personally with Louis Staunton about the certificate, nor with any of the prisoners. There had been more than one application for the certificate, but not to me personally. When I said there was hurry for the certificate, I alluded to these applications. I signed it when I was at dinner on the day following the death, about four o'clock.

Stiffness of limbs is not produced by paralysis. When paralysed they are useless. Paralysis deprives the limb of all muscular power. When a limb is paralysed it becomes atrophied.

The bites were produced during life; I have no doubt of that. The bite of a louse is like being pricked suddenly with a pin. Bites after death would not produce those appearances.

I thought poison might have been administered because of the congested state of the organs I have described. Congestion is an effect of an irritant poison, but might be produced by starvation or by eating after going without food for a long period. The appearances I saw in the eyes might be symptoms of narcotics, as well as the congestion. There was a general thinning, not only of the stomach, but of all sorts, which might be produced by emaciation. Any exhaustive disease that causes emaciation might cause a thinning of the stomach, but it is invariable in cases of starvation.

A patient suffering from diabetes would complain of all food, whether liquid or solid, turning to urine, and of the immense quantity of urine that would pass. This causes a gradual

Evidence for Prosecution.

wasting of the body, but it is a long time before it terminates **D. Longrigg** fatally, and that time varies very much. I have seen several cases of diabetes. The patient would also complain of great thirst. Extraordinary thirst is a frequent accompaniment of diabetes, but not an invariable one. If Mrs. Harriet Staunton had been suffering from diabetes for a considerable time I am sure those about her would have known it. The passing of an extreme quantity of urine is an invariable symptom of diabetes. The kidneys are also enlarged and spongy. On the post-mortem examination in this case we found that the kidneys were not enlarged. On the contrary, they were smaller than usual.

I have had no experience in Addison's disease. I believe it is a very rare disease. In ordinary language tubercular meningitis is an inflammation of the brain. There is a tubercular deposit. Tubercular meningitis will produce emaciation, but must exist some time to do that. If Mrs. Harriet Staunton had been suffering from that disease it must have existed for a considerable time, and she would have been in an enfeebled state for some time before her death, and the disease would have been more developed than it was. If she had suffered from acute tuberculosis the brain would be soft. My opinion is that her death was not caused by diabetes or tubercular meningitis, but by starvation. The doctors present at the post-mortem examination discussed the matter amongst ourselves, and we all agreed. Dr. Harman was there on behalf of the prisoners. If the patient suffered from starvation it might bring on a fit.

Dr. JOHN MEABURN BRIGHT, examined by Mr. POLAND—I am **J. M. Bright** a Doctor of Medicine of St. Andrews, M.B., C.S., and Licentiate of the Apothecaries Company. I live at Forest Hill, and have been in general practice for a period of fourteen years. I was present at the post-mortem examination of the deceased on the 19th of April. I was requested to attend on behalf of the relatives. I have heard Mr. Longrigg's account of the appearances presented by the deceased.

Has he accurately described them?—On the whole I believe he has done so.

Were there appearances which pointed to poison?—There were, and all the medical men agreed that there ought to be an analysis.

No poison was found?—None.

In your judgment what was the cause of death?—I have no doubt whatever that the cause of death, on the whole, was starvation and exhaustion. There was no fat whatever which we could detect.

Can you form an opinion as to the time this emaciation had been coming on?—It is difficult to say definitely.

79

Staunton Trial.

J. M. Bright   But, say, roughly?—I should say three or four months. I have had no personal experience of other cases of starvation, and I say this from my reading of analogous cases.

As a medical man you would say the condition must have been coming on gradually?—Yes.

And must have been apparent to those about the deceased?—I should say so.

The muscles were very much wasted?—Yes. Some time before her death, I should say, she had lost the power of motion.

How long before death do you think it would be when she lost the power to walk?—A week or a fortnight.

Her general condition was such as to require regular medical care and treatment, and also good nursing?—Undoubtedly.

You have heard that the night before her death she was taken in a wagonette, removed to a railway station, and afterwards taken a railway journey of 7 or 8 miles. In your judgment, would that accelerate death?—I should say undoubtedly.

Were the vermin bites you saw on the body of the deceased caused during life or after death?—During life.

Cross-examined by Mr. CLARKE—I noticed bites on the abdomen, and the insects themselves in the hair. In answering the question as to Mrs. Harriet Staunton's power to move before her death, I assumed she died from starvation. I am judging simply of her condition, the appearances before and after death. I only saw the deceased at the post-mortem examination, and my opinion is formed upon what I saw, and upon what Mr. Longrigg said. I formed my opinion then from the post-mortem examination, and from a history of the symptoms during life. I did not form any opinion as to the power of motion at the post-mortem examination.

I have no doubt the word " starvation " was mentioned there ; I do not recollect it, but I have been told so. There was but little conversation in the room; most of the conversation took place downstairs. I told Mr. Lewis[2] I did not hear the word " starvation " mentioned, and I referred to the time the post-mortem examination was going on. I never said death was caused by starvation alone. What I said was that the general appearances of the body were characteristic of starvation, but there were special appearances which led us to believe that an analysis was necessary. I did not suggest it was starvation and poison, in those words. I do not like the word " suggest." We all agreed on one point. I could not give an opinion as to the immediate cause of death. I expressed an opinion that she died of starvation. I could not form any opinion unless I had an analysis.

---

2 The solicitor for the defence.

Mr. Douglas Straight

Evidence for Prosecution.

J. M. Bright

I took notes at the time, and gave them to Mr. Longrigg two or three days afterwards. Mr. Longrigg, Dr. Wilkinson, and I had a meeting afterwards. My notes were read over at that meeting. They were discussed between us. I have them with me. I had a description of the symptoms before death from Mr. Longrigg. Those symptoms led me to the suspicion that the deceased had been poisoned by opium. They pointed in that direction, as I thought.

I then proceeded with the post-mortem examination, and on the stomach being opened there was a redness on the stomach, the small intestines, and the lower part of the bowels. That led me to the suspicion of an irritant poison. The matter was submitted to Dr. Rodgers.

I have not seen any case of starvation. I don't think my information scanty on the subject; I have tried to read everything upon it. After this matter I referred to Dr. Taylor's book on medical jurisprudence; it was a book which I borrowed. That is not the only work I have referred to with regard to starvation. I think that was the only work I had seen before I was examined before the magistrate. What I said before the magistrate as to the cause of death was accurate. I had only read Taylor's book up to that time. I said the information was very scanty in the book. I don't remember the exact words; if it is in my deposition it is quite true.

Cross-examined by Mr. STRAIGHT—At the close of the post-mortem examination I determined to defer my opinion until Dr. Rodgers' report.

Re-examined by the ATTORNEY-GENERAL—I think we all tacitly agreed that the symptoms pointed in one direction—that the general appearance of the body was most characteristic of starvation, but we all wished for an analysis of the contents of the stomach. Starvation would produce the emaciation that I saw in the body of this woman. The other symptoms that I saw would have been produced precisely if she had been kept for some time without food, and the emaciation caused in that way, and then poison had been administered to her.

I had a difficulty in coming to the conclusion as to the immediate cause of death. I thought narcotic poison would produce the appearances I saw in the eyes, and which were described to me by Mr. Longrigg. I think in a convulsion the distinction between opium poisoning and apoplexy is exceedingly difficult to discover. I was present and heard Mr. Longrigg examined. In my opinion this lady's death was not caused by diabetes. I cannot reconcile it with the view of tubercular meningitis or Addison's disease.

By Mr. CLARKE—There was urine discovered at the post-mortem examination. Undoubtedly, with regard to diabetes, the examination of the urine is the simplest and most perfect way of testing the presence of that disease. That is generally

Staunton Trial.

J. M. Bright considered the test symptom. The examination of the super-renal capsules can only take place after death. With regard to Addison's disease there are certain symptoms during life which are unmistakable. In examining for that disease after death I should feel it necessary to examine the super-renal capsules. I think in this case such an examination was overlooked.

I noticed tubercles in the brain myself. I made no microscopic examination. I remember they were put aside for examination with some of the matter of the tubercular deposit. I have no knowledge if they were ever examined. The presence of tubercles in the meshes of the brain and the existence of tubercular matter in the lungs was a very important coincidence taken together.

I have had the treatment of tubercular meningitis; it is a local disease to the brain, and very speedy in its effect. It is most frequent in children. As far as I can remember, all the cases I have seen have run too rapid a course for emaciation; the usual course has been from two to three weeks; that is almost the limit. It is not long since I had a case under my control. I have not been struck with great emaciation, though it may come on as the result of other conditions. Another disease may have produced emaciation, and then tubercular meningitis follow, which is very rapid in its effects. I can point out three things here which were inconsistent with death from tubercular meningitis; the very fact of there being some small tubercular deposit in the membranes of the brain led us to examine the brain very carefully, and there was a complete absence of three marked symptoms—first, the flattening and the bulging of the sides of the brain; secondly, the much more important, a complete absence of any effusion in the ventricles, in the chambers of the brain; and thirdly, the absence of any tubercles whatever at the base of the brain.

The characteristic post-mortem appearances of tubercular meningitis is the presence of tubercular deposit in the meshes of the brain, at the base of the brain. We examined the brain more carefully, because we thought we found some small deposit of tubercles on the convex surface that led us to examine more carefully. I made no examination with the microscope. I made a special note of there being a total absence of lymph, but I do not think I did so of the flattening and bulging of the brain. The presence of lymph is one of the most marked symptoms of inflammation; it becomes very serious indeed when there is lymph or pus.

The first stage of inflammation is a congested condition; we found that present. I must distinguish between the word congestion and inflammation, because the appearances of the brain were characteristic of intense congestion, and I could not use the word inflammation. The presence of lymph is the third stage in inflammation and congestion is the first. Con-

82

Evidence for Prosecution.

gestion was present in the brain. All the blood-vessels in the brain itself were remarkably congested. A very small quantity of fluid was found in the skull; I doubt if there was more than a drachm. I don't think it was actually measured. It will be found mentioned specially in my notes that there was an absence of effusion, but not, I believe, as to the quantity. I think that was remarkable from the absence of it. I do not remember making a written note, but I remember it perfectly. I recollect the appearance of the brain perfectly; we expected to find evidence of tubercular disease more marked, and we did not find it. I won't say that miliary tubercles never occur without lymph or effusion.

By the COURT—I said that I could not come to any decided opinion with regard to the immediate cause of death; I think there was enough upon the post-mortem examination to enable me to come to a conclusion, and I think the right answer would be that the post-mortem appearances of the body were not inconsistent with starvation. There were reasons why I thought there might be in the first instance a narcotic, and afterwards an irritant poison. The difficulty we had was to account for the immediate cause of death. I ought to say the special appearances are not limited either to poison or to starvation; there are certain appearances common to many diseases. in the stomach and so on.

FREDERICK WILKINSON, examined by the SOLICITOR-GENERAL—I am an M.D., and a member of the Royal College of Surgeons of England. I attended at the post-mortem examination at 34 Forbes Road on the 19th April. I have been present in Court while the post-mortem has been described. In my judgment the appearances were correctly described by the witnesses who have been examined.

The cause of death, in my opinion, was starvation. I have considered the various suggestions that have been made as to meningitis and so forth. I think there is no foundation for those suggestions.

I have heard both Mr. Longrigg and Dr. Bright express their opinion as to what would be the effect of moving the lady in the condition in which she must have been, and the way in which she was removed. I concur in their opinion that that arrangement must have conduced to her death. It was most dangerous in her condition, and must have accelerated her death.

Cross-examined by Mr. CLARKE—I agree with the doctors who have already spoken with regard to meningitis. I agree with their opinion with regard to the diseases, but not quite so as to their statements. I did not hear them all, but I agree with their opinions. I heard Mr. Longrigg give a description of the symptoms before death some time after the post-mortem.

Staunton Trial.

F. Wilkinson At the time I made the post-mortem I came with a perfectly clear mind, and without any knowledge at all of what had taken place. I refused to hear from Mr. Casabianca what he had to say about the matter. He came with a policeman, and asked me to attend the post-mortem, but I refused to hear him say anything about it; I told him I would rather go unbiassed.

At the examination the symptoms were put down to poison, but we thought we would have an exhaustive analysis, and sent the stomach to Mr. Rodgers. I was very dubious as to the symptoms; there was an inflamed stomach, and that was one symptom of poisoning. I concurred in the view of the other medical men in their wish to send them, and in the reasons for which they sent those things to Dr. Rodgers for examination.

I have had about thirty years' experience in the treatment of brain diseases. I have not practically had special cases with regard to brain diseases. I have had general scrofula, as you may call it, which is another name for general tuberculosis. I have also had cases of meningitis. Those diseases generally do not last sufficiently long to produce emaciation. Tuberculosis in the form of phthisis does so; tuberculosis has various forms; some lead to greater emaciation than others. The presence of tubercles in the brain, and tubercles in the lungs in that congested state of the vessels of the brain, was too small in quantity to produce any bad result of tuberculosis, I think.

There are three membranes of the brain—the dura mater, the pia mater, and the arachnoid. This deposit was on the arachnoid membrane, the size of about a fourpenny or a sixpenny piece. It was very recent, quite transparent, and had not produced any inflammation. There was no inflammation present; I did not even see any congestion. It was a perfectly recent deposit; there was no congestion in the organs of the brain; I mean, not connected with this tubercular deposit. There was some general congestion of the brain not dependent upon this tubercular deposit.

I have had persons under my care who were suffering from brain disease. They differed in temperament and manner and in behaviour. Persons who are afflicted with disease of the brain are very often affected in their temper, which makes them sulky. I have not had experience of persons who are under the control of warders in asylums, nor have I visited persons who have been confined in asylums, neither my friends nor patients. Vomiting is one of the things that may cause starvation.

By the COURT—Starvation might occur from three causes— from wilful refusal of food, from having food withheld, and from vomiting.

84

Evidence for Prosecution.

By Mr. CLARKE—I mentioned before the magistrate that F. Wilkinson vomiting might produce starvation. I never had a case of starvation under my care. I have had a case of starvation where a patient refused to take food. It was a grown-up person of weak intellect. It was a case of imbecility. The patient refused for some time to take food; it had to be forced down by the stomach pump. I saved the patients in that way, for I had two or three. A medical man is necessarily required to deal with a case of that kind.

In this case I saw some food on the back of the tongue of the deceased woman; she had already some in the stomach; some that had been recently given her seemed of the same kind. It might have remained there from her inability to swallow, in the state in which she was.

There are several writers on the subject of death from starvation. There is Kirk's "Handbook," Taylor's "Medical Jurisprudence," and Kasper's work, and one or two more, I think; and there is a long account published of the Welsh fasting girl's case.[3] Kirk does not treat it very lightly; he gives the weight of the organs and the way in which they lose weight.

I did not notice anything about the brain that might have been caused in early life. I noticed no old injury to the brain, but there was slight adhesion between the dura mater and the skull-cap. I did not think much of that.

Re-examined by the SOLICITOR-GENERAL—Kirk's "Handbook" gives inflammation in the stomach as one of the symptoms of poisoning. Inflammation of the stomach sometimes produced by starvation is given in Taylor's "Medical Jurisprudence" and Kirk's "Handbook" as one of the symptoms of starvation. I desired the contents of the stomach to be analysed in order to ascertain by exhaustive examination what was the cause in this particular case.

When poison is excluded as the cause of the inflammation, we have advanced one step towards ascertaining what it is not. Starvation is one of the things that produce it. The several diseases that have been mentioned are characteristic of those diseases. In Addison's disease you get the bronze skin, but I do not think the skin of this poor woman was anything at all of that colour; it was a more parchmenty state of skin, and with regard to diabetes, there is an enormous flow of urine which cannot be concealed, and an intense thirst. Life may be prolonged by medical treatment, proper diet, and so forth. There is an effect produced upon the kidneys themselves by diabetes. There was no symptom of that in this lady at all. The kidneys were healthy.

---

3 *Reg. v. Jacobs and Wife*, Carmarthen Summer Assizes, 1870; and see *Taylor's Medical Jurisprudence*, i. 645.

Staunton Trial.

F. Wilkinson

The tubercles were not in the substances of the brain but on the middle membrane, the arachnoid membrane, one of the envelopes of the brain. They did not fulfil the description of the symptoms which indicate cerebral meningitis. Those appear in the substance of the brain; they go through the membranes; they do not assume the form of tubercles; here was an isolated spot of tubercles on the surface of the arachnoid membrane, on the middle membrane, outside the brain.

By the COURT—There was one case which I had particularly under my notice, where a person had refused to take food, and where it had to be administered by the stomach pump. I have had three such cases. I did not find in either of those three cases that the patient had on any occasion taken some quantity of nourishment, but refused to take more; it was a general refusal to take any. If I found certain particles of food in the stomach, and other portions unswallowed resting on the tongue, I should infer that the patient must have taken it voluntarily. In the cases I have had under my notice there was no partial refusal; it was an entire refusal.

Alan Pigott

Mr. ALAN PIGOTT, examined by Mr. POLAND—I am a surgeon, and am in partnership with Mr. Longrigg. I was present at the post-mortem examination of this lady.

Have you formed any opinion as to the cause of her death? —Yes; starvation, accelerated by her removal from Cudham.

J. Bateman

JOSEPH BATEMAN, police sergeant, proved that he handed certain jars given to him by Mr. Longrigg to Dr. Rodgers.

J. E. D. Rodgers

Dr. JULIEN EDWARD DISBROWE RODGERS, examined by the ATTORNEY-GENERAL—I live at 38 Sussex Street, Warwick Square. I am Professor of Toxicology at the London Hospital. I received from Sergeant Bateman three jars. I made an analysis, but I did not find a trace of any poison of any kind.

Did you find any trace of fat in the internal organs?—There was an entire absence of it.

What, in your opinion, was the cause of death?—Starvation and neglect. Prolonged starvation, because there was an entire absence of fat. It would take several months to produce such a condition.

Does it take a long time to produce extreme emaciation?— Yes; I know of a case in which it was three months.

Should you say that the condition of the deceased in this case must have been known to those about her for some time before her death?—I should say for some considerable time. Undoubtedly they must have seen the condition in which she was. The patient some time before her death would be able to walk very feebly, and latterly unable to walk. In all cases I have known where starvation has been caused by disease

86

Evidence for Prosecution.

the shortest time to produce emaciation was three months; it must have been most certainly obvious to everybody that for ^{J. E. D.}
^{Rodgers}
some time before the death of this lady she required medical
attendance. The appearance of the stomach and other organs,
no matter from what cause, must have created suffering which
required medical assistance and great care. After a person
has abstained from taking food for a considerable time the
effect of taking food in any quantity would be congestion of
the brain. It is a very dangerous thing to do.

Did you see any evidence of excessive drinking?—None whatever. The liver had not the slightest appearance or indication
of habits of intoxication.

Do you think the condition of this lady could have been
produced by diabetes?—I do not think so. In diabetes there
is so much suffering that medical aid would have been required,
and, therefore, as no medical aid was ever sought, I believe
starvation was the cause, and not diabetes.

Is there excessive thirst in diabetes?—Invariably so. In
an experience of many cases of diabetes during forty years I
have never known excessive thirst to be absent.

Do you think death was due to tubercular meningitis?—No;
the symptoms in meningitis would have been far more urgent
in requiring medical attendance, and, therefore, as I have not
heard of any medical attendance, I keep to starvation.

Cross-examined by Mr. CLARKE—I was not present at the
post-mortem examination, but I had the notes of it sent to me
by Mr. Longrigg.   Here to-day I am not acting upon those
notes, but only upon the evidence I have heard in Court. If
there had been any evidence to warrant an opinion of intemperance, even for a limited time, it must have shown itself
in the internal organs.

Did the analysis in this case give you a great deal of
trouble?—Yes; because the appearances warranted the
suspicion of poison, and I had never seen those appearances
before without poison. Therefore, I took a great deal of trouble,
not only in analysing by the processes, but in verifying those
results. I proved the absence of any metallic or alkaloid
poison, and I then came to the conclusion that the cause of
death was starvation.

The case puzzled you up to the day before the inquest?—
Yes; because there were certain symptoms—the redness of the
stomach, duodenum, &c.—which I at first thought attributable
to poison, but which I ultimately ascertained were not, and
I then came to the conclusion that the appearances were due
to starvation.

Mr. THOMAS BOND, examined by the ATTORNEY-GENERAL—I ^{Thomas Bond.}
am a practising surgeon and Lecturer in Medical Jurisprudence
at Westminster Hospital. I have heard the medical evidence

Staunton Trial.

Thomas Bond in this case, and my opinion is that the cause of death was starvation.

Have you ever had an absolute case of starvation under your care?—Yes; it was that of a woman who swallowed some vitriol and got stricture of the gullet, and she was afterwards unable to take food except by injection. The patient ultimately died of starvation, after living three or four months.

Did you have a post-mortem examination in that case?—Yes; I made it myself, and the appearances were very similar to those deposed to in this case. There was congestion of the brain.

Do you think the deceased in this case died of diabetes, Addison's disease, or tubercular meningitis?—I do not think there are any symptoms spoken to which would warrant any such conclusion. If there had been diabetes I should have expected the kidneys to be enlarged and probably degenerated. In Addison's disease there is emaciation and very great lassitude, and it is a very long, slow disease. Nobody about her could have doubted that she was extremely ill if she had suffered from Addison's disease. In death from tubercular meningitis there is usually a good deal of fluid effused into the ventricles of the brain. There is also usually lymph effused at the base of the brain, and there is usually more evidence of tubercles than that described in the present case.

Would you say that long before her death the deceased would be able to walk about much?—I should say she would not.

Do you think the removal of the deceased on the night before her death accelerated that death?—It was a most injudicious thing to do, and, in my opinion, it would accelerate death.

Mr. CLARKE—Is it not the case, where a patient is suffering from a wasting disease, another disease may intervene and cause death?—Yes, I cannot undertake to say that Addison's disease was not present.

Do you find the record of the post-mortem examinations in this case complete?—It is not so complete and satisfactory as I should have made it. I should have recorded the weight of the brain and the quantity of fluid in the skull if I had found a large quantity; but, as there was very little of it, I should merely have recorded the fact. I should also have recorded the thinning of the coat of the stomach. The latter fact is an important one in a case of starvation. I apply the word starvation to mean a process caused by any disease which would prevent the nutrition of the body. I may say I have only seen the depositions and not the notes of the medical men.

Mr. JUSTICE HAWKINS—The depositions are taken by the magistrate's clerk, and he may not have recorded all that the medical men said. (*To Witness*)—If starvation had been going

88

Evidence for Prosecution.

on for some time would that lead to the deposit of tubercles?— Thomas Bond I am not prepared to say it would have led to sufficient tubercles to lead to tubercular meningitis, but it might lead to a deposit of tubercles either on the brain, lungs, or other tissues—if deposited in sufficient quantities they might produce the disease of tubercular meningitis. In a case of death by starvation I should expect a darkening of the skin caused by the loss of vitality and the dryness of the skin.

Mr. JAMES GIDEON CREASEY, examined by Mr. POLAND—I am J. G. a surgeon at Brastead, Kent. I know the Woodlands at **Creasey** Cudham. The Patrick Stauntons lived there. I knew Mrs. Patrick Staunton very well, Mr. Patrick Staunton very little. I attended there on 29th July in last year. It was for a very trifling ailment, I think, of Mrs. Patrick Staunton. Afterwards I attended from 23rd August to the 28th. The patient that time was a child.

Whose child was it?—I cannot say. I supposed it to be Mrs. Patrick Staunton's.

Did you ever attend any other person in that house after that time?—No. I knew the house as Woodlands. I did not know that it was formerly called Frith Cottage.

Have you seen Mrs. Butterfield this year?—Yes; I think it was in March. I saw her in a cab. She made some inquiry of me, and I afterwards received from her the photograph of a lady.

Were you in the habit of passing the Woodlands?—Often; sometimes daily, sometimes twice a week, and sometimes once a week.

Did you ever see in that house the lady whose photograph was sent you by Mrs. Butterfield?—No.

Did you ever attend her?—No; previously to 12th April I did not know any such person was living there. I did not know her child.

Did you know Mr. Louis Staunton?—Yes; he was living at Little Grays farm, or Woodside, as it was also called.

Did you know any lady living with him?—Yes; the prisoner, Alice Rhodes, though I did not then know her name.

What is the distance between Little Grays farm and the Woodlands?—Not very far—about a mile. Brastead, where I live, is about 2¼ miles from the Woodlands.

Is there any other medical man at Brastead?—No.

How far is Westerham from the Woodlands?—About 3 miles; there are two medical men there. There is a medical man at Riverhead within about 5 miles.

Mr. JUSTICE HAWKINS—Did you ever attend Harriet Staunton or anybody as the wife of Mr. Louis Staunton?—Never; I never went to his house; I was never asked to.

Staunton Trial.

J. G.
Creasey

Is your practice generally about the neighbourhood?—Yes; I am parish medical officer at Cudham, and I have a surgery a quarter of a mile from Little Grays farm, where I regularly attend once a week at a fixed hour.

C. E. Hoar

Mr. CHARLES EDWARD HOAR, examined by the SOLICITOR-GENERAL—I am surgeon to the Kent County Prison at Maidstone. Alice Rhodes was in custody there during the month of June last. She was delivered of a child on 28th June. It was a healthy child, and apparently at the full time.

T. Keene

Mr. THOMAS KEENE, examined by the ATTORNEY-GENERAL—I am a solicitor, of 32 Mark Lane. I acted as solicitor for Mrs. Harriet Staunton before her marriage, and afterwards for her husband.

Just tell me what her property was at the time she was married to Mr. Louis Staunton?—On 15th March, 1875, I received from the solicitors of her trustee £1177 15s. 2d. under a voluntary settlement she had made; on 22nd April, 1875, I received £639 4s. 1d.; and subsequently there was a further sum of £310 4s. 6d. received from the Court of Chancery on an order in the suit of Richardson and Beauclerk. This was in July—she was then married. She had reversionary interests in several other sums under the will of Lady Rivers, and on a sale these realised £1100, paid over to me on 23rd October, 1876, making altogether a sum of £3227.

When did you last see Mrs. Harriet Staunton?—On 23rd October, 1876, when she came to sign the deeds of assignment of these interests. She came to my office by appointment to meet the Commissioners for taking the acknowledgments of married women. Her husband came with her, but, of course, was not allowed to be with the Commissioners. He was in another room. I had no reason to doubt her being in good health. She was certainly not emaciated. I explained the deed to her, and asked her whether she really meant to give up the money.

Cross-examined by Mr. M. WILLIAMS—She came up twice to go before the Commissioners. On the first occasion she was taken unexpectedly before them, and she suffered from nervous hesitation of speech. The Commissioners thought it better that she should go away for a few day, and come again at another time. She had been examined on many occasions by doctors.

Third Day—Friday, 21st September, 1877.

The Court sat at 9.30.

CLARA BROWN, examined by the SOLICITOR-GENERAL—I was Clara Brown sixteen last month. I am first cousin to Mrs. Patrick Staunton and Alice Rhodes. I went into the service of the former in 1872 or 1873. My mother died in September, 1872. About twelve months after that I went into Mrs. Patrick's service.

Is your father alive?—No; he died in 1874.

Mrs. Patrick was living, when I went into her service, at 9 Loughborough Park, Brixton. The house, No. 8, nearly opposite, was occupied afterwards by Mr. and Mrs. Louis Staunton.

Do you remember Mr. Louis Staunton being married?— Yes; the house No. 8 was taken and furnished before he was married. I lived at No. 9 with Mrs. Patrick till she went to Cudham in November, 1875. There were no other servants in the house at Loughborough Park or at Cudham besides me. The family consisted of Mr. and Mrs. Patrick Staunton and their two children. One was about a month old when they went to Cudham, the other a year and a half. Dr. Russell attended the deceased in her confinement in 1876. Two or three days before that I came up from Cudham to No. 8, where I remained about a month. In the house at the time were Louis Staunton, Alice Rhodes, a nurse,[1] Mrs. Patrick eldest child, and myself.

Did you notice anything during the month in the conduct of Louis Staunton and Alice Rhodes?—I thought they were too affectionate to one another.

Did Alice Rhodes always sleep in her own bed?—I am not quite sure that she did.

Did you notice the bed of Mr. Louis Staunton, whether more than one person had slept in it?—Only by finding her night-dress in the chest of drawers in the room.

Did you hear Mrs. Harriet make any complaint about Alice Rhodes and her husband?—Yes; I have seen notes sent down by Mrs. Harriet to her husband. I saw Louis Staunton open one and read it. That was very soon after she was upstairs. After the month was over I went back to Cudham, where were Mr. and Mrs. Patrick and the children.

Mr. JUSTICE HAWKINS—When you went back did you leave Alice Rhodes at No. 8?—Yes.

Examination continued—Did Alice Rhodes, the baby, Harriet Staunton, and Louis all come down once to Cudham on a visit at the same time?—Yes; they came on the Saturday and left on the Monday.

---

[1] See p. 11, *supra*, and Appendix v., p. 301.

Clara Brown When was that?—About a fortnight after I had left Brixton.

When they left on the Monday did they take the baby back with them?—No; they left it with Mrs. Patrick. The baby was fed with the bottle. Mrs. Harriet came twice afterwards to see it, I think with Mr. Louis. I recollect Alice Rhodes staying at the Woodlands, but cannot remember the time; she stayed about a week, I think.

Did you hear anything pass between Alice Rhodes and her sister about Mrs. Harriet Staunton?—Yes.

What was it?—I think it was to ask if Mrs. Patrick Staunton would let Mrs. Harriet Staunton come down to the Woodlands for a week.

Did Mrs. Harriet come down?—Yes.

How long after?—About a month. Louis Staunton was also present, and I heard him speak to Mr. Patrick about his wife's hat and jacket.

What did he say?—"You had better put Harriet's hat and jacket away, or else perhaps she will come after me."

Did you see what was done with them?—I saw them put in a box and locked by Mrs. Patrick.

Did you hear Mrs. Harriet ask after them?—Yes.

When?—I don't know.

What answer was given?—That Mr. Staunton had taken them away with him.

Who gave that answer?—Mrs. Patrick. I have given her a similar answer to that myself.

Did Harriet Staunton ever leave the Woodlands, except on two occasions, until she was removed to Penge?—I don't recollect. On these two occasions she came back the same night.

Where did she go?—Once to London, she told me.

Did she tell you what about?—She said she had to go to Mr. Keene's office.

How long after was the second time?—About a week.

Where did she go then?—The same place—so I was told.

Who told you?—Herself.

Did you ever hear Patrick Staunton speak to Harriet Staunton about her going out of the house?—Yes, sir; I have heard him speak to her more than once. That would be after these visits to London.

What did he say?—I have heard him ask her where she had been to when she had been out.

I mean about her going out; not about having been out.

Mr. M. WILLIAMS—I must object to the Solicitor-General leading the witness.

Mr. JUSTICE HAWKINS—I see nothing improper in the question.

Examination continued—What did he say?—I have heard him say, "You will have to go to London to see Mr. Keene."

Evidence for Prosecution.

Have you heard Patrick Staunton speak to Harriet, and say she was not to go out of the house?—He did not say anything about leaving entirely.

I did not ask that, and I think you heard me. You must answer the question?—I never heard him say she was to leave.

I did not ask you that. Have you heard Mr. Patrick speak to Harriet as to whether she was to go out of the house or not? —I have heard him say, when she came back from London, she was not to go outside the house.

What did he say?—" You must not go outside for any one to see you."

Had he spoken to you on the same subject?—Yes, sir.

What?—" Don't let Mrs. Staunton go out so as to let any one see her." That has been more than once. At first Mrs. Harriet took her meals with the rest of the family.

Did that always continue to be so?—No.

When was there any alteration?—Just before Christmas.

What then?—She was sent upstairs more, and kept upstairs.

How was she provided with food?—It was sent up to prevent her coming down.

What food was she provided with? Was it the same always as the rest had downstairs?—Not always.

What then?—Sometimes pudding instead of meat, like what the rest had.

Has she complained to you at all?—Yes.

Of what?—Of not having enough to eat, and on several occasions complained of not having anything sent up to her.

Do you remember anything happening on one occasion when she made that complaint?—I have seen Mr. Patrick Staunton very angry.

Did you ever see him do anything to her?—Yes.

What?—I have seen him strike her.

Did the blow leave any mark?—Yes.

What?—A bruise.

Where?—On her arm.

Did you ever see her with another mark on another occasion? —Yes.

What?—A black eye.

How came that to pass?—He struck her.

Mr. M. WILLIAMS—Did you see him?—Yes.

By the SOLICITOR-GENERAL—Just describe what you saw?— I was upstairs. Mrs. Harriet shut the door in Mrs. Patrick's face, and Mr. Patrick struck her.

What did he do?—He struck her and pushed her down.

Where did it happen?—In the back room.

How was it furnished?—A chair bedstead, a bedstead, and two boxes.

Was there any basin or jug, or any other mode for cleaning herself?—No.

93

Staunton Trial.

Clara Brown   Were you there when the policeman afterwards examined the room?—Yes, sir.

Was it in the same condition as it used to be?—No; other things were put in it.

When had that been done?—After she had been taken away.

Where used the child to sleep?—Beside her in a bassinet.

What were the clothes to cover it?—A shawl, I believe.

You know?—Yes; only a shawl.

Where used the child to be kept?—Upstairs, in the back room.

About Christmas time did you see Patrick Staunton do anything to Harriet?—I saw him strike her just about Christmas. Mrs. Patrick was present. I heard her ask Mr. Staunton to leave her alone.

About this time what boots had Mrs. Staunton to wear?—She only had one pair of boots all the time she was there. When she was removed she had no boots on, but a pair of Mrs. Staunton's slippers.

What was the room like?—Rather dirty. I cleaned it about a month before she was taken away. I have heard Mr. and Mrs. Staunton tell Harriet Staunton not to come out of the room.

What was said?—I can't tell you; it was such foul language.

Mr. JUSTICE HAWKINS—But you must tell us what it was.

By the SOLICITOR-GENERAL—Tell us?—" You must not come downstairs, you damned cat, or else I'll break your back."

Have you heard that once, or more than once?—More than once.

What have you heard Mrs. Patrick say?—" Don't come downstairs, Harriet; we don't want you down."

Did she come down?—After that I don't recollect her coming down.

When she complained of being without food, do you know if she has been without it?—Yes.

For how long have you known her to be without food?—For a day.

How has that happened?—I have asked Mrs. Patrick to let me take it up to her, and she has said, " No; let her wait."

Was she ill?—She appeared to be getting very weak.

Suddenly or gradually?—Gradually; she had no fit or sudden illness.

Do you remember the child being taken to the hospital?—Yes.

What was Harriet's state then?—Very weak.

Did you hear if she was asked if the child was to go?—No. On the Sunday before Harriet herself was taken away she was very weak and bad.

Evidence for Prosecution.

Do you remember the Monday before she was removed?— **Clara Brown**
Yes.

Had she any food on that day?—Yes; a fowl was boiled for
her.

Do you remember the news being brought that the child was
dead?—Yes.

Did she take any notice of that?—No. She ate very little
of the fowl. She did not appear to understand anybody at
that time—that is, anything that was said to her.

Was she able to help herself?—No.

Do you remember Patrick Staunton getting some steak for
her, and cutting it up very small for her?—Yes. She tried
to eat it but could not swallow it.

When was that?—On the Tuesday.

Did they try to feed her with some bread and milk?—Yes,
the night she came away. She could not eat it.

When was she put in the trap to drive her away?—About
six in the evening.

Before that was anything said about keeping her later?—
Louis and Patrick said, " We should like to keep her later
for fear of the people at Portlands "—the name of the house
nearly opposite—" seeing her." Mrs. Patrick said, " You had
better take her at once, or she won't last the journey."

Where was Mrs. Harriet all this time?—In the kitchen, sitting
in a chair.

How did she get there?—Mr. Patrick carried her down in
his arms.

Was she propped up with pillows?—Yes; she seemed drowsy.
Patrick Staunton tried to rouse her several times.

Did Mrs. Patrick say anything?—She said, " You had better
let her sleep," and Patrick said, " If she goes to sleep she
won't wake up again, in my opinion."

Where was Louis Staunton living at the latter part of 1876
and up to the removal?—At the Little Grays, about twenty
minutes' walk off.

From time to time he came to the Woodlands. Did he see
his wife?—Not always.

Sometimes?—Yes.

Did you hear him speak of her, or say that he wished to
see her?—I don't remember.

Have you heard him speak to her?—Yes.

Who was living at Little Grays farm?—Louis Staunton and
Alice Rhodes.

Do you know if Harriet Staunton knew where her husband
was living?—No, sir; she did not know.

Or that Alice Rhodes was living with him?—She did not
know.

Do you remember picking up a letter and reading it?—
Yes.

Staunton Trial.

Clara Brown   What became of it?—I burnt it.

Whose handwriting was it in?—Louis Staunton's.   It was addressed to Alice Rhodes.   I found it in Mr. Patrick's bedroom.

At Cudham?—Yes.   Alice had been in the house, but had gone.

What was in the letter?—It began, " My own darling."

Well?—I think it was, " I was very sorry to see you crying so much when I left you.   It seems as though it never would be, but there will be a time when Harriet will be out of the way, and we shall be happy together." [2]

Anything else?—" Dear Alice, you must know how much I love you by this time.   We have been together two years now."

Did Alice Rhodes ever make an inquiry after the letter?— Yes, a week after, when she came to Cudham again.   She asked if I had seen a letter addressed to her.   I said, " No."

Where was the letter?—I had burnt it.   I found the letter at the first time that Alice came to stay for some days.   I cannot tell the date or the month when I found the letter. I think it was after I had come back to Cudham from Mrs. Harriet's confinement.

Do you know Alice's handwriting?—Yes, I think so.

Look if this is her handwriting?—(*Letter produced.*)—I think so, but I won't be sure.

To the best of your belief?—Yes.

By Mr. GYE—Have you ever seen her handwriting?—Yes.

Where?—At Cudham.

What sort of writing did you see?—A list of something, I think.

The SOLICITOR-GENERAL—We'll have the letter read.

Mr. AVORY[3]—It is dated, " Aug. 19, 1876," and is signed " Alice."

Woodlands, Saturday morning.

My dearest Louis,—I was extremely thankful to have a letter from you yesterday, as you must know it is extremely dull for me here, and baby is so fretful.   I have searched high and low for the lost letter and cannot find it, and I am sure Harriet has not got it.   So where it can be I cannot tell.   Come down to me as soon as you can if only for a few hours, for you cannot think how happy it will make me to see your dear old face again.   With affectionate love, and trusting to see you soon.   I remain. Yours affectionately,
ALICE.

Though absence parts us for a while,
And distance rolls between ;
Believe whoever may revile,
I am still what I have been.

---

2 For the explanation of this letter subsequently given by Louis Staunton, see Appendix viii., p. 317.

3 Clerk of the Arraigns.

Evidence for Prosecution.

Examination continued by the SOLICITOR-GENERAL—I was **Clara Brown** examined before the coroner, and made certain statements there.

Had any of the prisoners spoken to you about being examined as a witness before you were examined?—Yes.

Which of them?—All of them.

What did they say?—They told me to say everything that I did say. Between the death of Mrs. Harriet and the inquest I had been at Mrs. Bradford's.

Was what you said before the coroner true?—No, it was what I had been told to say by the prisoners.

Whilst you were at the Woodlands, did Alice Rhodes come over?—Yes; once or twice a week. She saw Harriet Staunton generally.

THOMAS KEENE, re-examined—The first occasion on which **T. Keene** Mrs. Harriet Staunton came up before the Commissioner was the 17th of October, 1876. The second was the 23rd of October.

CLARA BROWN, continued—I remember the day when Mrs. **Clara Brown** Harriet Staunton was removed. Alice Rhodes and Mrs. Patrick Staunton were present. Alice Rhodes came about 4.30, and Mr. Louis Staunton came afterwards with the trap. Alice Rhodes was not in the kitchen when the talk took place about Mrs. Harriet Staunton being sleepy; no one was present but Mrs. Patrick Staunton and myself. I think Mrs. Patrick remarked to Alice Rhodes about how bad Mrs. Harriet Staunton had been since she was there in the morning; how much she had changed.

Is this Mrs. Patrick Staunton's writing (letter produced)?—Yes.

March 5, 1877.

Mrs. Butterfield,—I hear from Alice who has been on a visit to me, that she met you the other day when in London, and you informed her that you thought of coming down here. I wish you thoroughly to understand that neither my husband nor myself will on any account see you. How can you think of calling on me after your disgraceful conduct towards my mother, Mrs. Hincksman, and my husband some months since? You also told Alice that you were coming down here to be faced with a revolver, my husband having said something about firearms. I have to deny that he ever said anything of the sort, and, another thing, I am sure he would not waste powder and shot on such a vile woman as you have proved yourself to be. ELIZABETH A. STAUNTON.

Cross-examined by Mr. WILLIAMS—I think Mrs. Harriet came to Mrs. Patrick's in August, 1876. I was the only servant in Patrick Staunton's house. I was in the habit of going out frequently, going errands, and seeing various people.

Since your statement before the coroner, did you make another on 29th May?—Yes, I believe I did.

Clara Brown And another one to Sergeant Bateman on 8th June?—Yes.
Another one on 20th June—a written one?—Yes.

Another one on 23rd June?—I don't recollect that one.

Can you say whether you made one on the 27th?—I don't
know the dates at all.

The ATTORNEY-GENERAL—You may take it that there was one
on the 27th.

Cross-examination continued—I was not called as a witness
before the magistrates at Bromley. Before the coroner did
you say anything about the hat and jacket?—I think I did,
but I am not sure.

Did you say anything about them before 23rd June?—I don't
recollect. I cannot say whether before the coroner I said
anything about Patrick telling Mrs. Staunton not to go out.
I did not say before the coroner that she had not had meat
for a whole day sometimes, and I do not recollect saying that
Harriet was in very good health.

Do you remember being asked if she always ate and drank,
and answering, "She always ate heartily"?—Yes. I also
said that my master and mistress and Mrs. Harriet always had
meals together.

Was that true?—No, sir.

Mr. JUSTICE HAWKINS—I don't want to check you, Mr.
Williams, but do you think it necessary to put these questions
after the answer to the Solicitor-General that what she had
said before the coroner was untrue?

Mr. WILLIAMS—I cannot take it in that way, my lord.

Mr. JUSTICE HAWKINS—I don't want to check you in the least
degree.

Cross-examination continued—Did you say that Mrs. Harriet
Staunton was always out, morning, noon, and night?—Yes. I
don't remember saying anything before the coroner about
Patrick striking her.

Were you asked what was the state of her flesh, and did
you answer, "Very clean, from what I saw"?—Yes, I believe
I did.

Did you make her bed?—Yes.

Were you asked what was the state of her bed, and did you
answer, "Clean"?—I don't remember.

I said that the night when she left the Woodlands she had
on a cloth jacket, an ulster, a blue shawl, and a rug. Before
she started I heard her husband say to her, "Will you go?"
I cannot answer whether I said that she appeared all right, but
she put her foot on the step, got hold of the brass railing, and
got into the wagonette; she sat in between Mr. Staunton and
Miss Rhodes.

I do not think I said one word before the coroner about
Patrick Staunton saying to her, "You must not come down-

stairs, you damned cat, or I will break your back." I might Clara Brown have made the statement before 23rd June.

I remember being asked if I considered that she was ill before she went away in the wagonette, and replying, " No, not very ill until the Thursday afternoon." I think I said it was between three and four o'clock, and that she had sat drowsy over the fire. I should not like to say that I heard my master ask her how she was on the day that she went away, and that she replied, " Pretty well." I cannot tell whether she answered or not; I might have said that she did. Mr. Patrick asked her in the morning, but I forget whether she answered him.

I heard my mistress say that the child was going up to the hospital. I believe I said that " Mrs. Harriet Staunton hoped Mrs. Patrick would be fortunate enough to get it in, as she hoped it would do it good." That was not true. Mrs. Harriet had not said so. It was not true when I said that I heard its mother ask that it should be taken to the hospital. Mrs. Patrick Staunton did not tell Mrs. Harriet that she would take the child to the hospital.

Mrs. Harriet Staunton did not know with whom her husband was living. I think I have said that Mrs. Louis Staunton knew that her husband was living with Alice Rhodes a little way off, and that she was passing as Mrs. Staunton. That was false; she was not aware of it. The prisoners told me to say so before the coroner. I swear that.

I do not believe I said one word about finding the letter beginning " My own darling, I was sorry to see you cry so," until the last time I gave a statement to the Treasury. I do not remember what the latter part of the letter was, but it was something about the death of his father. It was six or eight months before the death of Harriet Staunton that I saw the letter. I knew what it meant, and I understood what was meant by the sentence, " There will be a time, when Harriet is out of the way, that we shall be happy together." It referred to the death of Mrs. Harriet Staunton. I destroyed the letter; I do not think I ever said one word about it until I came to give my evidence to the Treasury.

Mrs. Harriet Staunton used to go out when she first came to Cudham. I have not said that she came home the worse for liquor. I might have said, " I have seen her the worse for liquor." I will not swear that I have not. I believe I saw her the worse for liquor at Brixton once; I am not sure. I went more by what I heard than what I saw; she seemed intoxicated to me. I have said that while at Cudham she went out on one occasion to a public-house in the village and told me that she had been there. I believe that was before she went down to stay at Cudham, on the first or second visit.

Staunton Trial.

Clara Brown Mr. Patrick Staunton was frequently out from Christmas up to April for hours together. Mrs. Patrick Staunton used to get out sometimes, not very often; she seldom or never went out shopping; she went out and about the Woodlands, the house and grounds, and she used to go to Little Grays. At that time Patrick Staunton was out too, and I and Mrs. Harriet Staunton would be left at home. I was attending to my work at home.

I have had some conversations with Sergeant Bateman since the inquest; I don't know how many conversations—a few, I should say. I cannot give you an idea how many; a good deal more than three or four; it may have been half a dozen. It was not much more than conversation; it was about this matter.

I don't remember making a statement to him on 8th June. I remember the end of the coroner's inquest. I don't recollect making a statement to him about a fortnight after the inquest terminated. I think I did make a statement about six or eight weeks afterwards. He asked me questions and I answered them. I remember his saying to me that I might get myself into trouble. I don't remember his doing so more than once. I think it was only on one occasion; that was some time before I made the statement to him.

I don't remember when it was that he said that to me. I don't think he said anything to me about penal servitude; I won't swear he did not. He did not say, " You had better take care or you may get penal servitude yourself." I will swear he did not say that. I don't recollect that he said anything about penal servitude. He said that if I went on in the state as I was then I might get into trouble, because he said he knew it was not the truth. I think he used the words " go to prison." I think that was some time before I made the statement to him.

Cross-examined by Mr. CLARKE—I remember being examined before the coroner. I was examined on more than one day. On the first day I was only asked a few questions, and the substantial examination was the second time. I think Mr. Patrick was in the room when I was examined on the second occasion. There were some witnesses downstairs, but I believe Mr. Patrick was upstairs. I believe but am not certain of that. I believe the others were downstairs. The witnesses remained out of the room, and were called in as they were wanted for examination.

I think Mr. Patrick Staunton had been examined the same day, before me. I was called up to the room when I was wanted for examination. I think the coroner, before my examination, cautioned me very strongly.

Do you remember on the second day the coroner saying,

Evidence for Prosecution.

to the Woodlands with fish and nuts and oranges. I went John Staples about half-past ten in the morning twice a week. I continued to go until after Christmas. On one occasion I saw Mrs. Harriet Staunton. I saw her on the Wednesday before Christmas. She was sitting in the kitchen. She had a child in her lap. She looked as if she had been very ill, or else half-starved. Clara Brown was with her. That was the only occasion I saw her.

ALFRED NICHOLLS, examined by the SOLICITOR-GENERAL—I A. Nicholls am fifteen years of age, and work with my father, a baker, at Cudham, in Kent. My father served the Woodlands with bread. He commenced to do so about 21st March this year, and continued until 23rd April. He called three times a week. I knew Clara Brown, Mrs. Patrick Staunton, and two children. I never saw another lady there, or knew that there was one living in the house.

OWEN DAVEY, examined by Mr. POLAND—I was assistant to Owen Davey Mr. Dalton, butcher, at Brastead. I know the Woodlands, and served Mr. and Mrs. Patrick Staunton with meat. I used to call for orders about four times a week. On the occasions of my going there I never saw Mrs. Harriet Staunton or her child. I never heard of such a person living in the house, or that there was a third child.

HENRY WEST, examined by Mr. POLAND—I am a baker at Henry West Brastead, and served the people at the Woodlands with bread up to March in this year. I knew Mrs. Patrick Staunton and Clara Brown. I never saw Mrs. Harriet or heard of her.

Fourth Day—Saturday, 22nd September, 1877.

The Court sat at half-past nine.

Clara Brown

CLARA BROWN was recalled at the request of the Attorney-General.

The ATTORNEY-GENERAL—There was in the back room where Mrs. Harriet Staunton used to sleep a fireplace, was there not? —Yes.

From Christmas to April were there any fires lighted in it?— I recollect only one.

When was that?—I cannot remember whether it was before or after Christmas.

Mr. STRAIGHT—With regard to the bed, does this drawing at all represent it when the curtains were up?—Yes.

Mr. JUSTICE HAWKINS—Was the curtain over the bed where you slept with the child?—Yes.

Mr. STRAIGHT—Your lordship will recollect that there was something said about a framework with curtains.

Mr. JUSTICE HAWKINS—Do you mean at the time Harriet Staunton slept there whether it was like this drawing?—Yes; when the curtain was hung over the framework, that is how it was.

You said Louis and Alice Rhodes used to come and dine on Sundays?—Yes; but I do not know how many times. Sometimes I and sometimes Mrs. Patrick used to give the orders to the tradesmen.

Mary Ann Weatherley

MARY ANN WEATHERLEY, examined by the ATTORNEY-GENERAL —Where do you live?—At Knockholt, and my father is a coal dealer.

Do you know the Woodlands?—Yes.

You used to go there?—Yes, with new butter.

Do you remember on one occasion being near the house?— Yes.

When?—I remember being near the house on Christmas Day last.

Was any one with you?—Yes; I was with a girl named Longridge.

What did you go for?—We were going to remain all the evening with Clara Brown.

Mr. and Mrs. Patrick being away at that time?—Yes.

Did Clara Brown open the door?—Yes.

And you went into the parlour?—Yes.

Did you hear anything?—Yes.

114

Evidence for Prosecution.

What?—We heard footsteps crossing the kitchen.

What was done?—Clara Brown went to the kitchen door.

Well?—She said, "Go back, ma'am," and turned the key in the door.

Did any one come into the parlour?—No one came into the parlour.

You did not stay?—No.

Why?—I said that we would not stay if Clara had some one with her.

Did you leave?—Yes; the other girl and myself left.

Did you know Mrs. Harriet Staunton?—No.

Did you know there was a lady living there with her child? —No.

Mrs. Patrick Staunton here rose from her seat and said—" She saw the child constantly."

By Mr. STRAIGHT—How many times were you at the Woodlands?—I don't know how many occasions.

Have you seen a child there?—Yes.

Were you told whose child it was?—Yes, Harriet Staunton's.

Who told you?—Clara Brown.

Has the child ever been brought to your house?—Yes; Mrs. Patrick has brought the child to our house for an hour or two occasionally.

Have you seen Clara Brown nursing it?—Yes.

Re-examined by Mr. POLAND—Did you ever see this child after Christmas?—No.

When did you last see it?—It was last brought about a month before Christmas, and stayed with us for the evening.

Mr. and Mrs. Patrick had some visitors?—Yes.

MARY ANN LONGRIDGE, examined by Mr. POLAND—I live at Knockholt, and am sixteen years of age. I remember on Christmas Day last going to the Woodlands with the last witness. I also heard some one cross the kitchen floor, and heard Clara Brown say, "Go back, ma'am." I did not see who it was. We stayed about half an hour chatting. That was the only time I was at the house.

Did you see a baby?—Yes, a little girl.

Who had it?—Clara Brown had it in the parlour. Our house is about a quarter of a mile off.

Witness was not cross-examined.

Mr. JUSTICE HAWKINS—I wish to point out that we have no evidence that the baby is dead or alive.

The ATTORNEY-GENERAL—We are going to prove that now.

FREDERICK C. COLEY, examined by the ATTORNEY-GENERAL— What are you?—I was formerly house physician at Guy's Hospital.

Staunton Trial.

F. C. Coley — Where do you live?—I live at Mordan Road, Blackheath.

Do you remember Sunday, 8th April?—Yes; I was at the hospital. I remember a child being brought there that day.

What time?—In the afternoon.

Who brought it?—A man and a woman. I could not recognise them again. They made a statement to me about it, and I ordered its admission into a ward in charge of "Sister Mary."

Did you examine the child?—I did.

Don't answer the question for a moment, but in what condition did you find the child?——

Mr. STRAIGHT—I object to the reception of this evidence on the ground that, while it prejudices the prisoners, it is not relevant to the subject-matter under trial. Besides, it might form the ground for a separate indictment.

Mr. CLARKE also objected to it.

Mr. JUSTICE HAWKINS—Take the case of four or five children under the charge of a particular person who is accused of causing the death of any one of them. Supposing evidence were offered to show that all the children had died from the same cause, would not that be evidence to show that the death of the child in question was not merely accidental? Would it not be just as good, as cogent, evidence to prove non-accidental starvation as to admit the evidence to which I have referred in a case of poisoning? As far as I can form an opinion, the evidence, if pressed, can be properly received.

The ATTORNEY-GENERAL—My object was not to show the cause of death.

Mr. JUSTICE HAWKINS—I can quite understand that.

The ATTORNEY-GENERAL—However, I will not press the question. (To Witness)—Do you know what became of the child?—It died.

When?—I was told——

Never mind?—I saw the body afterwards, and made the post-mortem examination.

Do you know whether a Mr. Staunton was in the hospital for some complaint in 1876?—I don't know.

S. Crockett — SUSANNAH CROCKETT ("Sister Mary") was called, but it was stated that she had not come down to the Court.

The ATTORNEY-GENERAL—I am very sorry, my lord, the witness is not here.

Mr. JUSTICE HAWKINS—How long had the child been ill before its removal?

The ATTORNEY-GENERAL—I think Susannah Crockett will be able to answer that from statements made to her.

W. S. Russell — WILLIAM SMYTHE RUSSELL, examined by Mr. POLAND—I am a member of the Royal College of Surgeons, and live at Cold-

Evidence for Prosecution.

harbour Lane, Brixton. On 23rd March, last year, I was W. S. Russell
fetched by the two male prisoners to Loughborough Park,
where a lady was near her confinement.

Is this photograph like her (*photograph produced*)?—Yes.

Was she confined that day?—She was confined that night of
a boy.

How long did you attend her?—I attended her for three
weeks.

Was she healthy and strong?—She seemed to be pretty
well, fairly nourished, and in good condition.

Did she get over her confinement all right?—She was weak.

Mr. Justice Hawkins—But in health?—Yes. I left off
attending her in about three weeks.

Mr. Poland—What was her weight?—From 9 to 10 stones.

Cross-examined by Mr. M. Williams—Was she up when you
first saw her?—Yes.

Susannah Crockett, who had now arrived, was then sworn, S. Crockett
and examined by Mr. Poland.

You are known at Guy's Hospital as Sister Mary?—Yes.

Do you remember a child being brought there on Sunday
afternoon, 8th April?—Yes.

By whom?—Mr. and Mrs. Patrick Staunton.

Were they strangers to you?—They were.

What did you say to them?—I asked Mrs. Staunton if she
was the mother of the child.

What did she say?—She said, " No. The mother has given
it me to take care of, and I have brought it from kindness."

Did you say anything about the child's clothes?—I told her
the child would require certain articles of clothing.

What did they say?—They said they would bring it some
the next day.

Did you ask anything about the father of the child?—Yes.

What?—I asked what the child's father was.

What was the reply?—They said a carpenter. She gave the
name of Henry Stormton.

Who did?—Mrs. Patrick.

Mr. Justice Hawkins—Was that the name of the father or
the child?

Witness—The child.

Mr. Poland—What address was given?—Frith Cottage,
Cudham, Kent.

Are you sure the name given was Henry Stormton?—Yes.

Why?—I spelt it over.

Mr. Justice Hawkins—To the persons?—Yes. I wrote it
down at the time. The name has to be entered in the books
of the hospital. The books are here, and it is entered as Henry
Stormton.

Staunton Trial.

By Mr. POLAND—Do you say the child was ill?—I told them that the child was rapidly sinking, and I asked Mrs. Patrick if she would stay.

What reply was made?—I don't remember.

Did she stay?—Oh no.

Did you ask the age of the child?—Yes.

Well?—Mrs. Patrick told me it was about twelve months.

How was the child dressed?—Not as a child should be at that age.

How was it dressed?—It was dressed like a child a month old. I took charge of the child. It was very ill.

How long did it live?—It died at nine the same night.

Suddenly?—It gradually sank.

Did it take any food?—It was not able to take food, and it did not make any noise. It was a male child.

Was anything said as to how long the child had been ill?—I don't remember. Mrs. Patrick said its mother was unable to look after it.

Did you notice the face of the child?—Yes, it had a bruise on the left side.

Whereabout?—On the cheek. The next day—on the Monday—I had a conversation with Patrick Staunton.

Did he and his wife give any names?—No. He came about five o'clock on the Monday. He had a parcel which, I supposed, contained clothes for a child. I told him the child died the night before, and I recommended him to go to the superintendent's office to arrange about the removal of the body.

What did he say?—He said that he had done it from kindness; the mother was a worthy woman.

Did he say who it was?—No; he said the child had nothing to do with him.

Did you see the child naked?—Yes.

Was it clean or——

Mr. CLARKE—I object, my lord.

Mr. JUSTICE HAWKINS—If pressed, the question is admissible.

The ATTORNEY-GENERAL—I will not press it, my lord.

Mr. JUSTICE HAWKINS—Very well. (*To Witness*)—Under such circumstances, is it not usual to ask the persons who they are?—No.

Mr. JUSTICE HAWKINS—Do you understand me? Supposing a perfect stranger brought an infant, would not some inquiry be made of the persons who brought it as to who they were?—We always get the name and address of the patient, but it is not usual to ask for the names and addresses of those bringing the patient.

Mr. JUSTICE HAWKINS—It seems strange that a child should be brought without any one asking who the persons were.

Evidence for Prosecution.

The ATTORNEY-GENERAL—The advantage of this hospital is S. Crockett
very great.

Mr. JUSTICE HAWKINS—Unquestionably. This matter shows
how ready they are to open their doors.

The ATTORNEY-GENERAL—I will recall Dr. Coley.

Dr. COLEY, recalled and examined by the ATTORNEY-GENERAL Dr. Coley
—I had a conversation with the man and the woman when they
first brought the child. They told me it was not their child,
that the mother of it was ill, had been ill for some considerable
time, and was therefore unable to attend to it. With regard
to the child they told me that it had only recently seemed ill.

Did the child seem ill?—Very ill. I omitted to state that
they told me they lived at some considerable distance, the
impression on my mind being that they said Penge, but I will
not be sure. I should not have admitted the child, only
that it seemed so ill, it not being usual to admit a child so
young, but I feared it might die before they got home.

ROBERT HOGG, examined by the ATTORNEY-GENERAL—I live Robert Hogg
at 30 St. George's Road, Southwark, and am an undertaker.
On 10th April last Louis Staunton came to make arrangements
about a child lying dead at Guy's Hospital.

What name did he give?—He gave me the name of John
Harris, and said that of the child was Henry Staunton.

Well?—He said the child must be buried inexpensively, as
the father of the child was away in the country.

Did he say anything about followers?—There would be no
one to follow the child. He said that at the hospital they
wanted it removed as soon as possible.

Did he say anything about the father of the child?—He
said the father of the child was employed at a firm whom he
represented. He did not give me the name of the firm.

Was anything said about the cost?—I told him the cost
would be 30s.

When did he pay you?—He paid me then.

Is this the receipt?—Yes; it is in my handwriting.

Was the child buried?—Yes; it was buried at the East
London Cemetery, Plaistow. I told him if he called in a
few days he could have a memorial card showing the cemetery
and the date at which it was interred. Some one called a
few days afterwards and received the card.

What name was given to you?—The name of the child given
to me was " Staunton," and it is so written in the receipt.

FRANK CHARLES JOSEPH, examined by the ATTORNEY-GENERAL F. C. Joseph
—I am a clerk in the superintendent's office at Guy's Hospital.
I enter the names of patients in the books. The name of this

Staunton Trial.

F. C. Joseph child was entered by me as Henry Stornton. I made the entry from a slip given to me by Sister Mary.

In August, 1876, have you the entry of a patient Thomas Henry Staunton?—Yes.

Read the whole of the entry?—" Thomas Henry Staunton, aged seventy-six, admitted to Guy's Hospital on the 26th June, 1876, under the care of Mr. Bryan, surgeon, in Job Ward; a married man; an Irishman; died on the 15th August in the same year; fifty days resident in the house; cause of death calculus cystitis. Address, 287 Coldharbour Lane."

The ATTORNEY-GENERAL—I put in the certificate of his death —the 15th August. I attach importance to this date.

Mr. JUSTICE HAWKINS—Very well.

The ATTORNEY-GENERAL—I also put in the certificate of the birth of the child, " Thomas Henry, son of Louis Adolphus Edmund Staunton and Harriet Staunton, formerly Richardson, born on the 23rd March, 1876."

George Wells GEORGE WELLS, examined by the ATTORNEY-GENERAL—I live near Knockholt, and am a flyman. On the 5th March last I took Mrs. Butterfield from Halstead to Little Grays farm. That is the nearest station; the drive is about 5 miles. I arrived there about four o'clock. Mrs. Butterfield got out and went to the door. She got out about 50 yards beyond the house.

Did you see any one in the house?—I saw through the window as I drove past the house Louis Staunton, Mrs. Patrick, Alice Rhodes, and two children. I turned my horse round and followed her up the road as far as the gate. She knocked at the door.

Who opened the door?—Mrs. Patrick let Mrs. Butterfield into the house. The door was closed after her. I went and stood near the window.

Did you see anything?—I saw Louis Staunton take up a knife from the table.

What did he do with it?—He flourished it about in the air.

What did you do then?—I went nearer the window.

What else did you see?—I saw that Mrs. Butterfield was pulled away from the door, when she made an attempt to go and seek for her daughter. I heard her ask to see her daughter.

Mr. JUSTICE HAWKINS—Did you hear her say she wanted to see her daughter?—Yes.

Mr. JUSTICE HAWKINS—Whom did she ask?—I don't know. It was either Mrs. Patrick or Louis Staunton.

The ATTORNEY-GENERAL—What next did you hear?—When she was pulled back from the door she said, " If you won't let me see her, let me hear her voice."

Evidence for Prosecution.

What did they say?—They said, "You shall not."   Then she said, "Let me see her hand on the bannister."

Mr. Justice Hawkins—Who said "You shall not"?—Louis Staunton.

Mr. Justice Hawkins—Did Mrs. Patrick hear that?—Yes, my lord. Mrs. Butterfield said, "Let me see her hand on the bannister; I shall be satisfied with that." Louis Staunton said, "You shall not. You never shall see her—not if you live for a thousand years."

Mrs. Patrick Staunton again rose from her seat in the dock, and, crying, said, "He was never in the house with the door open. She said she was sure her daughter was in a lunatic asylum. She never asked to see her hand on the bannister. It is cruel!"

The Attorney-General—Did Louis call her any names?—Yes.

What?—"You damned old bitch!" She was then elbowed out of the room by Louis Staunton into the passage, and Mrs. Patrick pushed her out of doors.

Did Mrs. Butterfield then do anything?—She went to the window and made some remark.

What did Mrs. Patrick say?—I don't remember all she said, but I heard her say, "You drunken old faggot!"

One of the prisoners, understood to be Louis Staunton, here exclaimed, "You villain!"

The Attorney-General—What next did you do?—I drove Mrs. Butterfield back to the station. On the way we met Dr. Creasey. I told Mrs. Butterfield who he was, and she spoke to him. I did not see anything of Alice Rhodes while Mrs. Butterfield was in the house.

Cross-examined by Mr. Straight—I was not examined before the magistrates, but I was before the coroner.

Who fetched you?—Sergeant Bateman.

That was on 19th May?—Yes.

Did you say, "I do not remember distinctly what was said"?—Yes; I did say that. I meant what was said inside the house.

Mrs. Butterfield appeared very excited?—She was very nervous. She was crying and spoke rather loudly. They all spoke loudly.

Did you hear Mrs. Butterfield say she was sure her daughter was in a lunatic asylum?—No.

Re-examined by the Attorney-General—You saw what passed, and have you told us what you have heard?—Yes.

Mr. Justice Hawkins—I think it is only right that the witness should be asked if he has said before what he has said to-day.

The Attorney-General—Did you give the same account

Staunton Trial.

George Wells before the coroner that you have given to-day?—Yes, to the best of my belief.

Mr. JUSTICE HAWKINS—That was only right. I have the deposition here.

WITNESS—Would you allow me to say that I did not hear the whole of the conversation? When I saw Louis Staunton with the knife I was in the main road, and when I saw the knife I went nearer to the house, as I thought I might be wanted.

The ATTORNEY-GENERAL—You thought you might be required?—Yes.

The FOREMAN OF THE JURY—Were the door and the window closed when the conversation was going on?—Yes.

The FOREMAN—And you heard all that was said?—Yes.

The FOREMAN—Were they talking angrily?—Yes, the voices were raised.

A JUROR—How far were you from Mrs. Butterfield?—The same distance as I was from the prisoners.

The JUROR—Were they inside?—They were inside, and I was outside.

Another JUROR—Were there any blinds?—There were not sufficient blinds to prevent me seeing them. I am not certain whether there were blinds at the bottom of the window or not.

Mr. JUSTICE HAWKINS—Did you hear anything said about where her daughter was?—No, I did not. If I did hear anything, I have forgotten it.

Sergeant Bateman

SERGEANT BATEMAN, examined by Mr. POLAND—I am a police sergeant in the Metropolitan Police force, stationed at Penge. On 14th April Mr. Casabianca, the brother-in-law of the deceased, saw me, and I went to Mrs. Chalklin, at 34 Forbes Road, Penge. The same day I saw Mr. Longrigg.

The next day I went to Cudham after having previously made inquiries at Bromley. I went to Little Grays farm. I went to the Woodlands first, but there was nobody at home there. I saw Mr. Louis Staunton at Little Grays. The servant opened the door to me. I was in plain clothes, and went in. I told him I was a police sergeant; no one else was then present.

I told him I had come to speak to him with reference to his wife's death, which had caused a little excitement in the neighbourhood. I said, " I shall want you to tell me something about the lady," and he said, " Yes." I asked him several questions, which he answered very readily. I said, " I will go back to the time you were married, and will trace the lady down to the present time," and I took the answers from him as I went on.

I cannot recollect the question I first put to him. I told him from what I heard I thought it ought to be brought under the notice of the coroner. I asked him when he got married,

Evidence for Prosecution.

and where he went to reside after he got married. He said, " I got married in June, 1875, and afterwards went to reside at No. 8 Loughborough Park." I asked him when he left there. He said, " I left about the end of May last and went to Gipsy Hill, Norwood." I asked him if his wife resided with him there. He said, " Yes, she did."

I asked him when he left there and came to Cudham, and he said, " I think I left about Michaelmas last." I asked him if his wife came with him, and he said, " Yes, she came and stayed a few days " or " a few weeks," I am not certain which he said, " but finding she was not able to manage my business I sent her to my brother's, and allowed him something for her maintenance."

I asked him if he had seen her since she went to his brother's. He said, " Yes, he had seen her several times." I asked if she visited at his house, and he said, " Yes, she visited me here, and I visited her at my brother's." I asked him if he had any family. He said, " One child, a boy." I asked if it was alive. He said, " No, dead." I asked him when the child died, and he said, " Oh, it only lived a few days. It was very delicate when it was born, and the doctor said it could not live."

I asked if a doctor attended her in her confinement, and he said, " Yes, a doctor in Coldharbour Lane." I asked him if the birth or the death of the child affected her mind or her health at all, and he said, " No, not at all; she always had an affection of the brain." I asked him how she was removed, and he said, " I removed her in my own trap." I asked if any one accompanied him, and he said, " Yes, my brother, his wife, and his sister-in-law, in the trap to the station."

I asked him how she had been, and he said there was nothing the matter with her until shortly before her removal. He said she had been rather poorly for a day or two. I asked him what she had to eat a day or two before her removal, and he said, " She had steak on Monday, fowl on Thursday, and she also had two slices of bread and butter, an egg, and a cup of milk on Thursday before her removal." He said no medical man had attended her down there. I asked him who attended on her at his brother's place, and he said his sister-in-law, Mrs. Staunton, and sometimes the servant.

. I asked him if she was a person likely to destroy her own life, and he said, " No, she was not." I asked him if there was any means of getting at a chemist's shop and getting anything likely to destroy her life, and he said there was not.

I asked him if Miss Rhodes had lived with him, and he said, " Yes, she lived with me at Brixton and Norwood. She remained at Norwood for three weeks after I left, and then she came here and managed my business for me." I asked him if his wife knew she was there, and he said, " She was per-

Staunton Trial.

fectly agreeable to that, as she was not able to manage my
business." I told him that the information I had received
I should have to lay before the coroner, and he would have to
decide whether it was a case in which an inquest should be
held. He answered my questions very readily; he hesitated
at one or two, but very little.

I asked him if any of the others could tell me anything about
her, and he referred me to the servant, Clara Brown, whom
he called into the room, and I put questions to her in his
presence. I asked her how long Mrs. Staunton had been at
her master's place—I knew she was the servant of Patrick.
She said she thought about four months. I asked her if she
had got any friends in the neighbourhood, and she said, " No,"
she had not. I asked her if she had been in the service of Mr.
Staunton before he came to Cudham and she said she had not,
nor had she known the deceased before then. She said, " Mrs.
Staunton generally attended to her, sometimes I did." She
said the deceased's state of health was generally very good.
I may have asked her about what she ate; I almost forget. I
asked her if she saw her removed and she said she did, and
that she got into the trap with assistance. I asked her if she
had heard anything further of her, and she said she had not.
I believe that is all I asked her.

I said I should like to see Mr. Patrick Staunton, and Louis
called him into the room. Louis remained. I asked Patrick
how long he had known the deceased, and he said for a long
time, several months, and she had been at his place about four
months. I asked him if there had been anything the matter
with her during the time she was there, and he said, " No,
except that she had an affection of the brain, or something of
that sort." He said, " She ate very heartily." I asked if
she had anything else the matter with her, and he said, " No,
there was nothing the matter with her." I asked him how
she was removed, and he said, " I removed her in my own
trap." He said she had been poorly a few days, and he
had advised her removal. I asked him again how she ate
generally, and he said, " Well, I was not always there." He
gave me some very evasive answers. I could not get answers.
When I asked him what she had to eat he said, " I was not
there, my wife would know better." I asked him if he was
generally in the house. He said, " Yes," his business, of
course, made him be indoors.

I saw Mrs. Patrick afterwards. I asked him if she could
tell me anything more about the deceased than he could, and
he referred to her, and called her in; that was at my
request. Just before she came in he said he did not see
the necessity for all this bother, as the doctor had given his
certificate.

When she came in I asked her how long she had known the

Evidence for Prosecution.

deceased. She said she had known her for a very long time.
I asked how long she had been at her place. She said she could not tell. I repeated the question, and she said she really could not tell how long she had been there. I asked her how her health was during the time she had been there. She said, " Very good." I asked her if she ate well. She said, " Yes, she ate, drank, and slept very well." I asked her if there had been anything at all the matter with her during the time she was there. She said, " No." I asked her who attended upon her. She said, " I did generally." She said she had been poorly for a day or two before the removal, that her feet had swollen. I asked her if anything was done for her in consequence of her feet swelling. She said, " Yes, they were frequently bathed." She said her feet had swollen for the last week or fortnight; that was in answer to my question how long they had been so.

I asked her if she saw her removed. She said, " Yes, I accompanied her to Penge." I asked her her state at the time she was removed. She said she walked very well, and got in herself. I asked her if the journey to Penge affected her in any way. She said, " No." I asked her if the deceased ever inquired for any of her friends. She said she did not. I asked her if any of the deceased's friends ever inquired for her down there. She said, " No, never." I asked her again if the journey to Penge affected her at all. She said, " No, it did not seem to affect her at all in any way; we took her to the bedroom in Penge, sat her on a chair, and she helped to undress herself; we put her into bed. She seemed very pleased, and thanked me for my kindness."

I asked her if she had anything to eat when she went to Penge. She said yes, she had some bread and butter and an egg. I asked her if there was any change at all. She said there was not until about midnight; that about midnight she seemed to get worse, and continued getting worse until the morning. She said the doctor was sent for, but he did not attend that night. He attended in the morning. I asked if she had anything to eat in the morning; she said she had some tea, but would eat nothing. I think that was all that passed.

She said the deceased had a great dread of her mother coming after her to put her into a lunatic asylum; that was said when I asked whether any of her friends inquired for her. I asked her the same question I had asked the others, about her going to a chemist's shop, and she said no, there was no means whatever of her getting to a chemist's shop. I asked whether she was likely to take her own life. She said, " No."

After asking these questions of the three, I asked Louis Staunton if Miss Rhodes could give me any more information than the others had given. He said, no, he did not

Staunton Trial.

think she could. I said, in consequence of the condition she was in at that time, I would not ask to see her. I did not see her. From inquiries I had made in the neighbourhood, I was told that she was very near her confinement, and that it was expected daily. That was all that passed, as far as I can recollect. This interview took place very near two o'clock on the Sunday. I reported to the coroner the following morning the result of my inquiries. There was then an inquest held at Penge.

The verdict was returned on 19th May, and on that day I went with Mr. Keene's clerk to the Ludgate Hill station. Mr. Keene had been the solicitor representing some of the prisoners, and had instructed counsel to attend the inquest on their behalf. I saw the two male prisoners near the station; that was by appointment. Mr. Keene's clerk took me there on purpose to see them. I said to them, "The coroner's jury have returned a verdict of wilful murder against you, and on that charge I shall take you into custody." They made no reply whatever to the charge. I then, in pursuance of an arrangement, went to London Bridge railway station and there saw the two female prisoners. Mrs. Patrick Staunton came on foot to the station from Walworth, I believe, about 6.30, and soon after that Miss Rhodes came up by rail from Norwood, I believe. I told Mrs. Staunton I should take her in custody on the charge. She said, "I am quite innocent of the charge." I told Alice Rhodes the same. She made no reply whatever. That was on Saturday, the 19th. On the next day, Sunday, the 20th, I went to Cudham. Before I went I spoke to all the prisoners together.

By the COURT—That was at the police station. They were all in the reserve room together. The two brothers had been put in one cell, and the two females were put in another cell during the night, and next morning they were brought out to have breakfast and a wash. If they are males we frequently put them together in one cell; it depends upon the number of persons we have, and the convenience. There is no rule about keeping prisoners, arrested on a serious charge like this, separate.

By Mr. POLAND—I told the prisoners that I was going down to Cudham to search their houses. Patrick Staunton said, "There is a key behind the clock at Little Grays, which belongs to a box at Mr. Bradford's; it was removed there for convenience, and was intended to be produced in Court, containing the clothes of the deceased person, but when we found how the case was going we did not think it necessary." That was all that was said. He did not say where it was removed from. I then went down to Cudham with Sergeant Philpot. Mr. Bradford met me at Little Grays farm.

I searched the house and found this draft letter (*produced*)

126

Evidence for Prosecution.

in a little drawer of a chest of drawers on the landing. I **Sergeant** found other letters there, the certificate of the birth of the **Bateman** child Thomas Henry Staunton, and a photograph of Louis Staunton and Alice Rhodes, in a group. I found the key referred to behind the clock where I was directed. These two papers containing the address of Mrs. Butterfield were found at Patrick Staunton's place.

The letter of Alice Rhodes of 19th August I found in the same drawer. I found it on that occasion. This is it; it is the one that was produced yesterday (*the envelope bore the postmark of 1st August*). I beg pardon, that is the wrong envelope. I don't think I found the letter in any envelope; it was the pencil letter that was found in the envelope, this was not. I afterwards went to the Woodlands that same day. I there found these two scraps of paper containing the addresses of Mrs. Butterfield and Mr. Hincksman. I found them in a drawer in Patrick's place. This pencil letter is what I found in this envelope in the same drawer as the letter of 19th August.

Letter read—

The Woodlands, Cudham, Tuesday.

My dear Louis,—I was very sorry to see it rain so soon after you left here yesterday morning. I am afraid you got very wet. It rained here incessantly until about 5 o'clock, and then I went as far as Roberts' to try and get some jam pots, but I could not get them anywhere. I had a good walk with Florie this morning to get Tommy's milk. You cannot tell how I missed my dear old sweety, and I hope he was not in mischief last night. Not that I think you would do it intentionally, but feeling dull might call on ——, and take strawberries and cream. I think myself it might be tempting. Come down as soon as you can, and then I shall have a great deal to tell you. Come down without Harriet if you can, when you take me home. The men have just come to make the hay here. Hoping I shall see my own darling soon, I remain his truly affectionate wife, Alice. I am not bad yet.

This is the draft letter found in the house at the Woodlands—

Mrs. Butterfield,—I really am astonished at your audacity and impertinence after your shameful and unnatural behaviour such as no mother in the whole world would have acted towards her own child. Rest assured I would cast myself into a lion's den to be devoured at once rather than come within arm's length of you, having come to the fullest determination to have nothing to do with you or your family. I have been again to my solicitor to-day, and we have given instructions for you to be taken into custody at once should you continue to molest me. With regard to the ill-treatment you allude to it is quite the reverse, having received the greatest kindness from Tom and Nancy since I have been in their house, and I must protest against such assertions.[1]

---

[1] This seems to have been a letter which Mr. Patrick Staunton intended to be copied by his sister-in-law; it was never sent. "Nancy" is Mrs. Patrick, whose second Christian name was Ann. I find no other allusion to Patrick being known as "Tom," but the reference can be to no one else; possibly it is a mistake of the reporter.

Staunton Trial.

On Thursday, 24th May, I went to the Woodlands again,
and found a letter signed "Harriet."[2] It was in the large
bedroom. It dropped from behind the washstand or dressing
table with some other papers when I moved it. I found some
castor oil and other drugs. I afterwards went to Mr. Bradford's and got the box that has been referred to; the key
referred to fitted the box. I made a list of the contents. I
also made a list of the clothing that I found at the Woodlands.

Cross-examined by Mr. M. WILLIAMS—The prisoners were
surrendered by arrangement. I made notes of the statements
which the different prisoners made the same night when I
returned; I have not got them here. I made a copy about
two days afterwards. I destroyed the original note. Louis
Staunton said that the child only lived a few days; he certainly
did not say that it had only died a few days.

I was present before the coroner when Clara Brown gave
her evidence; I heard her give it. I believe the coroner
cautioned her two or three times.

I have had several conversations with her since the inquest.
I put questions to her, I think, on two occasions. I did not
threaten her at any time, in any way whatever. I did not say
that she would be imprisoned.

I told her that I knew that the evidence she had given before
the coroner was wrong, and I told her that I had evidence to
prove that what she had said was wrong, and she had better be
careful; if she liked to persist in saying what she had said,
she could do as she pleased. I told her that for what she
had already said she would be liable to imprisonment. I said
if she went on in the way she was going on she would be
likely to get herself into trouble. I did not say she would,
only that she would be likely to.

She did not make any statement to me on 8th June; on 8th
June we were at the Bromley bench. To the best of my
recollection, I got no statement from her on 8th June. I
think she made a statement there to Mr. Pollard.

I remember Clara Brown saying, "I made an untrue statement with reference to the bedroom of the deceased and about
the food she ate. I now say that the food was put before her,
but whether she ate it or not I cannot say. What I have
said, both to the Treasury and before the coroner, I was told
to say by the prisoners themselves."

I do not remember when that statement was made. I
cannot tell you whether I told her of her liability to imprisonment before or after she made that statement to me. I have
no recollection of the date. I told her on two occasions of
her liability to imprisonment if she kept on in the way she

[2] See p. 50.

128

Evidence for Prosecution.

was going and stated what was untrue. The last occasion I told her so was 24th May. No, I cannot say whether that was the first or the last, but one occasion was on the 24th May, when she went to Cudham with me.

I do not know the date when I took her to live at Penge; it was fourteen or fifteen weeks ago. I did not then have a conversation with her on the subject, but I expect I had a conversation with her in respect to this charge. I did not tell her on that occasion that she might get herself into trouble. I took her to Penge because it was arranged that she should go there to live. She came from her aunt's at Heygate Street. She had no relations at Penge. A number of witnesses come from Penge. The Treasury paid her expenses, and I took her where I pleased. I live at Penge, and I took her there to be under my eye. She has been there ever since, and she came from there to-day.

Cross-examined by Mr. STRAIGHT—It was after she was examined before the magistrates that I took her to Penge. She came to Bromley by my instructions, and was there in attendance to be called as a witness; that was on 13th June. She had then made the statement which Mr. Williams has called my attention to. I did not write a statement out and forward it to the Treasury, headed " Bromley Police Station, 8th June." This is my signature to this document (*produced*), but none of the document is in my writing. It was written by Mr. Pollard, senior, but it is signed by me. Clara Brown was, I believe, in attendance at all the examinations before the magistrate.

I said before the magistrates, "I asked Mrs. Patrick Staunton how long she had known Mrs. Staunton; she said, ' For a long time.' I asked her how long she had been at her place, and she said, ' Some months.' " I asked Mrs. Patrick Staunton whether Mrs. Harriet had ever slept away from the house, and she replied, " No, not once "—that was referring to Mrs. Patrick's house.

Did you tell the magistrates that Mrs. Patrick Staunton told you Mrs. Harriet Staunton was very fond of a drop of spirits if she could get them?—I did.

Mr. JUSTICE HAWKINS—Then why did you not say that before? Was that fact in your original note?—It was.

Then let me tell you and others, once for all, that original notes ought not to be destroyed, but ought to be kept. The notes taken at the time the prisoners make statements ought to be kept, and not destroyed and merely copies retained. I hope I shall not hear any more of originals being destroyed and merely copies kept.

Mr. STRAIGHT—Did you not say before the magistrates that Mrs. Patrick Staunton said the deceased was generally in good

Staunton Trial.

Sergeant Bateman

health—that one day she was poorly and she gave her some castor oil, which was the only medicine the deceased ever had? Yes, that is so.

Did you not say before the magistrates that Mrs. Patrick Staunton said the deceased, the last day or two before her removal, did not care to eat without being forced to do so?— I did.

I asked Mrs. Patrick whether it was possible for her to get to a chemist's shop, and she said that it was not.

When I asked her about the state of health of the deceased lady the reply she made was, " She has not been ill, but rather poorly for a few days; the last day or two before her removal she did not care to eat without being forced to do so." I did not tell that in my examination-in-chief, because I did not think of it. I also said Mrs. Patrick said, " She was generally in good health; on Tuesday she was poorly, and I gave her some castor oil, which was the only medicine she had."

Mr. STRAIGHT—Then, really, why did you not say that here to-day in your examination-in-chief?—I had forgotten it.

Mr. JUSTICE HAWKINS—Of course, a witness, in giving evidence about a long conversation, may forget some things; but these are important omissions, and show the inconveniences of destroying original notes.

By Mr. STRAIGHT—Mrs. Judd, with whom I got lodgings for the girl, is not the wife of a policeman. I did not fetch her from there. She did not come up with me this morning. I saw her last night and saw her again this morning. I have read a very small portion of her evidence in this morning's paper, not a quarter of it. I read, or heard spoken of, the portion of it where it is said that I spoke about prison; I do not know which.

Re-examined by the ATTORNEY-GENERAL—It was a few days before 13th June that I was examined before the magistrate at Bromley; that was when we signed the depositions. I stated all I knew, and I was examined for a long time. After the coroner's inquest Clara Brown was taken to the Treasury. She went with Mr. Lewis's clerk on the first occasion, and I happened to be there at the same time. More than a day or two after she had been to the Treasury she made a statement to me, and I gave information that she had made such a statement. The statement was that she had not told the truth. She said, " I made an untrue statement with reference to the bedroom of the deceased and about the food she ate; I now say that food was put before her, but whether she ate it or not I cannot say; what I have said both to the Treasury and before the coroner I was told to say by the prisoners themselves." After she told me that, when Mr. Pollard, the elder, was at Bromley, he asked me if she wished to make a statement, and he called her in to make a statement. I told

130

Evidence for Prosecution.

him what she had said, but I cannot say when it was. I told him she had said, "What I have said to the Treasury and before the coroner I was told to say by the prisoners themselves."

After that I was instructed to get her away from where she was living, and I got her lodgings at Penge, because I was stationed at Penge. Since that time I have taken her two or three times to the solicitor to the Treasury at the Treasury. I knew from inquiries after she gave evidence before the coroner that she had not been stating what was true. When she was called upon to sign her depositions she said that what she had said was not true, and that when she came to give her evidence she would have to correct it all. It was in consequence of what she said before the coroner that I made the remark to her about getting into trouble.

Mr. E. CLARKE—I object to this style of re-examination. The matter referred to was not mentioned in the cross-examination, and it refers to what took place when the prisoners were not present.

Mr. JUSTICE HAWKINS—Beyond all question, what was said in the absence of the prisoners by anybody, at the inquest or elsewhere, is not evidence against them; but the witness has been cross-examined as to whether he told Clara Brown she might not get into trouble. That question could only have been put with one object, namely, to show that the witness was influenced by it, and surely, therefore, it is right for the Attorney-General to ask in re-examination, "Why did you tell her that?" and it is admissible for him to explain why he did, which, he says, was because he heard her before the coroner say her story was not true, and then he told her she would get into trouble if she went on in that way.

The ATTORNEY-GENERAL (To Witness)—Have you in any shape or way endeavoured to induce Clara Brown to give any statement which was not true?—No, sir, never.

ELIZABETH URIDGE, examined by Mr. POLAND—I am a widow, and live at Bromley. I am the owner of Grays farm, which consists of 22 acres. There are a farmhouse and buildings on the farm. The rent is £70. Some time last year that farm was advertised to let, and Louis Staunton took it and entered on it some time in October. He was to be my tenant from Michaelmas, 1876. He was my tenant till midsummer. He had a lease for three or seven years, at his option. I never went over the farm when he was there.

I saw Mrs. Butterfield in March, and found she was making some inquiries. In consequence of something I heard I telegraphed to her on Saturday, 15th April.[3] On the day

---

[3] See Appendix ii. p. 292.

Staunton Trial.

before that I was in a shop in Bromley, and Mr. Rose, the registrar of births and deaths for the district, came in and made a statement, in consequence of which I sent the telegram. Mrs. Butterfield had left her address with me.

By the COURT—When Louis Staunton took the farm of me he said that he was an auctioneer carrying on business at Gipsy Hill, Norwood.

HARRIET DAY, examined by Mr. POLAND—I live at Wrotham, in Kent. My husband is a gardener. We used to work on the farm at Little Grays. After Mr. and Mrs. Staunton came there I stayed there for some little time. I do not know Alice Rhodes by that name; she lived with Louis Staunton as his wife. They had no servant. I worked for them occasionally. There were four bedrooms in the house at Little Grays; only two were furnished, and only one occupied.

CHARLES JOSEPH CARTTAR, examined by the SOLICITOR-GENERAL —I am coroner for the county of Kent. In consequence of information given to me I held an inquest on the death of Harriet Staunton. On Wednesday, 18th April last, the inquest commenced. Harriet Butterfield identified the body of the deceased. Clara Brown was asked two or three questions, then an adjournment took place to 25th April. On that day Mr. Gye appeared on behalf of Louis Staunton, and then the inquest was further adjourned to 10th May to allow of the analysis. On the 10th May Mr. Gye again appeared and continued until the end of the inquest. Counsel was also there representing the Crown.

On 10th May Louis Adolphus Edmund Staunton was sworn and examined. I took down his evidence in writing; I have it before me now. Alice Rhodes was examined on the same day after he had been examined; she was the next witness. I have before me the evidence which she gave. On the same day Elizabeth Ann Staunton, the wife of Patrick Staunton, was examined. I took down the evidence she so gave. Then the inquest was adjourned to 11th May. On that day Patrick Llewellyn Staunton was called and examined. I have before me his evidence, which I took down in writing at the time. On the same day, after Mr. Patrick Staunton had been examined, Clara Brown was recalled. When all the evidence had been given the inquest was adjourned to the 14th. There were several adjournments, ten days, I think.

After the adjournment I appointed a day for the completion of the depositions. On that day neither of the four prisoners attended to sign their depositions. They did not answer to their names. On inquiry I was informed they did not intend to be present. In the interval prior to that Mr. Douglas

Evidence for Prosecution.

Straight appeared, representing one of the parties, Mr. Patrick C. J. Carttar Staunton, I think. Clara Brown attended to sign her depositions.

Cross-examined by Mr. STRAIGHT—These documents are not in my own handwriting, they are copied from my own notes at my dictation and my examination. I have the original notes at home, but these depositions are got up for all and each of the witnesses to sign. They were not read over because the prisoners did not attend, but the depositions on the various days on which Clara Brown attended were read over to her. The prisoners were not present. I asked the reason why. The learned counsel said they were not present in consequence of the alarm existing in their minds as to whether the multitude would not attack them, and further, that if they were present they would refuse to sign, under the advice of counsel.

[The evidence taken by the coroner was then about to be read by Mr. Avory, the clerk of arraigns, when Mr. Straight objected, on the ground that the depositions were not in the handwriting of the coroner himself and taken at the time. Those produced were only copies of the notes of the coroner.]

Mr. CARTTAR—I have not my original notes with me. They are at home; but I can verify every word in the depositions.

Mr. JUSTICE HAWKINS—If the objection be persisted in I will not raise a doubtful question, but will have the original notes here. They are not depositions until they are signed, only minutes.

Mr. STRAIGHT said he would not press the objection.

The depositions of the prisoners were then put in and read as follows—

" LOUIS ADOLPHUS EDMUND STAUNTON, of Little Grays farm, Deposition of Louis Staunton Cudham, Kent, farmer, sworn, says—' I have resided there since last November. From May to November, last year, I lived at No. 6 Corby Terrace, Upper Norwood. I was there an auctioneer. I married the deceased, Harriet Richardson, in June, 1875, at Clapham Church. There was no marriage settlement. One boy was born on the 23rd March, 1876. He died on 8th April, 1877, from convulsions. He died in Guy's Hospital. My wife was quite well up to Monday, 10th April last. She then complained of her feet swelling. I reside at the farm alone with Alice Rhodes. I have no servant. I have been separated from my wife since November last, by private arrangement. She lived at my brother Patrick's, at Frith Cottage, Cudham, about a mile and a half from my farm. I supported her, and allowed my brother one pound a week. I saw my wife two or three times a week there. I was on very good terms with her. She was

133

Staunton Trial.

addicted to excessive drinking almost daily; she drank spirits. I saw her on Saturday, 8th April; I had tea there. She was quite well. On Tuesday, 10th April, she was not so well, but she ate well; in fact, she was always craving for food. She was not allowed any spirits. Her face was swollen with a cold. I stopped there to tea and supper. On Wednesday I sent round some new laid eggs by Alice Rhodes, who brought word she was not so well. I immediately went there. She was sitting over the fire, and appeared very drowsy. I asked her how she was. The only remark she made was, ' Pretty well.' I asked her what she was going to have for dinner, if she could not eat a steak. She said, ' No, your brother has killed a fowl for me.' I then left. I went again in the evening and consulted as to what had better be done, as she did not appear to be getting any better. I suggested I should go up on Thursday morning and look for a place nearer London, where we might get advice for her. On Thursday morning Mr. Patrick Staunton came with me to Penge. We drove to Bromley, and came on by train. I knew Penge very well to be a place where they let a good many apartments, and also where there are a great many medical men. I saw apartments to let in the window of a house in Forbes Road from the train. I went there and took the apartments at 15s. a week and extras. I told the landlady it was for an invalid lady, and I thought it was a sort of paralysis. I said I would bring her about half-past nine that night. I paid a deposit of 5s. I did not say who she was. On Wednesday her memory appeared to fail her. My brother's household consists of himself and wife, two children (girls), three years and fifteen months old, and the servant Clara Brown, and my wife, and nobody else. I am told by my brother that Clara Brown is related to his wife. Up to Monday, 9th April, my wife was in a perfect state of good health. Mr. Richard James Bradford visited at my brother's. The mother and sister of deceased did not visit her. My wife declined to see her relations, because, before the marriage, they tried to make her out insane, and put her into a lunatic asylum, and it gave her such a hatred of them that she would never have anything to do with them since we were married. In fact, she had always quarrelled with her mother. I have seen Mrs. Butterfield at Brixton, when she saw her daughter. She has not seen her since. I saw Mrs. Butterfield myself about two months ago at Cudham. Mrs. Patrick Staunton was there. I did not tell her where my wife was. My wife was not at my farm. Mrs. Butterfield asked to see her. I told her on no consideration would her daughter see her, nor would I allow her to do so. I heard that inquiries were being made indirectly as to where she was. She wrote twice to her mother, once when living at Brixton,

Evidence for Prosecution.

requesting her never to call upon her again after her shameful conduct. My wife asked me to write a letter and date it from ' Brighton,' and to post it there to make her mother believe she was down there.[4] I wrote the letter, and I went to Brighton and posted it. In the same envelope there was a letter from my wife to her. It was about three o'clock on Thursday, 12th April, that we returned from Penge. My wife said she would get herself ready as soon as possible. I said I would be round about half-past six with my trap, a small wagonette with one horse. Alice Rhodes went to Frith Cottage in the afternoon. When I got there they were not quite ready. Deceased was in the parlour. They had dressed her once, but she had to be re-dressed again. She had the run of the house there. She had a private bedroom to herself. When ready I assisted her on one side, and my brother on the other, to the trap. She was able to walk with support. She assisted herself up into the trap, put up one of her legs and her hand out to catch hold of the rail. She sat on the front seat between me and Alice Rhodes. My brother and his wife went with us. It was dark. We drove to Bromley station. It was my intention to drive right up, but I thought it would save trouble taking the train from Bromley. We had a first-class compartment to ourselves. The train was just coming in. I asked them to stop the train as I had an invalid lady. The deceased was taken out of the trap and put into the train. We came to Penge. During the journey in the train she appeared very exhausted, was not able to speak. She got worse during the journey from Cudham to Bromley. At Penge a chair was got for her. Alice Rhodes and Mrs. Patrick Staunton went on to the lodgings to see that everything was ready. A cab was sent for and she was put into it by myself and brother. We could not get close to the house owing to the state of the road. The cabman assisted. She was not carried. The cabman did carry her from the gate up the steps into the house and into the bedroom. The front door was open. Mrs. Patrick Staunton and Alice Rhodes came up for the purpose of stopping with her while she was ill, at least Alice Rhodes was to have stopped. My wife was on friendly terms with Alice Rhodes—very friendly. She had been with us since six months after our marriage. Whilst they were undressing her I went to Mr. Longrigg's. He was not at home. I saw his assistant, and left word for Mr. Longrigg to come round at once, as my wife appeared so exhausted. I was told he would be in shortly. I then went back to the house. I did not seek any other medical man. I went again to Mr. Longrigg's, and his assistant said he would leave a note for him to come in immediately he

[4] See p. 273.

returned. I said, ' I will sit up for him all night.' About half-past eleven o'clock I went to the train and returned to Cudham. After she was in bed she appeared rather better, and said, ' I am tired.' That is all I heard her say. I took no advice as to removing her from Cudham, nor was she attended by any medical man there. Mr. Longrigg was a perfect stranger to me. I never said to Mrs. Chalklin or to any one that she had been attended by a medical man. I suggested on Wednesday to Mrs. Patrick Staunton that she should see Dr. Creasey. She said, ' He is no good; I have no faith in him. Far better take her to London.' I thought if any physician was wanted that I should sooner get him at Penge than I could at Cudham. Dr. Creasey lives at Brasted. I saw Mr. Longrigg the morning we took the apartments. I told him I wished him to attend her, and I did not exactly know what was the matter with her, her feet were swollen, and he seemed to understand the case. I did not tell him anything at all about the medical man having attended her, or that Dr. Creasey had seen her. I did not say that Dr. Creasey and other medical men had been attending her. I said the only doctor in the neighbourhood was Dr. Creasey, but he was so far off it would be better to bring her up. I told him I believed it was a sort of paralysis, that she had lost her memory, and shook a good deal. I returned on Friday at eleven o'clock. My wife was then insensible. My brother came with me. I found the nurse there. I remained until she died. I was not present in the room at her death. Alice Rhodes had left, Mrs. Patrick Staunton was with me. Her death was announced to me by the nurse. It was the drink that caused the separation between us. The marriage was not with the full sanction of her family. I had some property with her. I had derived benefit to the amount of between two and three thousand pounds. She was entitled to some reversion, which I have sold. The deceased herself wished to be brought up near to London.

" By Mr. POLAND—The child was brought up to Guy's Hospital, and died the same day. The child's name was Thomas Henry Staunton, aged one year. I paid the undertaker 35s. to bury it at Plaistow, in Essex. The child died on the 8th April last, and was buried on the 16th April. I did not attend the funeral. My wife was told of his death. I did not inform my wife's family. I never went to Guy's Hospital myself. I am twenty-six years of age. My wife was thirty-five years. Alice Rhodes is twenty years of age. My wife was not of weak intellect; I never noticed it. I did not hear the police were in search of her, or that her mother had been to the Bromley magistrates for their aid to find her. I know of no

Evidence for Prosecution.

one who ever saw her outside my brother's house. I cannot name any one who ever saw her the worse for liquor. I never noticed her emaciation until the Wednesday, 11th April. She was not neglected. She was always clean in her person and dress, but she has always since her marriage had lice in her hair, her false hair. There was nothing the matter with her but a cold. No box of clothes was brought with her; a hamper with some food. She dropped one of her slippers when carried from the trap to the railway carriage at Bromley station. She did not speak of supper. She was not conscious when I left Penge.

"By Mr. GYE—She would drink if she could get it. I have seen her outside my brother's house. She was a great eater. She was well clothed and had plenty of clothes. She never complained of not being comfortable. She wrote to her mother twice. Until the Monday she was not 'ill. In the trap a blanket was round her feet. She had her ulster on, and a shawl, and a rug. Alice Rhodes passed as Mrs. Staunton all the time we have lived at Cudham, and as my wife. I am not aware that my wife knew it. We left Norwood the last week in October. Deceased was at Cudham last summer for a short time. Alice Rhodes did not pass as Mrs. Staunton before we came to Cudham. I don't know whether Alice Rhodes is expecting to be confined. The deceased passed as ' a relative ' at my brother's."

" ALICE RHODES, of Little Grays farm, Cudham, single woman, says—I left Little Grays farm about three weeks ago, and I went to No. 3 Park Villas, Lower Norwood, at Mr. Bradford's, an auctioneer, where I am now staying. I have known him two years. I knew the deceased six years. I went to reside at Loughborough Park with Mr. and Mrs. Louis Staunton about six months after they were married. Deceased said she wished me to remain with her until she went to Norwood. About November she went to Cudham to Mr. Patrick Staunton's, and I went to Little Grays farm to keep house for Mr. Louis Staunton. I passed as Mrs. Louis Staunton there, but never before. I often saw the deceased. I did not know she was ill until Wednesday, the 11th April, and she was not very ill then. Mr. Staunton sent me to see how she was. I accompanied her to Penge on Thursday. Mrs. Staunton asked me to go with her; she sat between us in an open conveyance. The cabman carried her into the house, but she was able to walk. She undressed herself, and took out her own ear-rings, and was put to bed immediately. She took a little egg that night. In the morning she was a great deal worse. I did not remain until she died; I left about one o'clock. I do not know whether she knew about the death of her child. At Cudham she was not attended by any medical man; there

137

Staunton Trial.

was no occasion for it. She was in good health; her illness
came on suddenly; I cannot account for it. She was not of
weak intellect; she was a little nervous. I never heard of
her friends seeking to find her.

"By Mr. POLAND—I saw Mrs. Butterfield at London Bridge
station. She asked me how her daughter was, and where.
I told her she was at Brighton with her child and husband,
but I did not know her address. I did not tell her what name
had been given to the child. I did not tell her I had not seen
Mr. Louis Staunton for months. I knew the deceased was
not at Brighton, but at Cudham; I said it for a blind;
deceased asked me to tell her mother so. She said she had
written to her mother to say she was at Brighton, and advised
me to say the same. I never saw the deceased at any shops
at Cudham. She never cared to go out. Latterly she walked
down to Cudham, once or twice, not very long ago. I do not
know of any visitors coming to Mrs. Patrick Staunton's house.
I have seen her outside the meadow several times, and
generally alone. She did not want to see the tradespeople.
I should not say she was of weak intellect, but she was particularly nervous. She disliked being alone. I went to her
house, not to manage it for her, but to help her to manage
it, to assist her. She was not under the influence of other
persons, nor was she easily frightened when harshly spoken
to. She appeared to be very fond of her child, and nursed
it herself. I do not know whether she grieved at its death.
She was very weak the evening she left Cudham, but I daresay
she could have walked alone had she tried. She was too
ill to tell me why she was coming to Penge. She got worse
on the journey. She was not able to converse with me freely;
she was too ill. She helped herself to bed, and unfastened
her things as quickly as she was able. I did not see that she
was in a filthy state; I did not know that she was covered
with lice; I did not notice the dirty state she was in. I
have seen her the worse for drink, both at Loughborough Park
and at Norwood, and I think once at Cudham. I never
spoke to her of the death of her child, nor did she ever allude
to it; I thought that strange. Mr. Louis Staunton took the
child to the hospital. Mr. and Mrs. Patrick Staunton were
in the trap also. They came back to the farm, and said they
had left the child at the hospital. They stopped all night,
and went home on the Monday morning. I heard on the
Monday night it was dead. The deceased was quite able to
take the journey when we started from Cudham. We sat up
all night, expecting the doctor. I intended while we stayed
at that house to sleep with the invalid in the same bed."

"ELIZABETH ANN STAUNTON, wife of Patrick Llewellyn
Staunton, an artist, of Woodlands, Cudham, sworn, says—

Evidence for Prosecution.

The deceased came to us in November last in a perfect state Deposition of Mrs. Patrick Staunton of health. She had a wish to stay with me. She has been in good health ever since until Monday, 9th April last. On Sunday, 8th April, I took the child to Guy's Hospital. I gave there the name of Henry Staunton. I believe the child had another name, but I do not know it. The child was ill. My husband went with me. Louis Staunton waited at the hospital gate for us. We left the child about 4.30. On Monday night, 9th April, I heard of its death; my husband told me. He had been to take it some clothes, and found it was dead. It died on the Sunday night soon after we left it in the hospital. I went with the deceased to Penge. She was sitting by the kitchen fire before we started. I helped her to dress. She put her own ear-rings in. Her hair was always done every morning before breakfast. She always appeared very nice, and always had clean clothes. The cab-man helped to carry her in. She sat up and began to undo her dress. She thanked me, and appeared sensible then. I laid on the bed by the side of her after 3 o'clock a.m. We were expecting the doctor. I left the house about 5 o'clock p.m. I had previously told the landlady she was dead. The deceased requested me to come with her to Penge. Mr. Louis Staunton told the landlady and also the medical man that he was her husband.

"By Mr. POLAND—It was first arranged that the deceased should go to Penge on the Thursday. She had never com-plained. She was always a thin person. She always had her meals at the same table with ourselves. She was con-stantly out. The doors were always open. I have seen her out six times at least. I saw her write one letter to her mother. Dr. Creasey once attended my little girl about September last. We took a wicker basket to Penge with us containing clothes for the deceased, and a small parcel con-taining eggs and butter. I saw Mrs. Butterfield at Little Grays farm making inquiries about her daughter. I did not hear her say, 'If I could only hear my daughter's voice I would be satisfied.' I do not know whether the child was ever christened. The deceased was not at all a woman of weak intellect.

"By Mr. GYE—She always had meals at our table; plenty of food. She came down to breakfast daily and washed and dressed herself regularly. She did as she liked, and wore what she pleased. She had plenty of clothes, was always well dressed, and clean and fit to be seen. She had several dresses and jewellery. She could go in and out as she liked. My husband was not satisfied with Dr. Creasey when he attended our little girl. We had to hurry away on Thursday. We had no visitors at Cudham. I told Mrs. Butterfield I had

Staunton Trial.

dined with the deceased not twenty minutes ago. She said it
was a lie. I had directions from Mr. Louis Staunton not to
give deceased any spirits. I have not paid Dr. Creasey's bill;
I suppose my husband has. Mr. Louis Staunton did not
mention Dr. Creasey's name to Mr. Longrigg when he called
on him.''

" Patrick Llewellyn Staunton, of Woodlands, Cudham,
artist, sworn, says—I am brother to Mr. Louis Staunton. In
November last I agreed to board and lodge the deceased and
her child at £1 a week. She came in perfect health. She
partook of our meals at our table as a relation. My brother
desired me to prohibit the deceased the use of spirits, as she
had taken them too freely. I had twice seen her the worse
for liquor at Brixton, soon after she was married, and many
times since, indeed, constantly. I did not see any change in
her health until Monday, the 9th April, and then only knew it
from what she told me of her feet being swollen; her feet
were put in hot water, and she was then put to bed by my wife
and my servant. My servant waited upon her constantly and
regularly. I saw her as she was going up to bed, and afterwards when she was in bed; the servant told me she was awake,
and I went in to ask her how she was. She answered that she
felt all right, and the next morning she got up in the usual
way. I went the next day to see my mother, at Brixton, and
I told her the deceased was not well. I went to Guy's Hospital
on Monday, the 9th April. I started at ten o'clock; got
back about four. I drove to Bromley, then took the train.
At Guy's I went into the office and saw the clerk. I was told
the child was dead. I called at my brother's and told him
of the death. I stayed there about half an hour. I then
went home. I told the deceased, and she said, ' I thought as
much,' and she walked out of the room. I swear this
positively. She asked no questions, but walked out of the
room. Her husband came to see her in the afternoon. I
was not present. On Wednesday morning her husband advised
and I recommended her removal. She was consulted, and
consented to go to Penge. He and my wife went to take
apartments, and on their return I assisted her in and out of
the trap. She did not speak. I don't know that she was
insensible. I don't know that she was carried into the train,
as my brother was on one side of her and I on the other side,
and she put her foot on the ground. She was carried on a
chair from the train and put into a cab, and the cabman
assisted me to carry her into the house and into the room.
She seemed to be then more sensible. She did not speak. I
remained until half-past ten, when I accompanied my brother
to the doctor's. I left at about eleven, and returned to
Cudham. The next day I came up with my brother about

140

Evidence for Prosecution.

eleven, and was told she had had an epileptic seizure, but no information was given me that she was dying. I left about two o'clock, and went to my mother's to tell her she was very ill. On my return I found every one had left, and a message for me, and I went to Bromley. There I met my brother at the station. He had been to tell my mother. The child was born at Brixton—8 Loughborough Park. I believe it was registered. Dr. Russell, of Coldharbour Lane, attended at the confinement, and recommended a nurse, who remained the usual time—the month. The child was named Thomas Henry. The child was brought to my house at Cudham some months before the deceased came in November. It slept in a cot in our room, and my wife attended to it, assisted by the servant, Clara Brown. On Saturday, the 7th April, it had convulsions; it was always a thin child, almost all skin and bone. The deceased suggested that it should be carried to Guy's Hospital. No medical advice was had. On Sunday it was worse, and I and my wife and my brother went up with it to Guy's. My brother waited outside the hospital, and I and my wife went in and left the child with the doctor. I did not attend the funeral. I knew that Alice Rhodes was passing as my brother's wife, as Mrs. Staunton, but I did not know there was any criminal connection whatever. I cannot say whether she so passed for a deception or not. I took the Woodlands two years ago, leaving Brixton to go there on account of my profession. I was not assisted in taking the house in any way with money got from the marriage of my brother with the deceased. The child who died was the child of the deceased.

"Cross-examined by Mr. POLAND—Clara Brown was at Brixton in March, 1876, at the time of the confinement. In August, 1876, the deceased visited us at Cudham, and stayed a week with the child. She visited us four or five times; she was then living at Norwood. When with us she had perfect health; she was not a person of weak intellect, and was perfectly capable of managing her household and her own affairs. We had no visitors but Mr. Bradford. The deceased used to go out for walks. We have 7 acres of ground; she used to go in the wood and on the public road. I have seen my brother drive her out in a wagonette. I knew that Alice Rhodes passed as his wife; the deceased passed as a relation. My brother and Alice Rhodes came constantly to our house, three or four times a week, and deceased sat down at the same table with them and us, and partook of our meals, and made no objection and showed no jealousy. Deceased was in perfect health till the Monday, 9th April, washed and dressed her child herself. Deceased new Dr. Creasey had attended my child when it had been ill, knew that he had called five or six

Staunton Trial.

times, but she did not suggest he should be sent for to attend
on her own child.   She suggested it should be sent to Guy's.
She said, when told of its death, ' I thought as much.'   She
never asked where it was buried, nor the name of the doctor,
nor what ward it was in, nor expressed any wish to see the body
of the child, nor as to what members of her family should
attend the funeral.   Deceased was in perfect health.   I saw
no change in her till the Monday.   I did not send for Dr.
Creasey, as I have no faith in him.   It would take twenty
minutes to go to my brother's.   He had a wagonette which
could have fetched a medical man in half an hour, but no
medical advice was sought.   Deceased had a slight impedi-
ment in her speech on the Tuesday, a slight stutter.   Although
I knew that the child died immediately subsequent to removal
it did not occur to me to take medical advice previous to
removing the mother.   I suggested taking her to Penge, so
that a physician might be obtained, should the doctor there think
it necessary, but I did not consider her so seriously ill as to
require a physician.   I did not call on Mrs. Hincksman on
the Wednesday.   The distance from my house to the station
is about 8 miles, then there was the railway journey, making
it about 10 miles altogether.   I do not know how long it took
us to drive.   It takes me about an hour to drive it.   I met
Mrs. Butterfield at London Bridge one day, and she inquired
about the deceased.   She abused me, and got a great crowd
round us.   I had arrived from Cudham by the train.   I told
her that her daughter was quite well.   She said, ' No, she was
not ; she was confined in an asylum.'   I told her she was not
in an asylum, and she swore at me, and I walked away then.
I did not say, 'Damn your daughter.'   I never used such a
word.   She said, ' I am going to Cudham.'   I never said,
' If you do I'll blow your brains out, as I keep a loaded gun.'
I did not use that expression, nor any similar expression.   I
said I did not see what she could gain by going to Cudham.
I said she would not see her daughter, because I knew she
would not be allowed to see her.   I was at London Bridge
station ; the railway porters were there, and a crowd she
collected round us.   I did not know that she had applied on
the 9th April last to the magistrates at Bromley.   I never
heard of it.   The removals of the deceased and the child were
not in order to evade registering the deaths in the district or
to avoid inquiries.   I made no inquiry as to what district
Penge was in, nor did I know in what district it was.   While
in the trap the deceased made some remark about a dog, and
she also spoke to her husband.   She said nothing about the
slipper that was dropped.   I was not aware that she had lice
upon her, and I was much surprised to hear it.   When I first
knew her she was a very cleanly person, and she dressed as a
lady should.   I was at Penge on Sunday, 15th April.   I then

Evidence for Prosecution.

saw Mr. Longrigg. I went to see him to ask why the funeral did not take place after his giving his certificate; we thought there must be some mistake. I did not go to the undertaker's. The undertaker and Sergeant Bateman came to Cudham to my brother's, and by chance I was there. I undertake to say that I saw the deceased the worse for drink at least three times while she was in my house; I do not know how she got the drink.

" By Mr. GYE—The deceased looked after her child herself, washed and dressed it, looked after it in every way until its illness and removal. The child had plenty of clothes; clothes were brought to my house for the child several times by my brother. The deceased had plenty of clothes of very good description. She looked after her own clothes and the child's. My wife did not interfere. She was allowed to do just as she liked; she went out and about of her own free will; there was no sort of restraint put upon her, none whatever. The child had pretty good health, but was always thin; it had never had a like attack before. I was much dissatisfied with Dr. Creasey, and did not therefore call him in. Deceased understood the child was ill, and understood the purpose of its going to London. She was quite well up to the Monday. It was on the Wednesday she stammered, not on the Tuesday. She appreciated the suggestion that she should go to Penge, and was willing to go. I noticed nothing wrong with her, except the swelling of the feet, and she said her throat seemed a little sore; she said she thought she had a cold. She put one hand on my shoulder and the other on the rail of the trap, and put her foot on the step to get into the vehicle. She had list slippers, because her feet were swollen, and she had a blanket to keep them warm. Clothes were taken with her in a lady's travelling basket—a wicker basket lined inside. I did not pack it, but, as far as I know, that basket was full of clothes. There were no appearances in the deceased which, in my judgment, rendered it unwise to take the journey; none whatever. It took us about an hour and a quarter to drive. I had not the slightest idea that her death was so near, or that her state was in any way dangerous. She had no influence exercised over her to induce her to go. During the time she was in my house she was, in my opinion, capable of taking care of herself. I said Mrs. Butterfield would not be allowed to see her, not that she could not see her.

" Re-examined—Alice Rhodes saw Mrs. Butterfield on a different occasion. There was no particular reason for having the door of the lodgings at Penge ready opened; the landlady could have opened it if we had rung the bell. I contradict the statement of the landlady that she did not know until an hour and a half after we arrived that we were in the house; she knew it under the hour. I do not know whether the child

Staunton Trial.

had any godfather or godmother. It is about a mile to my brother's farm from my house; in twenty minutes I can walk it at an ordinary pace. The deceased was not kept secreted. I did not telegraph to my brother to warn him that Mrs. Butterfield was coming down. There were no precautions and no pains taken to keep the deceased private. I never knew the inspector and sergeant on duty at Sevenoaks were about my place. I swear positively that I neither directly nor indirectly had information of any application to the Bromley bench of magistrates. I presume Penge is in the county of Surrey; I did not think about what district it was in. We talked of driving all the way, but we did not know the road, and I think that was the reason we took the train. When I took the deceased there I did not think anything at all about what county it was in. I did not tell the deceased on the Sunday night about the child. I stayed at my brother's, as it was a pouring wet night. I told her nothing about it until I told her on the Monday night that it was dead. She was not restrained in any way, only with regard to the drink. I have not paid Dr. Creasey's account, unless my wife has."

C. J. Carttar

Mr. CARTTAR re-examined—Those statements were made by the prisoners as they are read—the statements contained in the depositions of Clara Brown are statements which she made, and they were read over to her and signed by her; there are three of them—she made an observation upon the signing which appears on the depositions.

Mr. WILLIAMS—The statements of Clara Brown are in with the rest of the depositions, but I do not propose to ask them to be read just now.

Mr. JUSTICE HAWKINS—The depositions are not in.

The ATTORNEY-GENERAL—I have no objection to put in the statements of Clara Brown.

Mr. WILLIAMS—I shall feel it my duty to call the attention of the jury to the discrepancies in those statements and her evidence during this trial.

Mr. JUSTICE HAWKINS (to the coroner)—Are these the statements of Clara Brown taken by you at the inquisition?—Yes; they were read over to her and signed by her.

Mr. JUSTICE HAWKINS—Very well. Then the statements of Clara Brown are now in evidence, and you may comment on them in your speech, Mr. Williams.

**Depositions of
Clara Brown[5]**

"18th April, 1877—I have never been in the service of the deceased lady. I have been two and a half years in the service of Mr. Patrick Llewellyn Staunton, of Cudham, an

---

[5] These depositions do not appear to have been read to the jury, but they are printed here as being part of the case for the Prosecution.

Mr. Montagu Williams

Evidence for Prosecution.

artist, who is the brother of deceased's husband. I first saw the deceased some time in last summer. She was then on a visit at my master's. She then remained two or three days only. She came again to stay a little before Christmas last, and remained until Thursday last, the 12th inst. She left about six o'clock p.m., in an open wagonette, with her husband, accompanied by my master and mistress and Miss Alice Rhodes, my mistress's sister.

"11th May (recalled)—I am first cousin to Mrs. Patrick Staunton and to Alice Rhodes. I have lived in the service of Mrs. Staunton, first at No. 9 Loughborough Park, Brixton, then at Cudham. Mr. Louis Staunton lived at No. 8 Loughborough Park. His household consisted of himself, his wife, and Alice Rhodes. The first time I saw deceased was at Brixton, soon after her marriage, in June, 1875, soon after I entered their service. In March, 1876, I went by chance to No. 8, and Mrs. Harriet Staunton was taken in her confinement, and then I stopped to do the downstairs work. The child was a thin little child. She did not suckle it. The nurse remained a month and I remained a month. Alice Rhodes was there the whole time. My mistress took charge of the child, and took it to Cudham about a month or six weeks before the deceased came to Cudham. The child was taken unwell on the Wednesday, 4th of April last, and the deceased said she would wish it to go to London to the hospital. The first attack of illness of the deceased was on Monday, the 9th of April last, when her feet were put in hot water. I carried up the water. The next day she had some castor oil. I heard her say she was going to the doctor's, and that she would rather go to London. She was not very ill till the Thursday afternoon, when she was drowsy, and sat with her head on a pillow, which was on a table, but she had her eyes open all the time, and said she was pretty well. She was about the same when she left in the evening, was able to walk, and got up into the trap. Her clothes were always very nice, such as a lady would wear. Her head and hair were very clean, and I never observed anything in it that was at all objectionable.

"By Mr. POLAND—The deceased was very fond of her child, washed it and dressed it herself. I knew that Alice Rhodes passed as Mrs. Staunton at Little Grays farm, Cudham. I never heard she so passed at Loughborough Park. I knew they were living together as man and wife at Cudham. So did the deceased. I have heard her speak of it. She showed no jealousy about it, and expressed no indignation, and showed no signs of hostility. The deceased was not a woman of weak intellect. She was frequently and constantly out of doors. Out every day. I had no orders to deny

Staunton Trial.

her to any one, and if her mother had called when my mistress was out I should have allowed her to see her. I cannot tell of any shop she ever went to at Cudham, or of any article of dress ordered by her. She used to ask me to bring her oranges and spirits. I got the oranges, but not the spirits, as I had strict orders not to do so. The tradesmen called at the house—the butcher, brewer, and baker. She used to amuse herself with her child, and with needlework; she did not write any letters. On Christmas Day Mr. and Mrs. Patrick Staunton went to London. The deceased was not locked up then. I know Miss Mary Ann Weatherley. She did not call on Christmas Day. I am quite sure I never turned a key on the deceased. She was not locked up. Miss Weatherley has called at the house. I noticed a change in the deceased on Wednesday. On Wednesday she ate some cold roast beef for dinner, and also at tea time, about a quarter past four o'clock. On Wednesday she had hot fowl for dinner at one o'clock (*sic*), and her appetite was pretty good. On Thursday she had a good meal of beef steak for dinner. Ate heartily.

" By Mr. GYE—She did not dress herself that Thursday morning; but she always dressed herself and the child during the time she was at Cudham, and did her own hair. Miss Weatherley lives at Knockholt. I washed the clothing. There was nothing different in the clothes of the deceased to the rest of the household. She had a good supply, in good condition, and they did not appear different to any one else's in the house. The tradespeople called, as is usual with tradespeople, and deceased might have seen them. She was not kept indoors, nor out of sight.

(Recalled)—On Thursday evening, 12th April, the wagonette was brought to the side door of the house leading into the little parlour, close to the door. The deceased was able to walk by herself. She was not assisted. She had no distance to walk, not across the meadow, only to the door. She got in herself. I state positively that she was not carried. She had been all day in the sitting room. She dressed in her bedroom. My mistress assisted her in putting on her bonnet. The ulster which she wore was her own, and she had two other dresses and a black silk skirt. I swear I never turned a key on her in my life. I always spoke to her the same as to my mistress. I deny using the expression, ' Go back, ma'am.' I did hear footsteps in the kitchen; the deceased was there. I did not go to the kitchen door. I swear I never said, ' She is no lady,' never said, ' Go back '; never said, ' She was deranged.' I swear I never said, ' She is no lady, she is only my master's sister.' When I heard the footsteps I did not do anything. There was a fire in the kitchen and one in the parlour, and a light in both. We were in the

Defence of Louis Staunton.

were not to go out sometimes to amuse themselves. On this occasion the doctor had gone to a supper party, and he did not return till a late hour—too late, he thought, to see the patient, who, he imagined, would by that time have been seen by some other doctor. It would have been better if he had imagined nothing of the kind, but had gone to her at once. When he did see her the next morning she was *in extremis*. Then we have the certificate of death, and this, in spite of the alleged filthy state of the woman and the vermin in her hair, was death from natural causes. There was no word of starvation. It was, in the first instance, a cerebral disease, and, secondly, apoplexy. A medical certificate of the cause of death must in all cases be given before the ground can be opened to receive the body, and who can doubt but that the certificate of Dr. Longrigg was an honest certificate? When he gave it he knew the state of this woman's body, both with regard to dirt and vermin in her hair, and it was a certificate of death from natural causes. Another question is, when did the doctors first think of starvation? Dr. Longrigg, Dr. Bright, Mr. Wilkinson, and Mr. Pigott, every one of them treated this case as one of poison. I say they may have had a notion of starvation, but they had a strong opinion at that time that the deceased woman met her death from poison, and hence the contents of the stomach were sent to Dr. Rodgers for analysis. So much for the Penge part of the evidence of Dr. Longrigg. Next, there is the nurse, and, again, there is no concealment from her. Then comes the undertaker, who was openly asked for. There is, I say, an absence in any shape, form, or way, of all concealment whatever. When the difficulty arose as to the funeral, Louis Staunton was quite ready to put it off for a day or two. It may be suggested that he could not help himself. But when a man is being tried for his life do not take everything against him, and I am sure you will not. Now, why do I call your attention to the absence of anything like concealment at Penge? It is for this reason, if this lady was to die, and if they knew she would die, and if they had schemed and plotted and contrived to bring about her death, why bring her to Penge? I am reminded, with regard to the nurse and undertaker, that Louis Staunton left word that if any one wished to see the body they were to be allowed to do so. Indeed, there was the very reverse of any concealment at Penge. If these persons intended to kill this poor woman, the one object of coming to Penge must have been concealment: but they did not conceal anything. With the exception of that question about Dr. Creasey, they truthfully told the names of the parties. You know they were not bound to go to Dr. Creasey. There were other medical men in the neighbourhood.

Staunton Trial.

Mr. JUSTICE HAWKINS—There were several medical men in the different villages within 5 miles off.

Mr. WILLIAMS—Under any circumstances a doctor must have been procured, for they could not have buried the body without a medical certificate. I ask, why did they move her unless their version of the transaction is a true one? I want to meet everything, and it may be said the intimacy with Alice Rhodes was the reason, but that is an untenable proposition. That cannot have been the reason, for Louis Staunton knew that Mrs. Butterfield was making inquiries, and only as late as 4th April he had written to her. He must have known that sooner or later his position with Alice Rhodes must have been discovered. Now, what do the prisoners say as to the reason for the removal? I will not give you what they said to the coroner or the magistrates, but what they said to Mr. Longrigg and the landlady at Penge. It was because Louis Staunton knew Penge, because he knew there were good medical men there, and he thought it better to bring her nearer to London. That is the statement they made at the time they go to Penge, and I ask you to reject the theory of the Crown that they went there for concealment—yet concealed nothing—but to believe that, getting frightened, Louis Staunton took his wife to Penge for the purpose of getting—unfortunately, too late, unhappily, too late—better medical advice. I say that from first to last there was absence of anything like concealment, and I say that the theory of the prosecution tumbles to pieces before the statement of the accused. But I take a higher ground, and say that in regard to the theory of the Crown and the statement of the prisoners, you are bound to adopt the statement of the prisoners. I have now dealt with the evidence at Penge, save as to the state of the body. There is no doubt this poor wretched creature was in a most dreadful state; no doubt, to a certain extent, she had been neglected. Who is responsible for that you will have to decide. Don't forget that Louis Staunton, although living away from his wife, and living disgracefully, I admit, was paying a sum of £1 a week for the proper maintenance of his wife. I know that, in a view my lord takes, it was not sufficient to pay £1 a week. He did not see his wife very often, but when he did see her in April, and saw the state she was in, he caused her removal, no doubt in a fright and hurry. This is important, because it then becomes an act of mere negligence, and reduces the crime to manslaughter. There is no doubt as to the state the body was in. How did she get into that state? She had been declared by her mother to have been of weak intellect, and there is no doubt that she was to a certain extent of weak intellect. What preys upon a weak intellect most? The knowledge that persons are trying to make the patients out

Mr. C. W. Mathews

Defence of Louis Staunton.

mad. That might have been the reason for keeping to her room. If this preyed on her mind, naturally the mind got weaker, and hence, as she was not properly looked after, the state of her hair. As to the vermin, where there is wasting, not only after death, but during life, vermin breed, and breed to a very alarming extent. She could not have been till very lately before her death in a state of vermin, because we have it that Clara Brown slept in the same room, if not in the same bed.

Mr. JUSTICE HAWKINS—Not in the same bed.

Mr. WILLIAMS—The child slept in the same bed.

Mr. JUSTICE HAWKINS—Clara Brown said that Patrick's child slept with her, and Mrs. Harriet's child in a bassinette.

Mr. WILLIAMS—The vermin could not have been there to any great extent before the removal to Penge, because there is Clara Brown sleeping in the same room. There is not a suggestion that Mrs. Patrick Staunton, unless she had been a fiend, would allow her child to be in the same room with a woman swarming with vermin. With regard to the absolute ill-treatment, the violence of Patrick Staunton—and I think, on one occasion, of Louis Staunton—upon this unfortunate woman, you have no absolute evidence—there is but the evidence of one person. You have the state of the body; you have the fact that the woman originally, according to mere guesswork, weighed 8 or 9 stones in all, and that she decreased one-half in weight. We say that is consistent with disease. But, beyond that fact, what evidence have you in corroboration of Clara Brown, who I will show you, and prove to you, is utterly, upon her own statement, unworthy of belief? Yes, you have a particle of evidence as to a mark in the face; and I want to call your attention particularly to that evidence— the evidence of Mr. Keene—and I also want to call your attention particularly to the dates. We have it in corroboration—I presume it is placed before you as corroboration—that upon 23rd October there was a mark upon this lady's face at the time she went up to Mr. Keene's, the solicitor.

The ATTORNEY-GENERAL—It was the 17th.

Mr. WILLIAMS—Either upon the 17th or 23rd. I am much obliged to the learned Attorney-General. This visit is made to Mr. Keene, and it is a most remarkable date. I think it was upon the second occasion, the 23rd. If it was upon the 17th it does away with the theoretical evidence—because it is only theoretical—of the man that was walking near the wood and heard the shriek of a woman on the 22nd. It would be utterly unsafe to rely upon that, because we do not know what persons were in the wood, or what they were doing in the wood; and it is only upon speculation you can connect the prisoners at the bar with any violence to the deceased on

Staunton Trial.

Mr. Williams that day. On the 17th or 23rd we find Mrs. Staunton having an interview—with whom? Her own family solicitor. She came up to consult him—for what purpose? For the purpose of signing certain papers relating to the selling of her reversion.

Mr. JUSTICE HAWKINS—I think you are in error in saying it was her own family solicitor. I think it was Louis Staunton's.

Mr. WILLIAMS—I think that is not so.

The ATTORNEY-GENERAL—He had been her solicitor when she was Miss Richardson.

Mr. WILLIAMS—I believe he had acted generally for both parties.

Mr. JUSTICE HAWKINS—Yes.

Mr. WILLIAMS—But on the 17th or the 23rd we have these visits, with this mark on her face; and yet, although she sees Mr. Keene, there is not one single word of complaint of any sort or description. That brings me to the evidence of Clara Brown. Now, what was Clara Brown's account of herself? I will take that first of all. Of course, it may be said she was very young. So is Louis Staunton; he is only twenty-four. Alice Rhodes is only twenty. But I think Clara Brown is as self-possessed a young person as you or I ever saw. She was not a person likely to be terrified, coerced, or frightened. And yet, what is the story she tells? Why, if her story be true, she is an accomplice. Putting the adultery on one side, she is far worse than any Alice Rhodes, because Alice Rhodes, save and except as a visitor, was not in the house. What is this girl's statement about herself? "I was a free agent. I was able to go out to the tradesmen. No control was ever put upon my movements. I went where I pleased, how I pleased, when I pleased, as far as consistent with my duties as a menial. I used to go out and see people, and yet I, knowing that these people were confining this poor semi-imbecile, for the purpose of compassing her death, never said anything about it." There is no doubt about that, and she must therefore have lent herself to it. I suppose she could write, but she never takes such trouble, and, even in a case like this, she never wrote a single line to protest against it. On the contrary, we find her on Christmas Day, when the two young women came to the door, saying, "Go back, ma'am," and shutting the door upon her. Then there is the lost letter. This, she says, is the effect of it—

My own Darling—I was very sorry to see you cry so when I left you. It seems as though it never would be; but there will be a time when Harriet will be out of the way, and we shall be happy together. Dear Alice, you must know how much I love you by this time; we have been together two years now.

She says that the construction she put upon the words that

Defence of Louis Staunton.

"Harriet will be out of the way" was that Harriet would be deprived of her life. Yet, with that knowledge, she never mentions the matter to a single soul. The first proposition is, whether her account of the letter is a true one. Were these words in the letter? She says that what she said before the coroner was false. She makes statements on 29th May and on 8th, 20th, 23rd, and 27th June, and it is not till 27th June that she makes mention of this letter. She has not the excuse that the prisoners urged her to conceal the letter. They had been taken into custody. Up to that time she had not said a word, so far as we know, as to the contents of that letter, and, with such a lying girl, are you of opinion that the words were in the letter at all? This man's life under this indictment is dependent to a great extent on the amount of credibility you give to the witness. Did the words exist? You have it that a letter had been lost, about the recovery of which Alice Rhodes was anxious. That might be, and yet such words might not be in the letter. If at that time Harriet Staunton was at Woodlands, if that letter referred to illicit intercourse between Alice Rhodes and Louis Staunton, they would be most anxious for its recovery. Supposing the words were correct, do they necessarily bear the interpretation that there was a suggestion and plot at that time to deprive Harriet Staunton of her life? Most certainly not. You must remember the dates again. At that time there was no Little Grays farm, because it was not till Michaelmas that it was taken. It is quite clear that Mrs. Harriet Staunton, to have found the letter, must have been present in the place where the letter might have been dropped. At that time Alice Rhodes was at Woodlands, because the letter alluding to the lost letter is dated Woodlands. Here is the letter which refers to the lost letter—

> Woodlands ; Saturday morning.
>
> My dearest Louis—I was extremely thankful to have a letter from you yesterday, as you must know it is extremely dull for me here, and baby is so very fretful. I have searched high and low for the lost letter and cannot find it, and I am sure Harriet has not got it. So where it can be I cannot tell. Come down to me as soon as you can, if only for a few hours, for you cannot think how happy it will make me to see your dear old face again. With fondest love, trusting to see you soon, I remain your affectionate ALICE.

> Though absence parts us for a while,
>   And distance rolls between :
> Believe, whoever may revile,
>   I'm still what I have been.

About the lost letter itself Clara Brown tells a parcel of lies. First of all, she says it was in her pocket when Alice Rhodes questioned her about it, and next she says that she told her

163

Staunton Trial.

Mr. Williams she had burnt it. If the statements of Clara Brown are to be believed, this poor woman was kept without food for days at a time; she was struck by Patrick Staunton; she was kept prisoner in a very miserable state in the room she occupied; and, in point of fact, the deceased was systematically ill-treated and systematically starved to death. Let us see if she is to be believed. I will not take up your time by going over all her evidence.

Mr. JUSTICE HAWKINS—Pray do not curtail any observations you may consider necessary; do not consider time for a single moment. I shall be willing, and I am sure the jury will, to hear all you wish to say.

The jury expressed their assent.

Mr. WILLIAMS—Thank you, my lord. Now, this is what took place before the coroner (reading)—" Are you related to Mrs. P. Staunton?—Yes, I am her cousin."

Mr. JUSTICE HAWKINS—The depositions before me—those of the coroner—are not in the form of question and answer.

Mr. WILLIAMS—I have only the shorthand notes. Will your lordship lend me the coroner's depositions?

Mr. JUSTICE HAWKINS (handing them down)—Certainly. I only mentioned the matter because the shorthand notes are not in evidence, and they must be proved.

Mr. WILLIAMS then proceeded in detail to quote the evidence of Clara Brown from the coroner's depositions, pointing out various contradictions. The learned counsel continued—

Can you believe her evidence? The Attorney-General told you not to rely upon it unless it was corroborated orally or by some fact bearing upon it. In the statement before the coroner she said that Alice Rhodes passed as Mrs. Louis Staunton, and insinuated that even while at Loughborough Park there was an adulterous intercourse between them. And she actually now has said the same thing in the witness-box. But what is the evidence to support it? No more than that a nightdress was found in a drawer in the room in which Louis Staunton slept. My lord put the question whether any other articles of her dress were found there, and she did not remember. I do not complain of the matter being improperly brought into the case, but it is calculated to prejudice the jury in coming to a decision. I felt this, and therefore asked if there was a chest of drawers in the room in which Alice Rhodes slept, and it turned out that it was the only one in the house, and her clothes, if in a drawer at all, could be nowhere else. I thank my lord very much for giving me these depositions. She is asked all kinds of questions, and she answers. She says she was inspired in her statements by the prisoners. How could her replies have been suggested in anticipation? In a question affecting the life of a fellow-creature, can you for one moment

Defence of Louis Staunton.

entertain as truthful the evidence which she has given in this Court? The prisoners must have had a wonderful intuition if they could have anticipated the questions which would be put by the coroner. I humbly and confidently submit that you cannot believe her, because, in addition to the two statements she has made, she has made other statements which she has kept until the last. I wonder whether she had seen the letter about the lost letter before she mentioned it? What do you think? She was having conversations with Sergeant Bateman, and, of course, he had the letter referring to the lost letter in his possession. I think we may speculate it was not until she had heard of that letter that she thought of making the statement she has done about it, especially when you take into consideration that she has made four or five different statements at various times. If she was unworthy of belief in the statements she made before the coroner, I say she is doubly unworthy of belief in the statements she has since made, and I hope I have successfully proved to you that she is a most unreliable witness, and a witness whom you would not be warranted in believing in such a serious matter as this. I do not care whether she told the coroner that her statement was untrue or not, but it is well you should remember she swore to it and signed the deposition.

Now, the other evidence which has been adduced is that of a number of persons from the neighbourhood of Cudham, and I will call it the Cudham evidence. There is the evidence of Quested and Hollands, the policemen; of Tucker, who watched the Woodlands after Mrs. Butterfield first began to make inquiries; and all the evidence is this, that at that time they saw no Mrs. Harriet Staunton. Now, if my theory is correct, the reason why they saw no Mrs. Harriet Staunton was not because of her absolute confinement, but because of her disinclination and inability to go out. The belief that insanity was growing upon her, and the fear of being locked up, was sufficient to keep her within the house in seclusion, moping and brooding over her wretched state. As to the evidence of the gamekeeper, that he heard the cry of a female on one occasion, I do not think much importance is to be attached to that, because Mrs. Harriet Staunton saw her solicitor, Mr. Keene, next day, and she made no complaint to him of having been ill-used, or any violence having been used to her. The evidence of Longridge and Wetherley I do not think is important, and, after you have the butcher and baker, I think you have exhausted all the Cudham evidence, the purport of their evidence being that no such person as Mrs. Harriet Staunton was visible; but that, on the part of the prisoners, is not denied.

I have not attempted to deal with the medical evidence in

Staunton Trial.

Mr. Williams this case. Mr. Clarke did so in cross-examination, but I may say that I believe certain medical testimony will be called before you to prove that deceased may have died from natural disease. The cross-examination of the medical evidence was put in two views. The first was that she died from natural causes, such as diabetes, Addison's disease, or tubercular meningitis, while the other view is that she was labouring from some natural complaint at the time her death is alleged to have been accelerated by her removal to Penge. Of course, if you are of opinion that there was no acceleration of death by any act of the prisoners, they are entitled to be acquitted. If, on the other hand, you are of opinion that death was accelerated by any act of the prisoners—wilfully accelerated—you have been told what your duty is as to the verdict you will have to pronounce. I am addressing you more as to the quality of the offence than anything else, and I hope I have made myself intelligible. You are asked on the first count to find the whole of the prisoners, or any one of them, guilty of murder, while you are also invited to find them guilty of manslaughter, and my observations are addressed to you in view of the latter, and I do not wish to be misunderstood in any way.

Now, there is another portion of the evidence, which, although it has no direct bearing upon this case, which is an inquiry into the death of Mrs. Harriet Staunton and nobody else, has been referred to—I allude to the death of the child. The evidence about the child has no bearing on this case, except so far as it affects the death of the mother. Now, the evidence respecting the child is by Dr. Coley, by the nurse, Sister Mary, and by the undertaker. With regard to Dr. Coley, he says he was the person who received the child, and that it was brought by Mrs. Patrick Staunton. A right name was given for the child, although it was spelled wrongly, being spelled " Stormton " instead of Staunton. Well, that fact ought not to weigh against the prisoners, and I will tell you why. Because they gave the right address of Little Grays farm, Cudham, and whether the name was spelled one way or the other, the fact of their giving the right address was sufficient, because they would be sure to be found there in case of inquiry. Therefore neither you nor anybody else, I am sure, will attach any importance to the fact that the name was spelled wrongly. Dr. Coley says the child was in a very bad state, and clothes were necessary. Well, next day Patrick Staunton arrives at the hospital with a parcel—which it is fair to assume contained clothes—when he learns that the child is dead. Therefore, we have a right name given to the child where there was no occasion to give a right name at all. Then there is a right address given where, if concealment was sought, a right address would not have been given. Louis Staunton's father had

Defence of Louis Staunton.

been in Guy's Hospital, and therefore he would probably know **Mr. Williams** what the rules were with regard to the admission of patients, and he would tell Mr. and Mrs. Patrick Staunton to do as they did, namely, give the right name and address. I am making these remarks in view of any suggestion that the child was improperly treated. As to the undertaker, there is no doubt lies were told to him, if his evidence be true.

Mr. JUSTICE HAWKINS—With regard to the child, there is evidence that Louis Staunton went to the hospital, but did not go in.

Mr. WILLIAMS—Thank you, my lord. I did not omit that fact purposely, but I overlooked it.

Mr. JUSTICE HAWKINS—I am quite sure you did not omit it intentionally. That is why I reminded you of it.

Mr. WILLIAMS—Well, no doubt, as I have just said, lies were told to the undertaker, it being told him that the father of the child was called Thomas Harris, and that he was a carpenter. But you must remember that people, with a view to save money, will sometimes do extraordinary things, and probably this was done with a view to reduce the expenses of the funeral, or for some other reason at which I cannot arrive, but I do not think you will attach very much importance to it. Well, then, there is the evidence of Sergeant Bateman. He was asked whether he did not threaten the girl Clara Brown that she would be taken to prison if she did not make a different statement.

Mr. JUSTICE HAWKINS—The statement that the name of the father of the child was Thomas Harris, and that he was a carpenter, was not made by your client, Louis Staunton; it was made by Mrs. Patrick Staunton.

Mr. WILLIAMS—I am obliged to your lordship for reminding me of that fact. Well, I was referring to Bateman's evidence. He admits that he told Clara Brown she might get into trouble. We now find that the girl is living down at Penge, and that she was taken there by Sergeant Bateman. She must be somewhere, and I do not attach too much importance to the fact that she has been living at Penge. It seems most natural that the place where the policeman himself lives should be the place to take the girl, so as to have her under his eye.

Now, gentlemen, I have dealt with all the matters as far as in my power lies, in this, believe me, very onerous case. The duty I have had to discharge is one of the most onerous I have ever had during the fifteen or sixteen years I have been in this profession. I have endeavoured to call your attention to the principal parts of the evidence, and I have endeavoured to wrestle, and, I hope, sometimes successfully, with the theories which have been placed before you by the Attorney-General on the part of the prosecution; and when I have done addressing you I shall have this satisfaction—and it is the only one—that

Staunton Trial.

Mr. Williams I have done so in discharge of my duty, and to the best of my very humble ability. My learned friends will have something to say for their respective clients, and the learned Attorney-General will then reply on the whole case. He is entitled to that reply, although we called no evidence whatever, by virtue of the high office he now fills, and I am quite sure that I speak with the concurrence of my learned friends when I say that he will discharge that duty conscientiously, and those who know, not only him professionally, but the goodness of his heart and the kindness of his disposition, will know full well that in the discharge of that duty he will say no word in exaggeration, and he will stretch no fact in aggravation. You will then hear the law as you are bound to take it from his lordship, and the summary of the evidence. Gentlemen, it seems almost unnecessary to remind you that the solemn, the most solemn responsibility of all will then devolve upon you, because if you are of opinion that one, or more than one, of these wretched prisoners is accountable for the death of that unhappy woman, it will be for you to say with regard to my client—and I will deal with him alone—with regard to the husband of the wretched woman who is no more; whether at the age of twenty-four—only a very small portion of the time, we are told, which is ordinarily allotted to men—he shall suffer a violent and ignominious death, shall be hurried into the presence of his Maker with that adulterous sin full heavy upon him; or whether, in years to come, when more matured by age and more wise in his generation, he shall have time to repent, and bitterly repent, the terrible offence that I, as his advocate, am bound to admit he has committed. Gentlemen, in choosing the alternative that you will have to take, if you think he is criminally responsible at all, I can only pray, in conclusion, that you may be assisted by a higher Power to whom this, which has been termed "the Penge mystery," has never been any mystery at all—that you may be assisted to come to a true and righteous conclusion.

Mr. Straight Mr. STRAIGHT then proceeded to address the jury on behalf of Mrs. Patrick Staunton.

My learned friend, Mr. Williams, at the close of his observations has referred to the anxiety and responsibility in regard to the duty which rests upon his shoulders in defending Louis Staunton. I may say, as far as I am concerned, and the other learned counsel associated with me in this defence, that we realise and recognise the importance and the difficulty of the task which is entrusted to us in this most momentous trial. Gentlemen, forgive me if I repeat what you have kindly said—that no time can be unreasonably occupied in the addressing of observations to you on behalf of the prisoners; and forgive me also if, in com-

Defence of Mrs. Patrick Staunton

mencing the remarks I have to make to you on behalf of Mr. Straight
Elizabeth Ann Staunton, I utter some words of warning to
myself and yourselves in respect to the discharge of the duties
which severally fall upon us.   There can be no question that
this case is one which has attracted much public attention
in the public Press, has been the subject of conversation and
comment, and has had drawn to it certain sensational aspects
of which it ought to be stripped, now that we are in a Court of
justice.   Whether it is to the advantage or disadvantage of
the public in these days of rapid and accurate reporting—in
these days of a large newspaper Press, when every occurrence
is transmitted to every centre where the journals circulate,
and is made the subject of notoriety and comment among all
classes—I will not say; but cases of this description provoke
feeling, and sensational headings are put to them in the public
Press, and people very often form hasty and inconsiderate
conclusions, partly because they allow their sentiments to get
the better of their judgment, and partly because they do not
read all the evidence which is published.   It would be idle to
conceal from you the fact, because it is beyond controversy,
that to you twelve gentlemen, ratepayers of the city of London,
has been relegated the duty which otherwise would have been
performed by a jury in the county of Kent, because it was
thought that a more calm, dispassionate, and unimpassioned
verdict would be given in the city of London than in Kent;
and I may remind you that you have the eyes of your countrymen upon you, and your own consciences to consult.   I am
perfectly satisfied, and I pay the compliment to you in no
false sense, and with no desire to ingratiate myself in your
good opinion, when I say that I have never had the opportunity
of seeing a jury which has paid deeper interest or attention
to the evidence brought before them than you have done, and
I know in the end, when you retire to consider your verdict,
you will arrive at a decision based upon fact, upon evidence
based upon reasoned-out conclusions, not animated by prejudice, not moved by emotion, and not brought about by
sentiment, but according to law.   As regards the manner in
which this case has been presented, I hope you will imitate
the fair and calm tone adopted by the Attorney-General.   He
has placed this case before you as the minister of justice
which he is, and I am sure to the end he will discharge his
duty in the same manner and with the same feelings.

It may now be convenient that I should trace out to you the
relationship of Elizabeth Ann Staunton to Patrick Staunton and
the deceased lady.   One of the facts we have to deal with is the
residence of the deceased at Cudham, and that she was not
allowed to go about as an ordinary person.   Now, what is
the story?   You heard on Saturday, and you may have heard

Staunton Trial.

Mr. Straight yesterday, because the spirit of the thing runs through that which you may have heard yesterday in your churches, about the duty of the wife to the husband. You heard, in respect of the relationship occupied by Elizabeth Ann Staunton to Patrick Staunton, the principle of law I endeavoured to urge in excusing her in this matter; and, notwithstanding the ruling of his lordship, I submit it is competent for me to argue that what Elizabeth Ann Staunton did may have been done under the coercion of her husband. By the law of God, and by their social relations, the position of the wife to the husband is recognised as a subordinate one; not that she is socially inferior, but from the time she enters into the contract with the man she promises to obey him; and when you are dealing with this case, always regulate your view by remembering that Elizabeth Ann Staunton was the wife of Patrick Staunton.

Prior to November, 1875, Patrick and his wife were living in the Loughborough Road, and I think they had one child born there. They lived opposite to the house in which Louis Staunton took a residence for himself and Mrs. Harriet Staunton. Now, with regard to the conduct of Mrs. Butterfield towards her daughter, is there one single thing in the history of humanity on which a woman entertains a stronger opinion than in reference to the interference of any person with her marriage to the man she wishes to marry? It is quite clear that Harriet Richardson was bitterly indignant against her mother for opposing her marriage to Louis Staunton. In the early or middle part of 1874 the deceased went to live with her aunt, Mrs. Ellis, who was the sister of Mrs. Butterfield, and she remained there some little time. Afterwards she went to Mr. and Mrs. Hincksman's, and there remained up to the time of her marriage. At the time she was there, you may take it, she was perfectly capable of controlling her own actions, and of judging whether she ought to get married or not, and she knew that no one but Mrs. Butterfield wished to prevent the marriage. Therefore, no doubt, at that time she had formed a strong opinion as to the course her mother was adopting, and this seems to me one of the most important parts of the case. A fortnight or three weeks after the marriage had taken place, Mrs. Butterfield comes down to the house. It is impossible that they could have been very good friends, considering how the latter had opposed the marriage. There was, of course, studied politeness, and it does not appear there was any disturbance on that day; but this is immediately after-wards followed by a letter from Louis Staunton, begging Mrs. Butterfield not to come to the house again, and it is hinted that there may be disturbance if she does come. Mrs. Butterfield appears to have been a kind of firebrand in the family. She had fallen foul of Mrs. Patrick Staunton, and of the

Defence of Mrs. Patrick Staunton.

Hincksmans, and all this was calculated to cause a good deal of angry feeling. I mention this to explain one part of the case. Of course, we must all sympathise with Mrs. Butterfield in this case; but we must not allow our sympathies to get the better of our judgment and the facts. Now, the marriage took place in June, 1875, and, as far as I understand, there is no element introduced into this case insinuating any guilty conduct on the part of any of the prisoners between June, 1875, and March, 1876, when Tommy is born. There is no particular stress laid upon what happened at the confinement. My learned friend Mr. Williams has dealt very fully with the statements of Alice Rhodes and her familiarity with Louis Staunton; but whatever may have been the views of Mrs. Harriet Staunton in 1875, it is quite evident when she wrote the letter she did her suspicions were at rest with regard to the condition of things of which she had formerly complained. It is also quite clear she was on the most affectionate terms with her husband, because she wanted to come back to him at home.

Leaving the confinement, we pass on to what seems to me the most material part of this case. In November, 1875, Patrick Staunton and his wife had gone down to Cudham to live. Occasional visits were made by Mrs. Harriet Staunton and by Alice Rhodes, sometimes together, sometimes separately; and about the beginning of August, 1876, Mrs. Harriet Staunton was down at the Woodlands paying a visit to Mr. and Mrs. Patrick Staunton, Mr. Louis Staunton being at Gipsy Hill. Whether Alice Rhodes was there does not appear material to inquire; but it is quite clear at that time there were means of access to Alice Rhodes by Louis Staunton. A letter was written to Louis Staunton telling him that the children of Patrick had been taken ill, and he at once writes back to say that Harriet had better come home, as she is not likely to be of much use as a nurse, and he will send Alice down. I confess there is no part of this case which has caused me greater anxiety, and there is no part towards which I have endeavoured to bring to bear such judgment as I possess more than that which arises now. Why was this lady confined and kept, so to speak, under control as she was at the Woodlands? Do you suppose Mrs. Patrick Staunton had any idea until August or September, 1876, that her sister, Alice Rhodes, was on the terms of familiarity with Louis Staunton which she was? It was brought to that woman's attention that Alice Rhodes, her sister, was in the family way, and they may have kept Mrs. Harriet Staunton out of the road in order that she might not know the fact—not with a view to starving her. In the letter of Alice Rhodes, with the postmark August 1, beginning, "My dear Louis, I was sorry to see it raining," you have, it

Staunton Trial.

Mr. Straight seems to me, the key of the whole mystery of what then occurred. That Alice Rhodes and Louis Staunton had been on too intimate terms then nobody can doubt, and what is the meaning of the postscript, " I am not bad yet "? What does that mean? It is quite clear that at the time that letter was written Alice Rhodes was under the apprehension that she was in the family way. She must make a confidante of somebody sooner or later, and whom could she but her sister? Was she to go to Mr. and Mrs. Hincksman, and let her shame and sin find an outlet there? What was to be done? It is true, as the Attorney-General says, that Cudham was a lonely place, although not such a cut-throat district as he would have you suppose. At any rate it is a very beautiful country. Now, Little Grays farm was to let, and Louis Staunton, having seduced this young girl under the eyes of his own wife, had the strongest motives for concealing her shame. I hope, gentlemen, in all this you will see that it might have occurred without any intention of causing the death of Mrs. Harriet Staunton. It appears to me there was the strongest motive for concealing her identity down at Little Grays. There were plenty of people in London who knew of the existence of Mrs. Louis Staunton; and if she were kept out of sight at Cudham she might not then interfere with Alice Rhodes passing as Louis Staunton's wife, which she did. Louis Staunton was in business at Gipsy Hill as an auctioneer. This he sells.

Mr. JUSTICE HAWKINS—There is no evidence as to his having sold the business.

Mr. STRAIGHT—I think it has not yet been proved, but it shall.[7] On 7th October he takes up his residence at Cudham, and this morning his lordship put a not unimportant question to Clara Brown. His lordship asked, " Was Mrs. Harriet Staunton ever at Little Grays? " and the answer was " No." Was it likely she ever should, if my theory is correct? Does anybody believe the story Clara Brown told at Penge, that Harriet Staunton knew of the intimacy between her husband and Alice Rhodes? On the contrary, every effort would be made to keep that fact from her knowledge. Of course, it was wicked and wrong, but we are not here sitting in a High Court of morals. We are sitting here in a Court of justice, and you have to deal with the facts of the case, and you are not here to deal with the case upon sentiment. I hope I make myself intelligible as to the origin and real character of the partial confinement of Mrs. Harriet Staunton at the Woodlands. It appears that Mrs. Harriet Staunton remained in residence at the Woodlands from 28th August, and never after that went to her house at Gipsy Hill. And now let me ask the prosecu-

---

7 It was not.

Defence of Mrs. Patrick Staunton.

tion when this conspiracy to cause the death of Mrs. Harriet Staunton was commenced? Is the point at which it commenced Christmas, 1876, or was it after the visit or visits to Mr. Keene in October, 1876? Christmas is apparently fixed upon. Now, what is the position of Mrs. Patrick Staunton? She is in a position of very great difficulty. As the wife of Patrick Staunton, she is bound to obey him; and she is the sister of Alice Rhodes. Now, ask yourselves what you would have done if you had been Mrs. Patrick Staunton at the time she first knew her sister was in the family way by Louis Staunton, entertaining towards her those feelings of affection which usually exist between children born of the same mother? Would you have proclaimed your sister's shame? Would you have gone on the housetops and proclaimed that she had committed adultery with her brother-in-law, and brought discredit on your mother, the common parent of both? Would you have told Mr. and Mrs. Hincksman? Would you not have kept to yourself as far as possible the secret which had come to your knowledge, and have done your best to keep it from the unhappy lady, Mrs. Harriet Staunton? I ask you, as men of the world, not to place too stern or harsh a construction on the acts of weak human nature. There is such sympathy and feeling towards those who are by blood dear to us that we sometimes do things on their behalf which are not right and proper.

Now, that is the state of things which existed about August or September, 1876. Of course, it was necessary that anything about this matter should be kept from Mrs. Harriet Staunton, and it was vitally important that Alice Rhodes should pass through her confinement under the sanction of the name of Louis Staunton; and I say all this may be perfectly consistent with the absence of any arrangement or agreement between these prisoners to bring about the death of the deceased lady. On 17th October, we have heard, Mrs. Harriet Staunton goes to the office of Mr. Keene, and, though abundant opportunity presented itself on that and another occasion, she makes no single complaint in reference to Patrick or Elizabeth Ann Staunton as to their treatment of her. From 23rd October to Christmas, which has been treated as the crucial point in this case, we know that no evidence was given as to what was taking place with regard to Mrs. Harriet Staunton. You have no doubt thought over and over again of this important point about the starvation. Now, it is a very extraordinary method to adopt for the purpose of causing death, unless you wish to attract suspicion. A day must come and an hour will arrive when investigation must take place. You can hardly suppose that these prisoners were so ignorant of the first elements of the law as not to know that before they could bury a person they must have a doctor's certificate. Would any but four

Staunton Trial.

lunatics have been guilty of what is attributed to the prisoners? These persons are accused of the deliberate starvation of a person, and on that person's body is to be found the evidence which is to convict them. We have the evidence of Clara Brown on that point, and I am going to ask you to test the process of fostering and manuring, so to speak, she has undergone before the coroner. My friend Mr. Williams had treated of many things she said, but there was one which has been omitted. She says—

On Thursday evening, April 12, a wagonette was brought to the side of the house, and the deceased was able to walk by herself. She was not assisted. She got in herself, and I state positively she was not carried. She had no great distance to walk, not across the meadow, only to the door. She dressed in her bedroom. My mistress assisted her in putting on her bonnet. The ulster which she wore was her own, and the two other dresses, and a black silk skirt. I swear——

I ask you to bear this in mind when I am presently making observations to you upon it—

I swear I never turned a key on her in my life. I always spoke the same to her as to my mistress. I deny using the expression, "Go back, ma'am." I did hear footsteps in the kitchen. The deceased was there. I did not go to the kitchen door. I swear I never said, "She is no lady." I never said, "Go back." I never said that she was deranged. I swear that two young women did not say to me, "Is that the way you speak to a lady?" I swear I never said, "She is no lady; she is only my master's sister." When I heard the footsteps I did not do anything. There was a fire in the kitchen and in the parlour, and a light in both. We were in the habit of having them every night. Weatherley and Longridge are both swearing falsely.

And yet this woman asks you to believe she is speaking the truth, and she comes subsequently into the witness-box and says the whole of her previous story is a fabrication from beginning to end. Now, why has she done this? God knows the motives which lead people to give false evidence in Courts of justice. I will explain why I think there is much which she says that you may rely upon, and much which she says which you must dismiss with contempt and contumely. Realise the position in which this girl found herself. No human being can doubt the excitement there was at Penge about this matter. To certain persons the affair was an extraordinary one, and after Clara Brown had given her evidence endeavours were made to get her to alter it, and while, on the other hand, she has the strongest sympathy and desire to help those who are related to her, yet there is a stronger element and feeling in her bosom arising from her having been threatened by the police officer that she may find herself in prison if she goes on making her statements. How have they dealt with her? After she was examined before the coroner, although she was continually in contact with the Treasury authorities, and under the eye

Evidence for Defence.

Pathology at St. Thomas's Hospital, an Examiner in Pathology J. F. Payne
of the University of Edinburgh, and the editor of "Jones and
Sieveking's Manual of Pathological Anatomy." I have had
a large experience of post-mortem examinations, and have been
engaged in the study of subjects relating thereto for several
years. A summary of the depositions of the medical witnesses
taken before the magistrates, and copies of the notes of the
post-mortem examination were submitted to me by letter by
Messrs. Lewis & Lewis—I forget the precise date, about the
end of July this year—it was before the last sessions of this
Court.

I was anxious not to be called as a witness upon general
grounds, but not with reference to this particular case. I
have been in attendance during the trial except the first day.
I was here on Thursday, and heard all the medical evidence on
that day.

I heard Dr. Longrigg say that the symptoms he discovered
were inconsistent with tubercular meningitis, and inconsistent
with rigidity of the arms. If I understood rightly, Mr. Longrigg
was asked whether the symptoms observed by him would be
consistent with a disease known as tubercular meningitis, and
he answered that if the disease were sufficiently established the
symptoms would correspond, with one exception, that exception
being rigidity of the arms.

In my experience, rigidity of the limbs, one or more, is very
common. The rigidity of one or more limbs is a very common
symptom of tubercular meningitis, in most cases, at all events.
I believe that symptom is mentioned in most, if not all, the
books on the subject.

The appearance in cases of tubercular meningitis of a flattening and bulging of the sides of the lobes of the brain depends
on the amount of fluid contained in the brain, and if the amount
of fluid is small that appearance is not produced. In my
opinion, the absence of it is consistent with the fact of death
being caused by tubercular meningitis. With respect to the
position of the tubercles found in the brain, they are found in
different parts of the brain, in different situations. Undoubtedly
they vary very much in number and appearance as well as
position. The symptoms spoken of, namely, the flattening and
bulging of the lobes of the brain, and the effusion into the
ventricles, vary very much. They are much more marked when
the tubercles are found at the base of the brain.

I think the fact of death from tubercular meningitis is consistent with the fact of no tubercles being found at the base
of the brain. I should add to that, no tubercles visible to the
naked eye. In the event of tubercles being found in the upper
part of the brain, it is very likely, by microscopic examination,
you would find that there were appearances which were not

J. F. Payne visible to the naked eye. If you found tubercles in one part of the membrane of the brain, there exists the probability that on a microscopic examination you would find others in other parts which were not visible to the naked eye. If you found some tubercles which were visible to the naked eye, it is possible by microscopic examination you would find more in other parts of the surface of the brain.

I heard the statement made by Dr. Longrigg in regard to the average weight of different portions of the body. Of some of them I took a note, but I am not sure that I did of all. I heard Dr. Longrigg say that the average weight of a woman of 5 feet 5¼ inches high would be from 9 to 10 stones. I think a much lower weight than 9 stones would be consistent with health. The weights of different organs of persons in health vary very considerably.

By the Court—In health, if you get persons of the same weight and the same height, the organs of the body would vary considerably in weight; that is what I mean.

By Mr. Clarke—I think the weight of the heart as stated in this case to have been 7¾ ounces is very much below the normal weight for a person in a healthy condition. I do not say below the average weight; I say below the weight consistent with ordinary health, but only a little below it. I understood the liver to weigh 2 lbs. 2 ounces. Whether that is correct I do not know. In my experience the average weight of the liver of a woman like the deceased as stated, viz., from 50 to 60 ounces, is somewhat too high. I should say probably 48 or 50 ounces, giving a rough estimate—about 3 lbs. It is very difficult to say what the lowest weight would be, compatible with health. I think the weight of the liver was much below the average. With regard to the spleen, which is said to have weighed 4¾ ounces, that is an organ the weight of which is very variable, so that no very great importance can be attached to it. With regard to the kidneys, the weights I took down were 3¾ and 4 ounces respectively. Those weights seem to me to be scarcely below the normal weights, a little below the normal, but very little.

I heard the statement that inflammation of the peritoneum was discovered on the post-mortem examination. I do not think that is a symptom which would arise from deprivation of food, taken alone. With regard to the congestion of the brain and stomach, and of the outlets of the body, I do not think deprivation of food, taken alone, would produce congestion of the brain or congestion of the stomach. With respect to the condition of the outlets, that is mentioned in several books as occurring in people who are deprived of food. I understand by that that the orifices of the body which are exposed to the air and to irritation, such as the lips, the nose, the anus, and,

Evidence for Defence.

so on, become inflamed. I have never seen it, but I have heard it described, or, rather, read the description.

The congestion of the brain I should attribute to the tubercular disease which is described as having been present there; the inflammation of the peritoneum I cannot explain, unless there were possibly tubercles present there also; in other words, I regard the tubercles and the congestion as a part of the same disease. This kind of tubercular disease in the brain, namely, the small miliary tubercles, accompanied by great congestion in most cases, indicates a general infection of the whole body, which we call acute general tuberculosis. My judgment as to that was greatly confirmed by the presence of tubercles in the lungs. With regard to the inflammation of the peritoneum, that, in my judgment, might be produced by tubercles invisible to the naked eye.

Bronzing of the skin is nearly always present in Addison's disease, and there is some approach to it in diabetes. I do not know of any other certain indication of diabetes than sugar in the urine after death. In Addison's disease I know of no other invariable symptom except the condition of the superrenal capsules.

I think the traces of intemperate habits are discoverable after death if the intemperate habits have lasted a long time. If they have only lasted for a few months, and had been discontinued, I think the post-mortem appearances would be fallacious. We have often had people in the hospitals who have formerly been intemperate. I have no doubt I have had post-mortem examinations under such circumstances, but I cannot recollect any particular one at the moment; after a few months' discontinuance there might be no trace.

Tubercular meningitis or tuberculosis does not so much produce emaciation, as it is a fact accompanied by it, and sometimes produced by it; it would produce it if it lasted long. It is not so much a consequence as an accompaniment and sometimes a precursor; it is not so much produced by it as preceded by it.

The loss of flesh is sometimes the only premonitory symptom of tubercular meningitis. It is often the only premonitory symptom, which comes before the outbreak of other symptoms. When it does manifest itself it is a rapidly fatal disease. By rapidly I mean from two days to a month perhaps. It is quite possible that up to the time the disease actually manifests itself progressive emaciation is the only symptom. In my judgment, if the post-mortem appearances are correctly described—of course, I am not responsible for the description—but if they are correctly described I think they are consistent with death from tubercular disease.

179

Staunton Trial.

J. F. Payne   With regard to the symptoms during life which have been
described as coma, unequal dilatation of the pupils, rigidity of
the arm, and stertorous breathing, I think they are quite
consistent with death from this disease. I think starvation
alone does not explain either all the symptoms before death or
all the post-mortem appearances.

In the course of my experience I have seen death result from
that disease in a considerable number of children and a considerable number of adults—not from starvation, but from this
disease. I may say that I have had considerable experience
of this disease at the hospital for children, where I was formerly
assistant physician. I have seen it chiefly in children, and
also in adults, the disease being far less common in adults
than in children. In the course of my practice I have seen
emaciation to a very great extent; I could not, however, say
to the same extent as in this case, without having seen the
thing myself. I am not prepared to express an opinion as to
the degree without having seen it.

I can quote a particular case from memory. It was the case
of a child, an out-patient at the hospital for children.   I
attended the child there, and afterwards at its own home.   I
made a post-mortem examination, and found that it died of
tubercular meningitis combined with some tubercles in the
lungs, and it was so emaciated that I remember particularly
a remark made by the mother, who was extremely affectionate.
She asked me to explain the death of the child, because she
said the neighbours accused her of starving it. I was told that
the condition of the child gave rise to the suspicion of starvation
in the minds of the neighbours.

I have never seen a case in which tubercles were present in
the pia-mater without producing some symptoms; more
especially, I should say, indicating disease in the head—head
symptoms.

I have seen cases of tubercular meningitis in which there
was not softening of the brain. They are not frequent or
common. After that disease it is stated that in some cases
the brain is found to be firm and not softened. The fact of the
post-mortem being delayed until after the patient had been
dead six days would not affect the possibility of drawing
accurate and safe conclusions on most points. There are no
points which have occurred to my mind in which the delay in
the post-mortem would throw doubt on the accuracy of the
conclusions—not on the material points which I have heard
mentioned.

Cross-examined by the ATTORNEY-GENERAL—Your view is that
death was caused by tubercular meningitis?—Yes.

From the notes of the post-mortem?—Yes, and from what
I have heard of the evidence.

Evidence for Defence.

When you speak of tubercular meningitis, you mean the J. F. Payne acute form of the disease?—I mean an acute disease.

What is the average weight of a woman of 5 feet 5¼ inches? —I am not prepared to say.

Answer the question generally?—I should say about 9 stones average.

So that if this woman were 9 stones on 23rd October, and on 12th or 13th April she was 5 stones 4 lbs., you would call that a case of extreme wasting and emaciation, should you not?—I should, undoubtedly.

You, I dare say, are of opinion from the evidence you have heard and the results of the post-mortem, it was a case of very extreme emaciation?—It was a case, from what I have heard, of extreme emaciation.

How long do you think, in your opinion, had this acute disease of tubercular meningitis been going on?—I think the post-mortem appearances do not supply the information.

But you say acute disease is generally fatal in a short time. You have given my friend from two or three days to a month? —Yes; the acute stage, one may say from the evidence, could not have been more than a few days. I cannot say more nearly.

Of course, the disease is more likely to make its appearance in a person of enfeebled condition of body than in a person in good health?—I should say so; in fact, I have no doubt about it.

If you had emaciation caused by any wasting disease, acute tuberculosis might supervene, might it not?—It does sometimes.

It would be much more likely to occur in a case of that kind than in a perfectly healthy patient?—More likely than in perfect health, undoubtedly.

Mr. Justice Hawkins—You say that in a person who wastes and becomes emaciated tuberculosis would be much more likely to supervene?—That would be so.

It would be much more likely to occur in a case of that kind than when the person was in perfect health?— Undoubtedly.

Now, supposing Mrs. Harriet Staunton had been reduced to the state described, would you be prepared to say that she would have tubercular meningitis?—Well, it is a rare complaint, so that I cannot say; but, taking a variety of cases of persons in an emaciated condition, I should say it is likely. Still, the disease is rare.

Supposing you had been called in when the wasting had gone on (because I assume it was gradual), and you saw that your patient was wasting away, what would be the sort of treatment you would recommend?—I should prescribe nourishment, tonic medicine, and so forth.

Staunton Trial.

J. F Payne   Would warmth be necessary—reasonable warmth?—Warmth is necessary in all such diseases.

It would be irrational treatment to subject such a patient to be without fire in winter?—It would be bad treatment.

In fact, it would be exceedingly dangerous treatment?—I don't suppose any medical man would recommend such.

It would be extremely dangerous, would it not?—Yes, bad, of course.

It would be extremely dangerous, is the question?—Yes.

The ATTORNEY-GENERAL—I suppose a patient suffering as we have heard described, emaciated from day to day, would be better for a little exercise and fresh air?—Well, that would depend upon circumstances.

You think that death was caused by acute tuberculosis or tubercular meningitis, and that that disease had not existed for more than a month, at all events?—Judging from the post-mortem it could not be more than that at the outside.

What, in your opinion, caused the emaciation?—I cannot tell that, without consideration of the history of the case.

But, of course, I need hardly ask you if a woman was supplied with insufficient quantities of food she would probably become emaciated?—Undoubtedly.

This disease that we have spoken of—I think you call the three coverings of the brain meninges, do you not?—We do.

I will not go into the names professionally. The disease is inflammation occasioned in this particular kind of disease by the deposit of tubercles?—Yes, probably the deposit of tubercles would cause inflammation, but that is a question of opinion.

Generally speaking, is the condition of the brain in tubercular meningitis a softening condition?—In the majority of cases.

You know Dr. Bristowe?—Oh, yes.

Is he a physician at St. Thomas's Hospital?—He is; and I am an assistant physician there.

Do you know his work?—Yes, well.

Do you agree with him in this (reading)—" Meningitis due to the presence of tubercles nearly always commences at the base of the brain, is often limited to the base, and is generally most intense there "? Do you agree with that?—I do. I agree with the word " nearly."

Does starvation ever cause congestion of the brain?—I am not aware that it does.

Does it ever cause convulsions?—It is said in the last stage to be accompanied by convulsions. Convulsions may occur in the last stage of starvation, but I am not prepared to say that convulsions will cause congestion of the brain.

If the patient has convulsions would you expect congestion of the brain at the vessels?—Not necessarily.

I do not say necessarily—would you be at all surprised to

182

Evidence for Defence.

find that there was congestion if you had convulsions?—I J. F. Payne should not be surprised.

Mr. Justice Hawkins—You do not know that starvation causes congestion of the brain—you say convulsions may occur in the last stages, and then if convulsions occur you would not be surprised to find congestion?—If, after death, I find congestion of the brain, I rather presume that the congestion caused the convulsions than that it was caused by convulsions.

The Attorney-General—But it might be either way?—I am not prepared to say that convulsions alone cause congestion.

Mr. Justice Hawkins—Are you prepared to say they would not be?—You might find, after death, congestion, because the convulsions and the congestion might have arisen from the same cause.

The Attorney-General—Will maniacal delirium cause congestion?—I think it would be rather caused by the congestion.

We have read very frequently of cases of shipwreck, where men have gone without food for a long time, have been exposed in an open boat, and have been delirious. Is that caused by starvation?—It may be, and by thirst as well.

Those are causes of maniacal delirium—a man becomes completely mad?—Very likely it is so described.

Now, about congestion of the stomach. Would you not expect that from starvation?—No.

If you had the case of a woman where there had been starvation for a considerable time and then food was administered to her in great quantities, you would expect congestion, would you not?—I should expect to find the stomach as it is during digestion, and the vessels full of blood.

If the vessels are gorged they are congested, are they not?—They are.

Supposing a patient had been without food for a considerable time, would you venture to give him any considerable quantity of food all at once?—I should give it to him gradually. I am not prepared to say what precise harm there would be, but it is a matter of experience that harm is done in that way.

If you had a man seized with paralysis, and deprived of the use of his arm, would you expect it to be stiff?—Certainly not. Paralysis does not produce stiffness of the limbs.

Would giving food to a starved patient be likely to cause inflammation of the coating of the stomach?—I do not think so.

Will you say it would not?—I should not like to say, I have not had experience.

Had you ever before you a case of undoubted starvation?—I have often seen cases where persons would not take food.

Have you found emaciation come on very rapidly?—Steadily, not always rapidly.

Staunton Trial.

J. F. Payne

You have listened to the evidence, and have learned the condition of this lady before she was removed from the Woodlands, and the evidence of Clara Brown. What do you say about the removal? Would it be likely to accelerate death? —I think it would.

Mr. CLARKE—Is the work of Dr. Bristowe one of considerable authority?—I think it is.

He is a great authority on this disease?—Undoubtedly; especially with regard to morbid anatomy.

J. S. Bristowe

Dr. JOHN SYER BRISTOWE, examined by Mr. CLARKE—I am a Doctor of Medicine and Fellow of the College of Physicians. I have not been consulted in any way in this matter before to-day. I sent you (Mr. Clarke) a private note in this matter. I am senior physician at St. Thomas's Hospital, and examiner in medicine at the College of Surgeons. I have heard the evidence that Dr. Payne has given, and I agree with it entirely.

In cases of death from tubercular meningitis it is a frequent thing to find rigidity of the limbs. That disease is very various in its symptoms; it is not infrequent that the acute manifestation of the disease is preceded by a period of progressive gradual emaciation—it may be a long period of emaciation.

Emaciation is one of the recognised symptoms of tuberculosis. In its acute form emaciation is often the only sign of the disease. The tubercles are often so minute as almost to defy detection; they sometimes require the microscope for their detection. I have never seen a case where there were tubercles in the pia-mater where there were no head symptoms during life. I have not looked up my experience for this examination as to there being cases of tubercular meningitis where there is no tubercle at the base of the brain, but I believe it does occur; I have seen cases where the tubercles have been limited to the upper part of the brain, but it is rare. There would in such a case be an absence of the flattening and bulging of the lobes of the brain and absence of effusion.

I have necessarily a large experience of vermin on the body at a hospital. It is a fact that where there are vermin at all on the hair they constantly spread immediately after death—they would spread over the body in a few hours; as the body cools the vermin spread over the whole body, over the trunk.

In the case of a post-mortem examination, where the body had not been washed after death, the presence of vermin all over the body six days after death would not necessarily indicate any great amount of filth before death; it would depend on the condition of the patient before death. If the patient had been bed-ridden or comatose before death, or had lain for several days or weeks before death, it is common to find even in a well-ordered hospital that the head is infested with vermin.

Evidence for Defence.

I should expect then to find them in great numbers. In any case, where there had been vermin in the head during life, and the body was left unwashed and untended during six days, the vermin might spread over the body, and I should expect to find them spreading.

Cross-examined by the ATTORNEY-GENERAL—Would you expect to find marks of the bites of vermin?—I don't think vermin bite the skin; I am not quite sure, but I don't think they do. They rather live on the scurf of the hair; they are scavengers.

You say this is a case of tubercular meningitis?—Yes; I entertain no doubt of this being a case of acute tuberculosis.

Now on 23rd October this woman was about 9 stones in weight.

Mr. CLARKE—That is not in evidence.

Mr. JUSTICE HAWKINS—We have evidence of her weight about the time of her confinement, and Mr. Keene said she looked well and about the same as usual on 23rd October.

The ATTORNEY-GENERAL—We are told that for a woman 5 feet $5\frac{1}{4}$ inches 9 stones is about the average. Is that so?—I think that is rather above the average.

Have you read the evidence?—Yes, I read it in the papers. That is all the knowledge I have of it.

Then you must have read that there was not a particle of fat found on any portion of the body. Now, what do you attribute the emaciation to? Is it from starvation?—I cannot attribute it to anything without knowing more of the case.

Is it consistent with starvation?—Yes, it may be.

Mr. CLARKE—Is it consistent with tuberculosis?—Yes.

The ATTORNEY-GENERAL—How long would acute tuberculosis take to produce great emaciation? About a month?—It might.

Would it produce emaciation as great as in this case?—It might; but I can't say.

Do you know a case of tuberculosis which resulted in such emaciation?—Yes.

Give us the particulars of that case?—I cannot do that. I have seen a case in which the body has been emaciated.

Now, you may have a person very much emaciated, say, from starvation, and then acute tuberculosis may supervene?—It is probable.

You may have a case in which emaciation has been going on for a considerable time, and then tuberculosis sets in?—Yes; but I cannot tell the cause of the tuberculosis or the cause of emaciation.

Emaciation may be caused by a variety of things?—Yes.

And then tuberculosis sets in?—Yes.

In that case you would not say that emaciation was caused by tuberculosis?—Not necessarily, and, on the other hand, I should not say that tuberculosis was caused by emaciation.

Staunton Trial.

J. S. Bristowe   Is it not a likely thing that tuberculosis should set in after emaciation—that the body being in an enfeebled state that disease might set in?—The majority of cases which I have seen were not emaciated, but we found evidence of tuberculosis. Tuberculosis might come on in a body in an impoverished state, but not as the result of previous emaciation or ill-health. Where that has been the case we have found evidence that there has been tubercle beforehand, before the acute symptoms manifested themselves. There is no connection necessarily between emaciation and tuberculosis.

If emaciation was the consequence of tuberculosis, and it assumed an acute form, how long do you think it would take to produce such emaciation as you have heard of in this particular case?—Well, six weeks, six months, or, it may be, a year. I have no means of saying.

But after an acute disease would you expect to find at the post-mortem an entire absence of fat round the omentum?—I believe I have seen such a case, in which there was an entire absence of fat. I should not expect to find it after death from acute tuberculosis only.

Do you still hold to the opinion expressed in your book—"Meningitis due to the presence of tubercles nearly always commences at the base of the brain, is often limited to the base, and is generally most intense there"?—Yes.

Would you expect to find effusion about the seat of the tubercles?—Generally.

In this case there was none?—So I read in the newspapers.

Re-examined by Mr. CLARKE—Do I understand you to say that the emaciation that existed in this case may have been produced by starvation or by tubercular or some other disease?—Yes. Other diseases would produce the same amount of emaciation. I have seen the same amount of emaciation in many other diseases—in diabetes, for instance, and Addison's disease—and patients who have been hysterical simply I have seen reduced to the last degree of emaciation.

In what length of time?—In the course of four or five weeks.

In that case, and in the case of emaciation, that produces acute development of tubercular disease, is there often no other sign than emaciation?—In the case of tubercular disease there may be no other sign. In the other there may be symptoms of hysteria.

You have been asked as to whether tubercular disease may not supervene upon mere starvation; do I understand you to say that it may be concurrent, but that you do not look upon its being consequent?—The cause of tuberculosis is not at all well understood, and I should be sorry to say that tuberculosis is produced by starvation.

The Court then adjourned.

186

Sixth Day—Tuesday, 25th September, 1877.

The Court sat at 9.30.

Dr. SMITH GREENFIELD was called and examined by Mr. S. Greenfield
CLARKE—Are you a Doctor of Medicine of the University of
London, a member of the Royal College of Physicians,
Assistant Physician and Lecturer and Demonstrator of Morbid
Anatomy at St. Thomas's Hospital?—I am. I have not heard
the medical evidence given on this trial. I have had the
depositions before the magistrates and the notes of the post-
mortem submitted to me, and I have given a written opinion.

Mr. JUSTICE HAWKINS—When was that?—About a month
ago.

Were the whole of the depositions sent to you?—The whole
of the medical depositions were, not the whole of the case. I
had Mr. Longrigg's notes, and the evidence and cross-examination of Dr. Wilkinson, Mr. Longrigg, Dr. Rodgers, Dr. Bright,
and Mr. Harman.

Mr. JUSTICE HAWKINS—It was material to know exactly
what was before the witness, as a word might make all the
difference.

Mr. CLARKE—I think, my lord, that he has mentioned the
names of all the witnesses.

Mr. JUSTICE HAWKINS—No doubt.

Mr. CLARKE—I think I have a copy of what was sent to
him.

Mr. JUSTICE HAWKINS—The originals——

The ATTORNEY-GENERAL—I don't object, my lord.

Mr. JUSTICE HAWKINS—I think you can guess what is in my
mind.

The ATTORNEY-GENERAL—I think I can, but I am content.

Mr. JUSTICE HAWKINS—To my mind this is a most unsatisfactory sort of evidence. The jury have to decide on what
is proved before them, and this gentleman is called here to
say that the conclusions of medical witnesses who at some time
appeared for the prosecution are wrong. He ought to have
heard their evidence here in this Court, and it is a most
unsatisfactory proceeding for it to be contradicted by a
witness who has not heard them, but who has formed an
opinion on something which is not before the jury. It is
the most unsatisfactory evidence I can imagine.

The ATTORNEY-GENERAL—Quite so. In a case different
from this I should have objected to it altogether.

Mr. JUSTICE HAWKINS (*To Witness*)—No one in the least
degree imputes any blame to you.

WITNESS—I have read the notes with the greatest care.

187

Staunton Trial.

S. Greenfield

Mr. CLARKE—I think I will examine the witness with regard to the post-mortem notes only.

Mr. JUSTICE HAWKINS—Where are the notes? (They were handed to his lordship.) Are these the originals?

WITNESS—Yes.

Mr. CLARKE—A copy was supplied to us by the Treasury.

Examination continued by Mr. CLARKE—Did you carefully read and consider the notes sent to you of the post-mortem?—I did.

Assume they accurately described the observations, have you formed an opinion of the cause of death?—I have formed an opinion that if the bodies described in these notes, as being in the membranes of the brain, were the tubercles of the acute form which I judged them from the description to be——

The ATTORNEY-GENERAL—There is no description before us.

Mr. JUSTICE HAWKINS—The witness ought to have heard the evidence, and then he might have been asked the question. He says, "If what is in there—— "

Mr. CLARKE—I think, after what your lordship has said, I will take upon myself the responsibility of withdrawing this witness.

Mr. JUSTICE HAWKINS—I don't wish to prevent you taking him as far as you in your judgment can legitimately go; but I am pointing out to you what I think is an unsatisfactory mode of procedure.

Mr. CLARKE—I will ask Dr. Greenfield to leave the box.

Witness here left the box.[1]

Mr. JUSTICE HAWKINS—I leave it entirely to you.

Mr. CLARKE—I am much obliged, my lord. This is the whole of the case for the defence.

The ATTORNEY-GENERAL—You spoke yesterday, my lord, about a nightdress.

Mr. JUSTICE HAWKINS—I want to know, first, where the nightdress came from that was put on the body; and, next, whether there was evidence of any clothes brought to Penge. I know there is evidence of a box containing clothes at Mr. Bradford's.

The ATTORNEY-GENERAL—I have a list here, if your lordship will allow me to read it. "The following is a list of articles in the possession of Sergeant Bateman, belonging to the late Harriet Staunton, 34 Forbes Road, Penge, and examined by Clara Brown at the Penge station, 30th May, 1877." The things in this list will not be the same as those in the box at Mr. Bradford's. Is Sergeant Bateman here?

---

[1] For the evidence which Dr. Greenfield came prepared to give see Appendix ix. p. 318.

Evidence for Prosecution.

Sergeant BATEMAN was recalled and examined by the Sergeant Bateman ATTORNEY-GENERAL—Did you, on 30th May, show a quantity of clothes to Clara Brown?—I did.

Where did you get them from?—They were at 34 Forbes Road.

Did you go to Forbes Road?—Yes.

Who gave them to you?—Mrs. Chalklin.

They were given to you as things belonging to the Stauntons?—Yes.

Is Mrs. Chalklin here?—She will be here soon.

Listen to the list—" One blue stuff dress, one black silk dress, two petticoats (one white and the other coloured), one crinoline, one black cloth jacket, one ulster, two breast improvers, one dress improver, one chemise, one nightgown, one pair of stays, one pair of stockings, one blue scarf shawl, one skirt, one fall, one pair of slippers, one neck ribbon, one bonnet, a purse, a towel, a sheet, a tablecloth, a tooth-brush, a reel of cotton, and a pair of ear-rings." Are those the things you showed Clara Brown?—There was only one slipper.

It is down here, " a pair of slippers." Those, I suppose, would be the things she wore. Mrs. Chalklin is not here?—I expect her.

A JUROR—Is the chemise taken from the deceased in the possession of any one?

Mrs. GOODINGE, the nurse, was recalled and examined by Mrs. Gooding the ATTORNEY-GENERAL—After the poor woman was dead, did you put a clean nightdress on her?—Yes.

Was that put on what you call a chemise?—Yes.

Had she on her before her death a chemise?—Yes.

What became of it?—I sent it to the wash.

Mr. JUSTICE HAWKINS (To the Jury)—That would not afford you the least assistance, it having been washed.

The JUROR—No, my lord.

Another JUROR (To Witness)—Did you find any appearance of skin disease?—No, sir.

The ATTORNEY-GENERAL—Did you find the chemise after it was washed?—Yes.

What did you do with it?—I gave it to the police.

Is that the chemise introduced in the list?—Yes, there was only one.

In what state was it before you sent it to the wash?—It was very dirty, as things are after death; but I told the woman to be sure and tell me if there was anything on it, and she said——

Mr. WILLIAMS—We cannot take that.

The ATTORNEY-GENERAL—Who was the woman who washed it?—She lives at Heath Grove, Kent.

Staunton Trial.

Mrs. Goodinge

You could find her if you went for her?—Yes.

The witness was not cross-examined.

The ATTORNEY-GENERAL—I do not suggest that she was not properly clothed at Penge. We have never suggested that.

Mr. JUSTICE HAWKINS—Do you propose to call that witness at Heath Grove?

The ATTORNEY-GENERAL—If the gentlemen of the jury wish it, but I cannot say her evidence would throw any additional light on the case. The nurse tells you the state in which the chemise was, and the other witness would tell you the same.

Mr. JUSTICE HAWKINS (*To last Witness*)—Was the deceased wearing both a chemise and a nightdress?—Yes.

The FOREMAN—The juryman, my lord, who asked the question said that he wished to ascertain how long, to all appearances, this garment had been worn—whether a few days or a few weeks.

WITNESS—Not a few weeks. It might have been worn a week, or a few days more.

Another JUROR—Was there any vermin on it?—I think there was not. I asked the woman who brought it home——

The ATTORNEY-GENERAL—Do not tell us that.

Mr. JUSTICE HAWKINS—The witness in her original evidence said, " The nightdress was as if it had been worn a week, or rather more, and there was dirt from illness upon it."

A JUROR—I remember that quite well.

Mr. JUSTICE HAWKINS—You can add nothing to that, I suppose.

WITNESS—No, my lord.

Mr. Clarke

Mr. CLARKE—May it please your lordship, gentlemen of the jury—I am very thankful that the moment has come when, after you have heard the whole of the evidence in this case, I have to discharge the duty of addressing you on behalf of Patrick Staunton.

I say nothing of the strain upon all of us, upon you and upon my lord, as well as upon those who sit around me, of the conduct of a trial of this kind. The interests that are committed to our care are so large that it is impossible one can discharge a duty of this kind without a feeling of the most anxious responsibility, and I say that I am thankful that the time at last has come when, having all the evidence before you, I can deal with it on behalf of Patrick Staunton, and press upon you, I hope in fair and reasonable argument, not only that upon the evidence before you there is no proof that he is guilty of the murder with which he is charged, but also that the evidence falls short, and falls far short, of bringing home to him

Defence of Patrick Staunton.

any such culpable negligence or misdoing as would entitle you to find him guilty of the lesser crime of manslaughter.

Gentlemen, I remember your kind interposition when my friend Mr. Williams was speaking, the interposition of yourselves, as well as of my lord, expressing your anxiety to hear all that was to be said, without grudging to the counsel who have to discharge this duty the time it may take them to deal with the complicated matters in this case. I believe I shall not have to occupy your attention long. My learned friend Mr. Williams on the one hand, and my friend Mr. Straight upon the other, have dealt, and dealt strongly, with many matters upon which I should have been called upon to say a word to you. I am perfectly satisfied to leave these matters as they affect Patrick Staunton in the exact position in which they have been left by the observations of my two learned colleagues, and I am quite sure that you will not think I am seeking to evade any point in the case because I simply abstain from repeating, and possibly weakening by repetition, the observations which were strongly made to you yesterday by those gentlemen. But before I address myself to the facts of the case with regard to Patrick Staunton, I am bound to say a word as to some observations which were made to you by my learned friend Mr. Straight towards the close of his speech as to the relation in which Mrs. Patrick Staunton stands with regard to her husband, and in what I say I am entitled to say here exactly, and am saying exactly, what I should have been instructed to say if I had been representing both of them instead of Patrick Staunton only.

My friend Mr. Straight has pointed out to you that in certain aspects of this case, the aspect in reference to the negligence, to the negligent administration of food, or the carelessness with which food was given to Harriet Staunton—that with regard to the question of manslaughter it will become a substantial question for you whether Mrs. Patrick Staunton was not acting under the immediate and direct control of her husband, and he has enforced his observations upon that point by recalling a witness and obtaining the statement that Patrick Staunton, violent as he has undoubtedly been shown to be in certain matters which are recorded in this case, was violent also to his wife, on one occasion even striking her. As the counsel of Patrick Staunton, so far from having anything to complain of with regard to my friend taking that line or bringing that out, I am entitled to and I do adopt it and enforce it.

Patrick Staunton undoubtedly must have been the person who made the arrangements for money to be paid for Harriet Staunton's being kept at Cudham. Patrick Staunton was not a person long and constantly absent from home; he was frequently, I might almost say constantly, at home. You have heard that when he went out his wife very often went out with

Mr. Clarke him. He was there during the day, painting, an occupation which would keep him at home for a considerable time, and I do not on his behalf complain in the least of the tone that my learned friend has taken; so far from complaining of it, I say to you that, as Patrick Staunton's counsel, I recognise and adopt the line which my learned friend took. Patrick Staunton, at least, has nothing to complain of with regard to his wife. He has nothing to say as to her, except that if she committed any fault, that fault was committed under his control and on his culpability, and if she made any false statements afterwards in the course of the case, those statements were made to shield him.

Gentlemen, the position in which Harriet Staunton was at this house must be looked at with reference to the statement which is before you that money was paid by Louis for her support, and with reference also to four letters which have been read to you once in the course of the case, but which seem to me so important that I shall read them to you again. They are the letters dated June, August, and September, 1876—letters in which Louis Staunton writes to his brother in affectionate terms, and especially with reference to Harriet Staunton being at Cudham, and I ask you in deciding, as you will have to decide amongst all the other matters in the case, the question, for what purpose was Harriet Staunton taken to Cudham or kept there? I shall ask you to remember those letters, which at all events were not invented for the case, found half a year or nine months after they are written, found when the persons are in custody, and letters which at all events you can rely upon as showing correctly what the relations and feelings of the parties were at the time these letters were written.

Gentlemen, on 28th June, 1876, Louis Staunton, dating from Gipsy Hill, writes to his brother this letter—" My dear Bay, many, many thanks for your kind letter. I am glad to say my hand is better, but no one knows, dear Bay, what I have had to put up with from Harriet the last six months. Her temper has been something frightful. I have talked to her for hours together and tried to reason with her, but it is of no use. From the time she gets up in the morning until she goes to bed at night she does nothing but try to aggravate me and make me as miserable as she possibly can. Although I say it, I have been quite disheartened, and cried for hours to think that I should have laid out money to have things nice and no one to take an interest in the place. I am truly unhappy; but, oh, dear Bay, I can never thank you and dear Lizzie enough for all your kindness to me, but rest assured I shall not forget it. I should have been glad to have been with you a few days, but am now afraid I shall not be able to, having had a few words with Bradford, which I will tell you about when I see you on Friday. I shall be at the hospital about three o'clock. Your

Defence of Patrick Staunton.

ever affectionate brother, Louis Staunton." The expression
" I shall be at the hospital " is explained by the postscript,
" I have not heard how dear papa is yet. I am going over to
Brixton to-day." At that time, undoubtedly, their father was
in the hospital, in which he afterwards died. On 28th August
he writes again to his brother, " Dear Bay, I was indeed glad
to get your letter this morning, and grieved to hear the two
children are still so ill, but trust they will get better. It makes
me quite miserable to think you and Lizzie are in such trouble.
I want you to send Harriet to me immediately; I am sure you
cannot be bothered with her now. Give my love to her.
I hope to see her soon, and, if possible, will run down. With
fondest love from your affectionate brother, Louis." " 1st
September. My dear Bay, I have received your letter, and am
sorry I said anything, but the fact is, I was very annoyed at the
time to think that Harriet had given you any trouble, for I
know you have enough already with the two children ill, but I
trust you will not say or think anything more about it. I had
hoped to see you all to-day, but suppose it will now be Monday.
With fondest love to all, your very affectionate brother, Louis."

Gentlemen, I have read these letters through because, amidst
the mass of doubtful material upon which you will have to
express an opinion in this case, this material is, at all events,
trustworthy, and these letters undoubtedly show that in the
months of August and September, 1876, the brothers were on
affectionate terms; that Louis so wrote with regard to his wife
to Patrick; that Patrick obliged him by taking care of Harriet
for such reasons as are suggested in these letters; and, at all
events, they are letters which you cannot read and believe that
there was any improper intention, if not plan or scheme, of ill-
doing to Harriet then in the minds of these two brothers.

Now, gentlemen, she goes down to stay at Cudham, and there
is one date upon which I want to make an observation in passing, because I think it is important to the whole case for the
defence, and my friend Mr. Williams will forgive me, I am
sure, if I refer to a matter which he himself has touched upon—
the letter of 19th August, which has been mentioned a great
deal, and which speaks of the lost letter. You are told by
Clara Brown—and you will attach so much weight to it as you
think her evidence in the case is entitled to—you are told by
Clara Brown that it contained an expression about Louis and
Alice being happy, or a better time coming, or something of
that kind, when Harriet was out of the way. It may be
suggested to you that at that very time Harriet was out of the
way at Cudham, and that, therefore, that must have referred
to something else than her being away from London. If that
is so, I think it is important to recollect the tenor of those
letters, which show conclusively that if she was staying at

Mr. Clarke Cudham at the time it was only temporarily; that, at all events at that time, there had been no permanent arrangement made for her to stay at Cudham. Well, now, gentlemen, she comes down and she stays at Cudham, and you have a mass of evidence before you with regard to the fact that she was, to a certain extent, concealed from observation. I am anxious to keep this part of the evidence separate from that part which relates to her actual treatment, and for this reason, it is given by a different set of witnesses. You have a certain number of witnesses who prove this beyond a doubt; they prove she was not in the habit of being about Cudham, out of the house, and they prove certainly that when Mrs. Butterfield was endeavouring to find out where her daughter was, her daughter's place was concealed from her. It is quite clear that Patrick in the course of the conversation denied that he knew anything about where her daughter was, and the same observation applies to other conversations at which the prisoners were present; but the important question for you—and one of the most important in the case—is this, does that concealment at Cudham necessarily imply anything more than concealment, than her being kept out of sight? Patrick Staunton denied that he knew anything of where she was, and at that time undoubtedly she was in his house. But see the reason for which he has taken her into his house; see the way in which it may have been put to him by the brother who wrote these letters to him with regard to Harriet Staunton.

The brother was not happy with her. He says in that letter he was anxious that she should go and live at Cudham. There was no question of taking a place in the country, and out of the way. At this time, when this correspondence is going on, Patrick Staunton has for a year been living and carrying on his profession as an artist in a little cottage in one of the loveliest parts of England. That cottage he had probably taken for the pursuit of his profession, and he is residing there, and, although there is not much room in the house, it is arranged that Harriet Staunton shall go down; but for reasons to which Patrick Staunton could not have been to any great extent a party. Louis was anxious that Mrs. Harriet Staunton should not be seen by her mother. Might it not be—you cannot tell; you have no evidence on either side after what took place in London—but might it not well be that Mrs. Staunton herself was anxious that her mother should not find her? Let us deal with the position she is in. Let us remember the fact that her mother had given evidence and attempted to prove that she was insane. One of my friends pointed out to you the horror that one who is conscious that something is the matter with the brain would feel of anybody who attempted to put her into a lunatic asylum. Let us remember that her mother had not

Defence of Patrick Staunton.

seen her for twelve months before her marriage, and we know that when she did come she had a conversation for a few minutes, which my learned friend Mr. Williams commented upon, and may it not well have been that Harriet Staunton herself was desirous not to be found by her mother? You have her own sentiments in the letter she wrote to her mother so soon after that interview, in which she expresses the wish that she should not see the mother again, and in which she said her husband was desirous that the mother should not come. Does it come to anything more than this, that, in the first place, she should not be found by her mother, and, in the next place, that there was some other reason for it? It would be incomprehensible if there really were this plan and plot of murder which has been shadowed out to you. Strangely enough, Louis Staunton, whose one object, if he had been a party to a conspiracy or combination to destroy his wife, would be to keep himself as far as possible from the place to which she was to be taken, and at which this terrible resolve was to be carried out, arranged to go down and live with Alice, choosing the place only about twenty minutes' walk from the cottage where his wife is staying; and so long as he was down there, so long as his being there was concealed from the knowledge of his wife, every time she went out into the village, every walk she took about the place, might have revealed to her the fact that her husband was living down there with Alice Rhodes, and there comes at once a second reason for her being checked and not being allowed to ramble about the place near which, for some inscrutable reason, Louis Staunton has actually come down to live. If she goes out she may meet him or Alice Rhodes, or may be given the information that he is living within a mile of the place in which she is kept.

Now, gentlemen, if Patrick Staunton did deny the fact of her being there, was she checked and prevented from going out? Upon what Clara Brown said, with regard to that part of the case, I shall have a word to say presently; but, so far as any evidence goes, there is only the general evidence of the man who tells you that, in a tone and with a manner from which he thought he was joking—he thought it a joke at the time—Patrick Staunton one day said to her outside the house, "Here is a policeman, and he will run you in." The man thought it a joke. I think, with that exception, there is no direct evidence that she was checked or limited at all with regard to going out of the house.

One observation I should like to make at this moment, because it comes in order of time, although I confess I do not attach much importance to it. It must be admitted that Harriet Staunton was concealed from observation down there. I leave the suggestion with you. I have suggested to you that

Staunton Trial.

Mr. Clarke that was not merely in order to prevent her being found out by Mrs. Butterfield, but also to prevent her finding out the place where Louis was living, and where he was living with Alice Rhodes as his wife. But you will observe when you come to the evidence which has been given by persons who say they watched the place, or were passing near the house, that they did not see her about at any time. I only want to call your attention to this observation, that a good deal of that evidence relates to the last month or two months during which she was at Cudham, and that with regard to that there is an explanation of her not going out, which certainly does not require the interposition of Patrick Staunton. It may have been that during that time the emaciation, which was afterwards so extreme, was gradually coming upon her, that she was wasting away and becoming weaker. There would be a reason in her own bodily condition. I do not say " health " for a special reason; but there would be a reason in her bodily condition, as well as in the wish entertained by Patrick Staunton and his wife, that she should not go out.

That being so, let me point out to you that if there is that explanation of her being kept concealed, one can understand but cannot sympathise with it; of course, one cannot approve, it is impossible to approve it, but you are not asked to do so; but one can understand, perhaps, the way in which Patrick Staunton would act, and understand that he would, for the sake of his brother, help to keep the wife in some sort of concealment there.

But the next step you are asked to take is a tremendous one. You are asked from the evidence in this case to conclude that, if not at the time when Harriet Staunton first went to that place, at all events at some time while she was living in that house, there was either a combination between these persons to do her to death slowly by starving and neglecting her, or that there was that intention on the part of some one, with the knowledge and without the interposition of the other.

Mr. JUSTICE HAWKINS—Or to do her grievous injury, grievous bodily injury; if they did that the probable consequences of which would be to reduce her to such a state as that death would be the probable result, or if they were doing acts which they were aware, and reasonably ought to be aware, would lead to that result, that would be equal to murder without the actual absolute intention.

Mr. CLARKE—I will neither try to repeat, nor comment upon, anything my lord says. I know well he will lay down the law in his summing up.

Mr. JUSTICE HAWKINS—I mention that in order that you may deal with it before it comes to be too late, and that I may not conceal from you anything that is passing in my mind.

196

Defence of Patrick Staunton.

Mr. CLARKE—I am very much obliged to your lordship, but
I think there are different aspects of the case which are present
to my mind, and I propose to deal with them in their order.
You, gentlemen, are asked in this case, and asked on the
authority of one important bit of evidence, to believe that in
August there was the intention that she should be done to death,
not merely that she should be ill-treated, concealed, neglected,
but that she should be got out of the way; and there was no
doubt about it, because you heard what Clara Brown said,
and what the interpretation was that she put upon that letter,
an interpretation which suggested that there was the deliberate
intention that she should be put to death.

I will deal in their order with those facts of the case which
would throw upon Patrick Staunton the burden of having been
negligent, or having been a party at a later time to neglect
which would cause her death, or to a combination, whatever
it may be. I will deal with the whole evidence, but at this
moment I am asking you to consider this point, that with
regard to the whole current and tenor of the conduct of Patrick
Staunton in assisting to keep her in a certain sense concealed
in his house there is an explanation, there is a possible motive;
but it is a motive which fails to be sufficient when you come to
the larger crime with which the prisoners are charged.

It might well be that from the affection which appears to
have existed between the brothers, and which would induce
him to do those very matters which I do not approve or defend,
it might well be that Patrick Staunton would consent to help to keep the lady concealed; but can it
be that he lent himself to the deliberate intention
that he would put her to death, that he would be a
party to her being murdered by starvation and negligence in
his own house? Is it possible to explain his conduct upon any
such hypothesis as that? Why, gentlemen, what was the
motive? In his case it was no motive of money. So far as
there was money, if money was of any importance in the poor
little household which seems to have existed in that little
cottage at Cudham, so far as money would be of value, money
was paid to keep her, and it was by her life and not
her death that he would profit. As for the gratification of
passion, he has not been implicated in the tragedy
of guilty passion which runs in this case alongside
with the terrible tragedy into which you are inquiring. And is it conceivable that without either of these
motives, so far as one can see, without any motive of adequate
strength, that he would lend himself to a scheme which would
destroy the happiness of his own home, and bring the victim
of the crime which they were about to commit into daily and
hourly contact with himself, where he could not fail day by

Mr. Clarke day, in the presence of his wife and children, to see the progress of the crime he is supposed to have been committing, and where in that little house there was necessarily either an accomplice or a spy, for there was a servant, upon whose secrecy or upon whose concurrence in the plot the lives of himself and his wife must depend. Surely it is monstrous to suppose that, without motive, he should lend himself to a plan so difficult in its execution, so horrible in its progress, so far as he himself is concerned, and so certainly fatal to him in the fact that it must at last, either by the speaking out of the witness, who was present in the house, or by the appearance of the dead when death had been accomplished, have been brought home to him. If this death was actually worked out in that way, if Harriet Staunton, in fact, was wilfully brought to her death by the deprivation of food in that house, then for days, for more than a month, Patrick Staunton must have had before him every day and every hour, present to his nightly dreams and to his waking thoughts, a crime which one could scarcely contemplate so long without an unutterable horror, which must surely have turned him from his dreadful purpose.

Gentlemen, apart from this question of concealment, there are only three matters with which I think I shall have to deal; starting with the absence of motive, there are three sets of evidence in the case upon which I must address you. The evidence against all the prisoners divides itself fairly enough into these three classes. There is the evidence of the statements that the husband and the wife themselves have made; the direct evidence, which is only that of Clara Brown; and the evidence of the medical witnesses; and excluding, as I desire to exclude after what I have said, the question of concealment, and the witnesses who referred to the fact of the lady not being seen about Cudham, I think you will find that the evidence is fairly summarised in the other classes I have mentioned.

With regard to the statements, of course my learned friends and I feel the responsibility, representing, as we do, the different prisoners, of going through the statements, and of seeing how far each prisoner is affected by the statements that were made. There were important conversations, for instance, like the conversation with Mrs. Chalklin and Dr. Longrigg on the night of the 12th. At those conversations Louis Staunton and Mrs. Patrick Staunton were present, Patrick was not.

Mr. Justice Hawkins—In the morning, you mean.

Mr. Clarke—Or in the morning. I was thinking of the conversation with Mrs. Chalklin, which I think took place that night or the following morning, and Mrs. Chalklin did not see Patrick or have any conversation with him till a quarter to six on the Friday evening. At all events, gentlemen, I

Defence of Patrick Staunton.

was indicating that as a conversation which I may have incidentally to mention in connection with Dr. Longrigg. But so far as Patrick is concerned, the only statements I remember which are contained in the case are, first, the account of his conversation with Mrs. Butterfield at the station, when he met her and denied knowing anything of Harriet Staunton (and with that I have dealt in dealing with the question of concealment), and the statement which was made to Sergeant Bateman when he went down and made inquiries at Cudham. It is also said that Mr. Patrick went to the hospital with Mrs. Patrick Staunton when the child was taken there, but that he took no part in the conversation, and the nurse said that she did not know he was within hearing. It is true that he said something to the doctors at the hospital, describing the child, and it was put in evidence, though I do not suppose it will affect your minds upon this question. It is true it was mentioned at the hospital that the wife had nothing to do with it, that the mother was a worthy woman, and that is a statement which is really to a certain extent true concerning Harriet Staunton. I need not make any observation about that. It was not his child, as a matter of fact, but there are people who have availed themselves of the magnificent charity which the hospital offers, and who have availed themselves of it without fair reason. It may be so in this case, but I am not anxious to acquit him of that; at all events I am confident you would not desire that I should burden you with observations on circumstances which are incidental, and upon irrelevant conversations.

Then, with regard to Sergeant Bateman. He made a statement to Sergeant Bateman which I shall ask you to accept and to say was true. He made a statement to Sergeant Bateman that she had been there for some months, and that there was nothing the matter with her except a little brain disease. Gentlemen, I think you will find upon the whole evidence of the case that the statement which was made to Sergeant Bateman was a true statement, substantially a true statement, and I say substantially because when you have to deal, after my lord has called your attention to it, with the whole of that statement, I think you will find very fair ground for caution before you accept it at all points. One of my learned friends has already spoken of the conduct of Sergeant Bateman in going down and asking questions in the way he did. I cannot imagine how it is allowed that a police constable should go down to persons in this way, that he should call them one by one into a room, should examine and cross-examine them, and then should go and give evidence at the trial, unfortified by any notes which he made at the time, and liable, as was shown to you by the example of Bateman himself, to lapses of

Mr. Clarke memory, which may prevent his repeating matters of the gravest and most vital importance to the prisoners. There was a great case in this Court not many years ago, the case of the Lewisham murder,[2] when I remember the then Lord Chief Justice Bovill spoke very strongly indeed with regard to inquiries made by policemen, and reports which they brought as to the statements which had been made to them; and I do ask you to remember this in dealing with the evidence of Sergeant Bateman, that my learned friend, Mr. Straight, in listening to the evidence he gave here, and referring to the notes of that which he had given before, was able to suggest to him matters of grave importance to Mrs. Patrick Staunton, which he had innocently, I have no doubt, and from the defect of the human memory, left out in his statement here.

The observation I make is not in any way one of censure. I suppose he took the ordinary course, and you may take it that I do not impute to him any breach of duty. But the observation I make with regard to that brings me naturally to another which I heard made by the Attorney-General himself in the very fair and temperate speech in which he opened this case. He pointed out to you himself that at Cudham there were only five people in the house who could give direct evidence as to what had taken place there. He pointed out to you that, of those five people, four were silenced because they were in the prisoners' dock.

Now, gentlemen, this trial, of course, has to be conducted according to the rules of procedure as they at this moment exist. This is not a place to rail against the practice of condemning prisoners to silence, and allowing them to sit in a dock, day after day, as if they were spectators of some highly interesting game which the counsel on both sides played out with their lives at stake. This is not the place to complain, though one may hope that the day will soon come when something may be done to strike out from our criminal procedure what is its last remaining barbarism.[3] But I think, so long as the practice lasts, I am bound to point out to you that in this case the prisoners are suffering not only the disadvantages of this practice, but the disadvantages of another practice without having the advantage which would then be given them. It is urged against prisoners being allowed to give evidence on their own behalf that they would be liable to cross-examination; but these prisoners cannot give evidence though their cross-examination is before you.

Mr. JUSTICE HAWKINS—The coroner's duty is not to cross-examine; the coroner's duty is to say, " What have you to

---

2 *The Queen* v. *Edmund Pook*, July, 1871.

3 This was effected by the Prisoners' Evidence Act of 1898, 61 and 62 Vict. c. 36.

Mr. Edward Clarke

Defence of Patrick Staunton.

Now, gentlemen, bearing in mind that evidence given by Clara Brown, which I now pass over with those observations, asking you to look at the evidence to which you are referred, it is conceded that Clara Brown's evidence, so far as it is uncorroborated, is not evidence upon which you would act in this case. You have not been so warned by me, but by the prosecution in this case. I have asked you to carefully consider as a matter of logic where corroboration begins and what you strictly can call corroboration; and when you have heard Clara Brown's evidence and considered how that evidence broke away under your feet at every step, you are thrown back upon the medical evidence in this case, and I must come to the evidence which Mr. Longrigg gave with regard to the matters which were before him in life, and also in the post-mortem examination.

Now, gentlemen, upon this point there is a conflict of evidence before you. It has been my duty in this case (and my learned friends have confided it, somewhat too trustfully, perhaps, to me) to deal with the medical evidence in the case, and to the best of my ability I have endeavoured to grapple with the questions which have arisen; and I now want to point out to you the inferences which have been drawn from the appearances in life and from the post-mortem examination, and to prove to you, not on the evidence of the witnesses I have called, but upon the admission of the doctors who have given evidence for the prosecution in this case, that the examination and the record of the examination are imperfect, and that the inferences are inconclusive and untrustworthy.

I deal first with the evidence of Mr. Longrigg. He is consulted about the patient, he is told that the lady is very ill; and here I must for a moment refer to a statement in the conversation with him. He says it is only a matter of recollection on his part—there is no note of it. He says that when he was talking to Louis Staunton and Mrs. Patrick Staunton they told him that a doctor had been attending her, and that he asked the name, and was told Dr. Creasey; and on suggesting it was Dr. Creasey, of Gravesend, he was told no, it was Dr. Creasey, of Brastead. There was a Dr. Creasey at Brastead, so that to that extent, if they were desiring to conceal anything from Mr. Longrigg, they took the worst course: they gave the name and address of the doctor, where he could be found and actual inquiries made.

That is his recollection, and if it is accurate with regard to that conversation it is very important. There were two persons who were present with him during the conversation. It is so important that he had to be pressed with regard to the exact words spoken, and he said in cross-examination that he could not state the exact words which were spoken in that

Staunton Trial.

Mr. Clarke conversation. Now, gentlemen, in the report of a conversation of this kind, everything depends on the exactness of his recollection. The mere form of the sentence, the mere form of the question as he addressed it to one of these people, would make the whole difference between on the one hand a true statement of that which had taken place, and on the other a falsehood, or what you might consider as a falsehood designed to lead him off the scent and prevent investigation. He was speaking to these two persons, he wanted to ask them a question about the doctor; he tells you he cannot recollect the exact words he used. He asked if a doctor had been attending her and they said, " Yes." Is the answer untrue? If he asked them (and is it not the usual form of a medical question?) Have you a doctor there? and they said " Yes," it would be true. Upon that small difference in the exact words in which the question was put by Mr. Longrigg depends the whole difference between the truth or the falsehood of that statement, and let me just say that what immediately follows in that conversation is an almost conclusive indication that Dr. Longrigg's memory is failing him, and what was really said was, " Have you a medical man? " because they tell him that she has been only ill for a few days, and they tell him that this doctor lives 7 or 8 miles off. Is it not a great deal more likely that the statement by them was, " We have a doctor, and he is not attending, for he lives 7 or 8 miles off," than that they told him he had been attending and went on to say that the doctor lived 7 or 8 miles off? What was Dr. Longrigg's impression of the matter immediately after? He is speaking now from imperfect recollection, but what was his impression immediately afterwards? Why, gentlemen, surely his impression must have been that there had not been a doctor attending her, for this reason : he treats the case—he does not ask to send for the doctor—he treats the case, he does not ask anything about the treatment. One would think if he was told that a doctor had been attending he would have asked what medicine had been taken, and " Did you give her stimulants? " or something of that kind. H does not ask anything of that kind; but there is something more than that, he attends the case, and within a few hours, apparently, the patient dies.

Mr. JUSTICE HAWKINS—When he had that conversation about the medical man he had not seen the patient.

Mr. CLARKE—When he had that conversation he had not seen the patient, but he attends the case, and in a comparatively few hours the patient dies. If he believed that the medical man at Cudham had been attending that lady, is it conceivable that a man exercising ordinary care, having seen so little of the patient as he had, having had so few opportunities of

210

Defence of Patrick Staunton.

testing the cause or the nature of the disease, is it conceivable
that he would give a medical certificate without taking the
ordinary precaution of writing to the other medical attendant
to inquire what the former symptoms had been? No. Not
only that, but when he gave the certificate, and Casabianca
comes and tells him there is foul play, it does not seem to occur
to him then to communicate with Dr. Creasey with regard to
the matter.

Gentlemen, I hope I do not seem to be labouring this point
too much. That conversation is an important one in this
most important respect. From that conversation and from
the exact form of this answer is there not a reason, as well
as from the account of what else was said, to doubt the
accuracy of Dr. Longrigg's memory, and to believe that the
question really asked was the question, " Have you a medical
man? " and that the answer to that question was truly answered
by the statement that Dr. Creasey lived at Brastead, but with
the explanation that as he lived some miles off they brought
the patient up to London.

And what was the conduct of the people who bring the
patient there? Directly they get to the place they go twice
that night to urge Mr. Longrigg to come. I am not going to
say anything in the way of censure upon Mr. Longrigg for
not going that night. Certainly it occurred to one, as the
house was little more than a quarter of a mile from his own
house, and as it was a case in which, so to speak, he was
retained, as the people had been twice in the course of the
night to tell him that the lady was worse, and to beg him
to come as soon as he came in, it did occur to one that
whenever he came in, whatever time of night it was, it would
have been a reasonable thing for him to have gone those few
hundred yards to see how the lady was. However, he did
not. The next morning he went, and the next morning
undoubtedly this poor lady was beyond the reach of medical
aid. But there is one important piece of evidence that he
gave you in favour of the prisoners. He says—" I noticed
nothing in the appearances inconsistent with their account.
I noticed nothing in their behaviour which was in the least
suspicious. I noticed nothing about the patient herself, or
the behaviour of the people around her, which gave me any
cause to suspect at all." He came to a conclusion he fairly
enough defends to a certain extent, and I am not here to
dispute it. There was truth in the certificate that he gave,
but then came Mr. Casabianca. Mr. Casabianca gave him
a history which we know may have been a romantic one,
probably it was a very serious one, of the members of the
family to which the deceased lady belonged. Mr. Casabianca
told him that there was foul play, and upon that Mr. Longrigg

Mr. Clarke was led to another conclusion. His first conclusion was stated in the certificate; his second conclusion was narcotic poison, because he tells you that directly he was told that there was foul play, the symptoms which he observed during life were of course present to his mind, and he formed the opinion of narcotic poison. Upon that a post-mortem examination was ordered, and a post-mortem examination took place.

Now, gentlemen, upon the accuracy and completeness of that post-mortem examination very much indeed depends. Who conducted it? Mr. Longrigg. He examined the viscera, I think, and he examined the brain. Mr. Wilkinson also examined the brain. Who recorded it? Curiously enough, in the first instance, Mr. Longrigg, who was the responsible person in the case, and who took notes, who was the principal, therefore, practically having attended the patient. He took notes in a little book of his own—a private memorandum book. He may have filled, I think he says, two and a half pages, or something of that kind in this book, but all the notes that he took at the post-mortem examination were contained in that memorandum book, and that book, unfortunately, is lost. The notes which we have now, and which we know as Dr. Longrigg's notes, are notes that he made afterwards with regard to the appearances that he had observed. Well, now, was that post-mortem examination a complete one? It is perfectly clear that it was not. That, by the confession of the doctors who have been called upon the other side, was not the case. The brain was not weighed, the urine was not tested, the suprarenal capsules were not examined, the microscope—and perhaps this is the most important of all—was never used.

Now, gentlemen, how can we explain this? How is it that the three or four doctors of some experience in the matter, going to look at this body and to study the appearances presented by it, how is it that they allowed a post-mortem examination to remain incomplete? Is not the answer obvious, and that in the early stages of the post-mortem examination they were, I won't say directed to a conclusion, but were led to entertain a belief which, so to speak, threw them off the scent? Early in the post-mortem examination they found redness of the intestines, and upon that the theory was suggested to Mr. Longrigg and to the other medical man who was conducting the post-mortem examination, that although there may have been poison it was not a narcotic poison such as Mr. Longrigg inferred from the symptoms during life, but that it was an irritant poison which would have effect in that way upon the coating of the intestines; and upon that, discussing the matter amongst themselves, having that suggestion presented to their minds—for I will put it no stronger than that—their examination, like

Defence of Patrick Staunton.

the examination of Dr. Rodgers, when the matters were submitted to him afterwards, was an examination directed to the
presence of poison.   If it had not been so, is it not obvious,
gentlemen, that they would have filled up the gaps that I have
pointed out in this medical examination?   Were there not
appearances there which should have led to further examination?   My learned friend the Attorney-General called one
witness who was not present at the post-mortem examination,
and a witness whose ability, I suppose, is known to all who
are practising in this Court.   Mr. Bond was called into the
witness-box, and gave certain evidence in regard to this matter,
and, in cross-examination, do you remember what Mr. Bond
said with regard to this post-mortem examination?   He admits
that it was incomplete, and the evidence which he gave points
to two, at all events, special evidences of this incompleteness.
Mr. Bond tells you this, " There are two diseases which cause a
bronze skin."   He says, " I know of no other disease which
causes a bronze skin.   In diabetes the skin is slightly bronzed.
In Addison's disease the skin is a great deal more bronzed,
and, therefore, if I find a bronzing of the skin, that would
lead me to the suspicion that either diabetes or Addison's
disease might be present."

Now, suppose that to be so.   In this case there was a
bronzing.   Mr. Longrigg says, " The skin was bronzing."
Then that would lead to the inference that one of those two
diseases was present, and with regard to each one of those
diseases there is only one unmistakable symptom to be discovered after death.   In the case of diabetes that one
unmistakable symptom is the presence of sugar in the urine.
With regard to Addison's disease, the one unmistakable
symptom is the condition of the supra-renal capsules.   I asked
the doctors with regard to this post-mortem examination, " Did
you find urine?"   " Yes."   " Did you test it?"   " No, there
were 3 ounces of it, and it was not tested."   " Did you
examine the supra-renal capsules?"   " No, they were overlooked."   There was the indication on the appearance of the
body that one of those two diseases might probably be present,
and with the opportunity of making sure of that fact with
regard to each of them by an appearance which they could
easily have tested, they did not test either.   Is not that one
explanation, the explanation that I have suggested to you,
that their minds had already gone off on the suspicion of
poison, and that, with that view in their minds, it did not
occur to them to follow up the other evidences that were
present before them?

But this is still more important according to the view of
the case which I have ventured to take.   There is a still more
important omission upon their part, and that is the omission

Staunton Trial.

Mr. Clarke of the use of the microscope. They find in the lungs a certain amount of tubercular deposit. They find in the meshes of the pia mater a certain number of granules or miliary tubercles, tubercles which connect themselves with tubercular disease, and connect themselves either with a chronic state of disease, tuberculosis, which would be acute and general, or with the local disease, meningitis. Now, these indications are found in the brain, and the doctors who were called on behalf of the prosecution say that they did not attach much importance to these tubercles on the brain, they were not sufficient in quantity and they were not in the right position. Some of them seemed to consider that the important point was that there was not enough of these tubercular substances; another, Mr. Wilkinson I think it was, seems to think that they were not important because they were not at the base of the brain.

Now, gentlemen, of course the very important question for you is, not whether it is proved that the death of this lady was caused by any of the diseases I have mentioned, but whether her death, with the symptoms I have described, is consistent with her having died of one of those diseases; because I am quite sure you would demand, before you acted upon it to the prejudice of the prisoners, that the medical evidence given before you should be consistent with the hypothesis of their guilt, and with that hypothesis only. If you find that all the appearances here are consistent with her having died from a fatal disease, a disease not necessarily produced by privation of food, then surely you could not be asked to say that you were satisfied that the crime of murder had been committed by the wilful deprivation of food.

Well, now, how about this disease? What do we hear? In the first place these doctors, one or two of them who have given their evidence on the part of the prosecution, I suppose now must admit themselves to have been mistaken, after the authority, the great authority, which has been produced in this case with regard to the question of tubercular meningitis and tubercular disease. Mr. Longrigg and Dr. Bright would probably hardly persist in the evidence which they have given, and which has been contradicted. I asked Mr. Longrigg whether there was any sign in the appearances which he noticed which was inconsistent with the symptoms occurring from tubercular meningitis, and he mentions one; he mentions the rigidity of the arm as the symptom which shows him that it is not tubercular meningitis.

The ATTORNEY-GENERAL—I think you are mistaken.

Mr. CLARKE—It is so really.

The ATTORNEY-GENERAL—I think he mentioned paralysis.

Mr. CLARKE—My lord will correct me by and by if I am wrong.

214

Defence of Patrick Staunton.

Mr. Justice Hawkins—I have carefully abstained.   I keep Mr. Clarke silent.   I do so, not because I assent to everything.

Mr. Clarke—I quite understand that, my lord. Of course, gentlemen, I am speaking under my lord's correction.   There is my lord's note.   One of my friends has been kind enough to take a note for me, and this is what he has—" Considering the rigidity of the muscles of the upper extremity, tuberculosis was not sufficiently established.   If it had been established, it might have caused the other symptoms."   That is Mr. Longrigg's statement—that if tuberculosis had been sufficiently established, it might have caused all the symptoms except the rigidity of the arm.   That was, at all events, in my mind to ask him, and I believe I did ask him, and that is on the note.

Thus Mr. Longrigg stated that the rigidity of the arm was inconsistent with tuberculosis. We have called witnesses in the box to put the matter beyond a doubt, referring not merely to their own experience but to their knowledge, the high scientific knowledge of Dr. Payne and Dr. Bristowe.   They are the authorities for the proposition that so far from its being inconsistent with tuberculosis, it is one of the consequences and frequent signs.

Now take the other suggestion, that because these tubercles were not at the base of the brain, therefore they could not have produced the disease and produced the emaciation which existed.   Gentlemen, the answer to this is the evidence of Dr. Payne, evidence which is endorsed by the authority of Dr. Bristowe, and is of the greatest importance.   I asked Dr. Bright, you will remember, in cross-examination, with regard to the symptoms that he saw, whether those were not consistent with tubercular disease, and with being caused by that tubercular disease.   He said, " No, there were other appearances that one would have found, namely, tubercles at the base of the brain, flattening and bulging of the lobes of the brain, and effusion into the ventricles."   Now, then, I asked Dr. Payne, and his opinion is supported by Dr. Bristowe, and he said, " It is quite possible to have the disease produced without having tubercles at the base of the brain, that would produce the appearances which Dr. Bright conceived should have been presented if the disease was there at all; but in the absence of tubercles at the base of the brain those appearances will not be presented, and yet there will be the tubercular meningitis which would cause the emaciation and the death."   Therefore, upon those points the differentia indicated by these doctors, as showing that it was not tubercular meningitis, are proved by the evidence which is before you to be perfectly consistent with that disease.

Now, gentlemen, there is another important part of the evidence, and it is this, there is evidence of appearances in the

Staunton Trial.

Mr. Clarke body which are inconsistent with death being the result of starvation only, and that is the inflammation of the peritoneum, and upon that point did not the evidence of Mr. Payne, given in the witness-box yesterday, make you regret that there had not been more care in this post-mortem examination and a more careful resort to the appliances of science to solve the difficult question? Dr. Payne says, "I cannot explain the presence of the appearances of inflammation of the peritoneum unless, in fact, it was caused, as it might have been, by tubercular deposit not to be detected by the naked eye, but yielding to the examination of the microscope." And Dr. Payne says this further, which is of the greatest importance, "If I find the existence of tubercles in the brain discoverable by the naked eye, I should consider it probable that in the other organs of the body I should, by microscopic examination, be able to discover further marks of tubercular deposit."

What, then, was the condition of the body? There is one matter that I must mention before I sum it up, and that is the state of the brain. This is very important. In cases of starvation Mr. Longrigg admitted that the brain was pale. In this case it was not pale. Mr. Wilkinson says that in cases of tubercular disease he should not expect to find the rest of the brain healthy; but Dr. Payne, backed again by Mr. Bristowe, who endorses that medical opinion, and supported by medical authority beyond and apart from his own experience, says, "There are cases in which the disease does exist, and in its fatal form, and yet the residue of the brain would be found healthy."

Now, gentlemen, what was the fact? In examining this body they found tubercles in the meshes of the pia mater in the brain. Let them look further and see whether those tubercles were matters to which no importance was to be attached, or whether the presence of tubercles in another part of the system showed that there was great importance to be attached to it. Looking further, you find a patch of tubercular deposit on one of the lungs, and although they found it, although there were these tubercles in the brain, and this tubercular deposit on the lungs, that must have guided them to the suspicion of disease, they did not call to their aid the microscope, which might have enabled them to detect, at the base of the brain or on the coating of the peritoneum, the still further and conclusive evidence of the presence of the tubercular meningitis which might have produced this death.

But, gentlemen, there are two more matters with regard to which the evidence of Mr. Longrigg and the other doctors is of great importance. In cross-examining Mr. Longrigg, I hope I did not seem unfair to him for a moment. Certainly there was no intention on my part to be unfair to him with regard

216

to the notes that he took, and I think you will bear me witness, **Mr. Clarke**
directly he complained of the matter, I was only too glad
that the notes should be in his hands, and that he should
have an opportunity of examining them. But there was an
important question, and important to put in a particular way;
and in cross-examination one exhausts the recollection of a
witness before helping it, in order to test it, and I asked him,
" Have you told us everything that you noticed with regard to
the coating of the stomach?" He said distinctly, " Yes."
Then I asked him, " Did you make a note of it?" " No, I did
not." He examined his notes, and there was no trace of it.
Another of the doctors was asked solely about the thinning of
the coats of the stomach; but Mr. Longrigg admits that there
are two indications, almost necessary indications, of death by
starvation: one is the thinning of the coat of the stomach, and
that the doctors never noticed and never noted. If Mr. Longrigg
did notice it himself, or noticed something which he thought was
thinning, he made no note of it. The other inevitable symptom
is the paleness of the brain, and in this case the brain was not
pale at all. With respect to the thinness of the coating of the
stomach and the paleness of the brain, you have the absence
of both these invariable symptoms.

The ATTORNEY-GENERAL—Who proved that paleness of the
brain was a symptom?

Mr. CLARKE—I believe I examined Mr. Longrigg about it.
I think you will find I am right. He said, " It was neither
pale nor wasted."

The ATTORNEY-GENERAL—I do not say that was not stated,
but who proved that it was a symptom of starvation?

Mr. CLARKE—The same witness that I asked.

The ATTORNEY-GENERAL—It is not so, I think.

Mr. CLARKE—He says, " I expect to find it pale in cases of
starvation."

Mr. JUSTICE HAWKINS—Whom are you alluding to?

Mr. CLARKE—Mr. Longrigg. In my cross-examination he
says, " The brain was neither pale nor wasted. I should expect
to find it pale, but not wasted."

The ATTORNEY-GENERAL—If that was the note, so be it. We
hear nothing of that kind from Mr. Payne.

Mr. CLARKE—Gentlemen, the point that I was upon—and
I am quite satisfied now by the notes of my learned friend that
I was right about the statement that I made—the point that I
was upon was this, that, by the evidence of the doctors who were
called by the prosecution, there are two symptoms of starvation;
one is the thinness of the coating of the stomach, the other paleness of the brain; and in this case, so far as the other doctors
beside Dr. Longrigg were concerned, there was no thinness of
the coating of the stomach. And he only admits that thinness

Mr. Clarke when it was suggested to him, although he made no memorandum in his notes, and although he had already said that he had told us all that he remembered about the condition of the stomach. He admits that he said the organs, with the exception of the lungs, were in a healthy condition. Then, gentlemen, if you get two symptoms that would be there in starvation, they are absent.

Mr. Justice Hawkins—Not that they of necessity would be there, Mr. Clarke, in all cases of starvation.

Mr. Clarke—Well, my lord, they would expect to find it.

Mr. Justice Hawkins—I mean to say, Addison's disease has the bronzing of the skin as in diabetes; it is not an essential.

Mr. Clarke—I am quite content. If there is one thing that I am anxious about in this case, it is that I should not overstate or exaggerate propositions which are not so familiar to me as they are to the gentlemen who have been in the witness-box, but which are very important for your consideration in the case. At all events, there are two symptoms one would expect to find in starvation, and neither of them is mentioned in the record of the post-mortem examination. There is the symptom of the inflammation of the peritoneum, which you would not expect to find in cases of starvation, and which you do find here. There is something more. Mr. Payne was examined with regard to the matters which were found, and which he thinks were inconsistent with death from starvation only; and I want to call your attention to the evidence that he has given in the cross-examination to which he was subjected.

Mr. Payne says that the rigidity of the arms would not be caused by starvation alone. He says that congestion of the stomach and congestion of the brain would not be caused by starvation alone. My learned friend the Attorney-General, in cross-examination, suggested to him two matters, one the matter of a person dying in convulsions. Now, so far as I know, there is no evidence in this case of any convulsion prior to death. So far as I know, the symptoms which Mr. Longrigg noticed with regard to the dilatation of the pupils and the stertorous breathing, the head symptoms, as I may call them, were symptoms noticed by him actually some time before the patient died. Then another question—I won't call it far-fetched, that would be disrespectful, but it was certainly a question I did not expect to hear put to Mr. Payne; it was this, " Don't you know that, in cases of shipwrecked sailors who have become maniacs and have died, the brain is congested?"[4]   One would not suppose that anybody has had any very long experience of shipwrecked sailors who died maniacs, from absence of food and of drink, and there is no evidence in this case, from

---

4 See p. 183.   Mr. Clarke's condensation does not agree with the Attorney-General's question as reported.

Defence of Patrick Staunton.

beginning to end, that the privation, if there were privation, to which this lady may have been subjected, assuming for a moment the suggestion of the prosecution to be true, there is no suggestion of any maniacal excitement or convulsion, or anything of the kind. Mr. Payne gave important evidence. He told you he had read the depositions. He had read the notes of the post-mortem examination. He had sat here and listened to the examination and cross-examination of the doctors who had been called into the box, and he gives you his opinion that the deceased was killed by tubercular meningitis. He gave you his experience that this tubercular disease had for one of its frequent and early symptoms the slow and gradual emaciation, and an emaciation which is unaccompanied by any other sign of disease.

Now, of Mr. Payne's eminence in his profession one need not, I think, speak. The less necessity is there for my doing so, because in a curious and remarkable way he was corroborated by evidence to which the Attorney-General himself appealed. It is the Attorney-General's own witness in one sense that I next call into the witness-box, in order to test the accuracy of Mr. Payne's evidence with regard to these symptoms of obscure diseases. My learned friend had had handed to him, I suppose by the scientific gentlemen who are instructing him in dealing with this case, a book, as a book of authority, upon which he might rely, and by which he might test evidence. It was Dr. Bristowe's book, and in cross-examination he puts that to Mr. Payne. He seeks to modify Mr. Payne's evidence by appealing to the dicta which he finds in Dr. Bristowe's book, and Mr. Payne admits that Dr. Bristowe's book is acknowledged to be a high authority, and that Dr. Bristowe himself is one of the highest living authorities upon these subjects. It must be so, because my friend has used it as an authority. It so happens that I have the good fortune of Dr. Bristowe's personal acquaintance, and it so happened that Dr. Bristowe, having nothing whatever to do with this case, and dealing simply with me as a private friend, made a communication to me, and at the moment when Mr. Payne was challenged with that book, and referred to Dr. Bristowe's authority, Dr. Bristowe himself was sitting here.

Mr. JUSTICE HAWKINS—You really must not state anything that he has not stated.

Mr. CLARKE—But he has stated it, my lord.

Mr. JUSTICE HAWKINS—I mean you must not state what he has stated to you.

Mr. CLARKE—I am not doing that.

Mr. JUSTICE HAWKINS—You said something about his being a private friend.

Mr. CLARKE—I am only stating what Dr. Bristowe stated

Staunton Trial.

Mr. Clarke in the witness-box, that he had not been retained in this case, and had no communication with the other gentlemen in the case. It was in consequence of a private letter to me that he was here. At all events, at the moment when his authority was appealed to—and my friend called it a high authority—he was here, and he was in the witness-box yesterday. He endorsed the opinion which Mr. Payne had expressed, and he endorsed it in the answer to the questions of the learned Attorney-General, saying that he felt confirmed by that opinion in the judgment that he had formed with regard to this case.

Gentlemen, upon that point have I not produced to you evidence which is worthy of consideration, and worthy of respect? The matters with which you are dealing in this case are matters with which Mr. Longrigg may well be forgiven for not being very conversant. A general practitioner at Penge, however able he may be, however good his practice may be, cannot be supposed to have that knowledge of the most recent results of scientific investigation which belongs to gentlemen who occupy the position of those whom I called into the witness-box yesterday. I am not asking you to find affirmatively a verdict as to the disease which caused this lady's death. I am quite aware that with regard to one of the diseases mentioned—diabetes—my learned friend the Attorney-General may put that out of view, because I am quite aware that disease would bring with it a symptom during life which could not be mistaken, and which would easily have been noticed. But it is only necessary for me to show, as I hope and believe I have shown upon the evidence that I have called before you, that the symptoms which were observed during life or on the post-mortem examination were consistent with death from a disease which produces gradual and great emaciation, which is ultimately fatal, but fatal after being in its acute form possibly for only a few days, and the history of which disease is therefore consistent, not merely with the appearances during life and the post-mortem examination after death, but consistent—and this is all-important to me—with the account that the prisoners themselves have given of the condition that Harriet Staunton was in whilst she was remaining at Cudham.

Gentlemen, if this was a case of tubercular disease, assuming on the Monday this acute form, there is an explanation of the whole of the symptoms that have been stated and the gradual emaciation going on. And here let me call your minds—for at this moment it seems to me of the greatest possible importance—here let me call your minds to the observation I made with regard to one thing that you do not find in the course of this evidence. You do not find any complaint of suffering or any complaints of disease. These scientific men tell you that one of the symptoms of this tubercular disease is that

220

Defence of Patrick Staunton.

preceding it there may be a long period of gradual wasting leading to very great emaciation. Dr. Bristowe vouched for having seen cases in which the emaciation was as great as it was in this case, the disease having no symptom other than this slow and gradual emaciation. Now, if during the two or three months that had preceded this lady's removal from Cudham she had been gradually becoming emaciated without any painful symptom to herself, without any other symptom noticeable by the persons in the house, no symptom other than the gradual wasting of her frame; if this disease became acute on the Monday that she was removed to Penge, you find then that the account of the prisoners is consistent with the current of the disease, and you find that when you come into the presence of medical science every symptom of the brain and on the body, which after death is observed in the patient, is consistent with the presence of this disease.

.Now, gentlemen, I confess I hope and believe that this evidence puts it beyond a doubt that you will refuse to return a verdict of wilful murder, based upon the idea that Harriet Staunton was wilfully and systematically starved. When you recall the way in which you are asked to believe Clara Brown only if she is corroborated, is there not force to all of you in the observation I venture to make, that, although, if the medical evidence were clear and decisive, it would be a satisfaction to your minds to have seen Clara Brown in the witness-box, and have heard her story for what it is worth given out before you, if you found reason for doubt and hesitation upon the medical evidence, the value of Clara Brown's evidence is gone altogether? If the medical evidence is consistent with either of the two hypotheses, the one hypothesis the hypothesis of innocence, the other the hypothesis of guilt, I am quite sure you would never allow the evidence of Clara Brown to force you to accept the hypothesis which is inconsistent with the innocence of every prisoner at the bar. But I think it carries it a little further than that. I am not content to challenge your verdict with regard to the question of murder or not murder. I do not repeat any of the definitions or endeavour to repeat any of the definitions of the different stages or different forms of the crime which will be laid down to you by my lord. I think my lord will quite understand that, while I am anxious to deal fully with the facts, I do not think it part of my duty to put before you propositions of law when those propositions of law will come with the fullest authority to you from the bench. But I do say that I am carried a step further here. It is suggested that there was manslaughter at all events in this case, that there was the neglect to provide the medical attendance and the comforts which the prisoners, I suppose it will be suggested, must have seen were needed,

Staunton Trial.

and which they ought to have provided. The medical attendance is the only thing which presses upon me with regard to that matter, for as to the question of the comforts, that entirely depends upon the evidence of Clara Brown, and to that extent I am content to leave it. But with regard to the medical attendance, is there not an explanation, and a reasonable and fair explanation, in that medical evidence to which I have just called your attention?

Gentlemen, it is not a mistake, it is not an act of carelessness which the law brands as a crime and would punish, for the law is not so inhuman. The delay that a father weeps for when his child is dead, and when he thinks and thinks, in the bitterness of his sorrow, that if he had gone a little sooner, if he had called the doctor earlier, if he had wrapped the child up and taken it to a doctor he might have saved it; that is not the sort of thing which constitutes a criminal offence. And even if these people were negligent and careless, if you think they would have done wisely and properly when this gradual wasting, with no other symptom, was going on, to have called in Dr. Creasey or some medical attendant, and did not; you would not necessarily say that there was such an amount of neglect and carelessness on their part as would entitle you to find a verdict of manslaughter against them.

So far as the indisputable evidence goes, it seems clear that when they did move this lady, when they thought she was ill, and when they were going to take her to a medical man, so far as their conduct was concerned with respect to Penge, I say that conduct is consistent with the readiness to bear the fullest inquiry and investigation, and with the greatest care and attention to this unhappy lady. The doctor speaks of the distress the women were in who were attending to her, the surprise that they expressed at the illness from which she was suffering. He says that Alice Rhodes—I think it was he or the nurse, I am not quite sure which—that Alice Rhodes was attending and doing all she could in the matter. Then again and again to the doctor; twice that night they sent for the doctor. They leave the urgent message for him to come. They go, and it was Alice Rhodes who goes and waits till he comes. Louis Staunton goes to him later. The true name was given, the address was given. I heard some suggestion at the beginning of the case of their going to Forbes Road, as if that was not in the same registrar's district. I do not know whether anything is to be made of that, but it seems to be in evidence that Forbes Road is in two districts, and that No. 34, the place they took, was in the district which would be registered at Bromley, the very place it would have to be registered in if the death had occurred at Cudham. This is a matter of very trifling importance, and I only mention it to

Defence of Patrick Staunton.

get rid of the idea of suspicion or concealment at all. This Mr. Clarke death takes place, and after the death what happens? Is there any behaviour on their part as if they knew they had hurried this unfortunate woman to her grave, and were afraid of the deed? They had gone in by chance, as it were, where "Apartments to let" was in the window. They took the apartments from a person they never knew before, and from that person they accepted the recommendation of the doctor, of whom they had never heard until that day. From the doctor there came the nurse, a perfect stranger. The undertaker was sent for afterwards. And what do they do? Why, they go away from the place, and they leave a key with the nurse, or at the inn where she was then being employed, with instructions that she is to show the body to any person who comes; and when there is a suggestion of a difficulty with regard to the medical certificate, Louis Staunton says—"If there is any question about it at all, I should rather you waited. Do not hurry the funeral."

Gentlemen, from beginning to end, are not the circumstances of the removal consistent with the story which they have told, and which they tell, that there was a sudden illness which surprised and alarmed them, which made them think it necessary, instead of having a doctor who lived some distance off, that they should take this lady where the best medical skill could be constantly at hand? And was there not in the whole conduct of the transfer from Cudham to Penge a manifestation of solicitude and care in the way in which they took the lady, and a manifestation of the most perfect openness and freedom with regard to the publicity of all the proceedings in which they took part?

Now, gentlemen, I believe I have almost finished the observations that I have to make to you. I urge upon you that there is no evidence which would justify you in bringing a verdict of guilty of murder against the man for whom I appear in this case. And I do urge it upon you most seriously, in asking for your anxious consideration, that there is no evidence that he is guilty of the crime of manslaughter. I am anxious to urge this upon you, for I beg you not to look upon it as if manslaughter were a crime involved or necessarily to be decided by the other. When you have dismissed, as I hope you will dismiss, the charge of murder against him, it is for you then carefully to consider whether there is evidence against him of this negligence, and carelessness, and recklessness, as to which my lord will direct you. I have no desire to anticipate a phrase which would entitle you to find a verdict of manslaughter. Is not there only the mistake—the honest mistake of which I have spoken, the mistake for which he has suffered the most terrible punishment, gentlemen, to be

Staunton Trial.

Mr. Clarke for months in gaol awaiting his trial for life, to know that, while he lay in one cell of that gaol, in another cell of that shameful birthplace his wife is bringing forth the child of their love; to have to give up everything that he possesses to supply the means of facing a criminal trial like this; to sit—I was about to forget the worst of all—to have to sit for five or six days listening to these discussions going on, and I fear very much, thinking now and then how much was being left unsaid that should be said for him, how much was being left unasked that might have brought an answer in his favour? All this would have been to him an unsupportable agony, it would have constituted to me in this trial a responsibility almost too great to bear, if he, and I as his advocate, had not been sustained by the knowledge of the way in which a jury deals with a question of life and death.

Gentlemen, in a case of this kind, would you venture as Christian men to pronounce a verdict of guilty unless you were satisfied beyond reasonable doubt by evidence which was accurate, and clear, and trustworthy, and satisfied you to the hilt of the matters which were alleged, and with which you were asked to deal? Will you venture to rely thoroughly upon the controverted conclusions of the doctors who have dealt with the medical evidence, or upon the shameless evidence of that girl who came into the witness-box admitting herself a perjurer before the coroner, and proclaiming herself in this Court to be the accomplice of the crime which she denounces? Gentlemen, human justice is depicted as blind. It is not given to human justice to see and to know, as the great Eternal knows, the thoughts and feelings and actions of all men. She has to depend upon what she hears. She must depend upon recollection. She must depend upon testimony. She must depend upon inferences. How should she deal with the irrevocable issues of life and death unless those recollections are exact, that testimony trustworthy, those inferences uncontradicted? How should she lift the sword to strike—and you, gentlemen, guide her hand to-day—while at the moment that the accusing voice is in her ear denouncing the crime, the echo of that very voice is heard proclaiming that the prisoners are innocent, and when passionless science steps to her side to warn her that there may have been in truth no crime committed?

Mr. Gye Mr. GYE—Gentlemen of the jury, in addressing you on behalf of Alice Rhodes, though I approach the case with the most anxious care and with the strongest sense of responsibility devolving upon me, I have the advantage of following my learned friends who are engaged with me in this case, and they have called attention to the main points generally. They have dealt fully with the question of the guilt or no guilt of

224

Sir Henry Hawkins and his dog Jack

Photo by W. H. Bustin, Hereford

Defence of Alice Rhodes.

my own as regards the matters to which they have alluded
I could usefully occupy your time, or attempt to add to the
arguments which they have used. They have also dealt
with the circumstances of the case as bearing on the Stauntons ;
but many of these circumstances also bear upon the case against
Alice Rhodes. The medical evidence has been particularly
called to your attention. That evidence applies precisely and
in the same manner to the case of Alice Rhodes, and has the
same bearing in her case as it has in that of the Stauntons.
The facts relating to all that was done with regard to medical
attendance also equally apply in the case of Alice Rhodes.

[*At this point the prisoner Mrs. Patrick Staunton was seized
with a violent fit of hysteria. Her husband, who was sitting
next to her in the dock, immediately turned to her aid, as did
also the female warders and the governor of Newgate, who
were in attendance. At the suggestion of the learned judge
the prisoner was removed, and the other prisoners were also
allowed to leave the dock. In about five minutes Mrs. Patrick
Staunton returned, looking very pale, and the other prisoners
having been brought in,*]

Mr. GYE proceeded—I was saying to you that the medical
evidence has the same bearing on the case of Alice Rhodes
as upon the case of the Stauntons, and that evidence has been
so fully gone into that I feel if I were to call your attention
to it I should only repeat the arguments which have been
already used, and with which you are perfectly conversant. I
shall therefore ask you to take the medical evidence on
behalf of Alice Rhodes in precisely the same manner as it has
been applied to the case of the Stauntons, and with all that
has been said on their behalf I fully and entirely concur and
adopt. Do not let it be misunderstood between us that this
question of the intimacy between Alice Rhodes and Louis
Staunton has been denied. It has been admitted throughout
by my learned friends and myself in the entire conduct of this
case. It has been admitted by the prisoners throughout the
whole proceedings from their very first institution. At the
inquest, acting without advice, they all made statements. I
am not here to say one single word in excuse or justification
of the intimacy between Alice Rhodes and Louis Staunton.
It was wrong, it was most improper, and most wicked if you
like ; but there may be circumstances about it which, upon
consideration, will cause you to take a more lenient view of
the conduct at least of the parties concerned. There is no
doubt that this intimacy has given rise to an enormous amount
of prejudice against the prisoners. The examinations to which
they were subjected lasted some considerable time, and the
case was published in all its details in the newspapers, and the

Staunton Trial.

Mr. Gye prisoners have been judged severely throughout the country. The case has been discussed far and wide, and many persons have not scrupled to say this intimacy justified the charge against the prisoners. Besides this, the prisoners have been cruelly hooted, and held up to execration by excited crowds utterly ignorant of the principles of justice. In fact, the conduct of some people can only be likened to that of savages, having no civilisation at all. Well, gentlemen, I hope you will put any of that prejudice aside. It should not be forgotten that intimacies of this immoral kind exist in every class and every creed of society. They exist amongst persons who know full well what they are doing, and know that at any moment they may be found out, their proceedings brought to light, and a lifelong punishment await them; yet they are willing to run the risk for the gratification of passion. But I do not think there are many who would consent to commit such a cold-blooded murder as that which is alleged in this case, even for the gratification of passion. Therefore, if motives are to be searched for to explain the commission of this alleged murder, I hope to find a reason why you will go beyond the intimacy of Alice Rhodes and Louis Staunton. I will now endeavour shortly to call your attention to the evidence as against, and subsequently as in favour, of Alice Rhodes. The evidence against Alice Rhodes begins at the date of the confinement of Harriet Staunton, in March, 1875, and it rests only on the testimony of Clara Brown, and simply on the words, " I am not quite sure that she always slept in her own room." That is the whole of the evidence at this stage of the case against Alice Rhodes, except that about the nightdress; and, gentlemen, you may depend upon it, if more could have been got out of that witness, it would have been. A mere slanderous insinuation from a witness who had admitted her own untruthfulness need not take up any more time; and with regard to the nightdress found in a drawer in the room in which Louis Staunton slept, it is capable of an easy and natural explanation. Louis Staunton, on account of the confinement of his wife, was obliged to dress elsewhere, and it happened that on that floor there was only one chest of drawers, and thus Alice Rhodes had no other place for her clothes. The learned judge asked Clara Brown if there was any other of the clothes of Alice Brown in those drawers, and she did not remember; so that the whole story is not worth a moment's consideration. The next point is that arising out of Harriet Staunton being sent to Cudham for a week. That is naturally accounted for on the hypothesis that they wished her out of the way while they pursued the intimacy which no doubt at that time existed between them, and which has never been denied.

The next thing urged against Alice Rhodes is what she said

Defence of Alice Rhodes.

when she met Mrs. Butterfield at London Bridge station. No
doubt she told a falsehood as to the whereabouts of Mrs.
Harriet Staunton; but, if there was any criminal intention at
that time, why did Alice Rhodes make use of statements which
were not calculated to allay, but rather to arouse, the suspicions
of Mrs. Butterfield? Mrs. Butterfield complains of Alice Rhodes
wearing a brooch belonging to her daughter. That is a mere
trivial matter. The brooch itself was of trivial value, and
may have come into the possession of Alice Rhodes in many
different ways consistent with honesty. It might be that in
reward for what Alice Rhodes had done for her during her
confinement she had given the brooch to her. If the prosecution intend to attach any value to details of this kind, their
case against my client must be very weak indeed. Then we
have the fact of Harriet Staunton going to live at Cudham.
Now, gentlemen, what are the probabilities of Alice Rhodes's
knowledge of the condition of Harriet Staunton? At the time
they were at Cudham together Harriet was in a good state of
health, as we know from the evidence which Mr. Keene gave
us as to her appearance in October. I come now to the "lost
letter," which was said to have been found by Clara Brown.
An oral version of a written document ought always to be
received with great caution, even when given by an honest
witness. Clara Brown does not remember one word except
that which affects the prisoners; and I urge that it was only
when she knew a lost letter was mentioned in another letter
that she thought of this one. The lost letter, according to
Clara Brown, said, "There will be a time when Harriet is out
of the way, and we shall be happy," but the alteration of a
word will give a widely different meaning to those words. I
contend that the words may not be correctly remembered—that
is, supposing there was such a letter—and if the words read,
"There will be some time," or "some times," it may be well
taken to allude to the opportunity of Louis and Alice seeing
one another only, and not in any way connected with Mrs.
Staunton's death. Then, just consider who and what Alice
Rhodes was at that time. She could scarcely have been more
than nineteen years of age—a weak girl with all the impulses
of youth strong in her. What is more likely than that, knowing Louis Staunton well as her sister's husband's brother, she,
however unwillingly at first, at last yielded and fell, and,
having once fallen, there is no retraction of the step.

[*The prisoner Alice Rhodes here wept very loudly and
bitterly.*]

Mr. GYE—It is said, in corroboration of the finding of the
lost letter by Clara Brown, that Alice Rhodes wrote a letter
to Louis Staunton, in which she said, "I have searched high
and low for the lost letter, and cannot find it. I am sure

Staunton Trial.

Harriet has not got it." Now, at the end of this letter there is some poetry which I should like to call your attention to. It is as follows:—

> Though absence parts us for a while,
> And distance rules between,
> Believe, whoever may revile,
> I am still what I have been.

Now, that refers to the intimacy which existed between them, and why I call your attention to it is to show that Alice Rhodes was a weak and foolish girl, and she puts in these lines, which are not poetry, to show her affection for Louis Staunton. As to the pencil letter with a postscript, " I am not bad yet," that is dated 1st August last year. It has been suggested that that sentence had some reference to the pregnancy of Alice Rhodes, but that can scarcely be the case, because she was not confined until June 28 this year. As regards all the correspondence, you must remember you have only one side given you, because the mouths of the prisoners are closed. Then you have the period during which Mrs. Harriet Staunton was at Cudham. You have it from Clara Brown that Alice Rhodes was there from time to time, and there is no doubt that whatever may have been the state of that house, Alice Rhodes saw it up to a certain period. Whenever Alice Rhodes was there, you have it from Clara Brown that the deceased's meals were taken upstairs to her. It is quite clear that up to very late in November you have what was the state of Harriet Staunton's health. Mr. Keene's evidence shows that in October she was in a perfect state of health; therefore, you may dismiss what Clara Brown says about her health. Clara Brown says she observed her to be ill a month or six weeks before the date of her removal, and then, in answer to a question from the learned judge, you have it that Alice Rhodes was there and dined there the Wednesday before the removal. That was only one day before, the removal having been on the Thursday. His lordship put a question later on in the case, which may be used, and which no doubt will be used, as against Alice Rhodes, in order to show that she was there after that period. The first answer of Clara Brown was, " I noticed her being ill a month or six weeks before the date of her death "; and then the next answer was, " Alice Rhodes dined there on the Wednesday." Now, gentlemen, you have the presence of Alice Rhodes up to that time, but you have no evidence except that evidence of Clara Brown as to the state of Harriet Staunton's health up to that period. Now, when Alice Rhodes and Louis Staunton went there it would be natural they would not like Harriet Staunton to be present. We have it that she was usually in her room, that she preferred to be there, and that Patrick Staunton had to call her down occasionally to her

Defence of Alice Rhodes.

meals. What more natural than that she should stay up there sometimes?

I am dealing now, and have dealt up to the present time, only with the evidence as against Alice Rhodes. We now have the question of the removal, and upon that a very material question depends. Alice Rhodes came there on the Wednesday. At that time all questions as to the removal were settled and definite. It had been decided that the woman must go to London or elsewhere to see a physician. At that time Alice Rhodes therefore could do nothing, and whatever remonstrance she might have made would have been of no avail. Alice Rhodes could not prevent the Stauntons doing what they pleased with the deceased. There was no duty on Alice Rhodes to look after this woman, or her necessities, or to take any steps with regard to her food or clothing. The doctor had been procured, the lodgings taken, and even the room taken which she was to occupy. If there had been any criminal intent then to kill the woman, I do not see how it is possible to reconcile it with the facts that then existed. The doctor, I say, had been engaged, and the time arranged when they were to come into the rooms. Then I do not see how, at that time, any criminal intent could have existed. If it did not exist it is clear that Alice Rhodes could take no part in it; and if it did exist, it must be shown that Alice Rhodes knew of it, and took part in it. It may well be that although she participated in that removal she did not participate in the felonious design, if felonious design there were. When they get to Penge, what is done? Is their conduct there consistent with the existence of crime, or the guilty knowledge of putting this woman away? It cannot be. She is there, it is true; but her conduct is entirely consistent with the greatest care and solicitude. Everything is done for the poor woman. The two Stauntons go for the doctor, Alice Rhodes stays with Harriet, and then goes herself and brings him back with her. The nurse and Dr. Longrigg say she exhibited the greatest care and solicitude for the patient. Is that consistent with a criminal intention at that time to do away with this poor woman? One of the many things urged for the prosecution is the discovery of these letters. The phrases in those letters were, if anything, in favour of the prisoners. They knew from the first what the charge was that would be brought against them, and if they had for one moment conceived that the contents of those letters referred to the crime of murder, they would most assuredly have destroyed them; they would, in fact, have searched for every bit of paper in the place which might have referred to any of those misdoings of which it had been said they were guilty. The sole desire

Staunton Trial.

Mr. Gye of Alice Rhodes was to keep the knowledge and the intimacy between her and Louis Staunton from the world at large. Try and see if you cannot reconcile these statements with the fact that all she did was to conceal herself from shame and infamy, and not that she ever contemplated the commission of the awful crime of murder. The intimacy with Louis Staunton is the key to the whole of her conduct; for, can you believe that if a man was designing slowly, foully, and deliberately to murder a woman who stood to him in the relation of a wife—if he had courage and wickedness enough for such a villainy—would he take for his confidante such a girl, and that a girl of her age would consent to take a tacit part, much less an active one, in such horrors? You are asked to believe she went to Cudham with this guilty knowledge, and that she sat down to a well-spread table, and ate her fill, while she knew that in a wretched room upstairs there was a poor creature craving for food—imploring those about her to bring her anything to stay the pangs of hunger. Believe that if you can. The prisoner is in your hands. You will do what you will with her. It is for you, and you alone, to pronounce for her condemnation or her release. I know that you will act fairly, that you will not undertake the task lightly, and I am sure that you will arrive at a conclusion in accordance with right, justice, and mercy.

Attorney-General The ATTORNEY-GENERAL rose at seven minutes past three to reply upon the whole case. The hon. and learned gentleman said—Gentlemen of the jury, in the course of the five days of this momentous trial you have had placed before you with the greatest care all the evidence that can be produced, both on the part of the prosecution and of the defence. The evidence for the Crown and the medical evidence for the defence have been elaborately commented upon by the counsel for the prisoners, especially by my learned friend Mr. Clarke. Gentlemen, it is my duty now to reply on the whole of the case, and, as I shall have to comment upon evidence which jeopardises the lives of some of my fellow-creatures, I feel that my duty is both responsible and painful. But to me is confided in some degree the administration of justice in this country, and I, no more than my lord or you, cannot avoid the duty imposed upon me. I hope, therefore, I shall be perfectly clear and temperate, but I hope, at the same time, that I shall be firm in obeying the behests of duty. You have heard the speech delivered by Mr. Clarke. I do not think a Court of criminal justice is exactly the place to bandy compliments, or a trial of prisoners for murder exactly the time, but I cannot help saying that a more able speech it has scarcely ever been my good fortune to listen to. At the commencement of that speech my learned friend complained bitterly of the judicial system

The Attorney-General's Reply.

of this country, and thought it a great hardship that prisoners were not allowed to give evidence under the sanction of an oath. And he said that the refusal of that was a barbarism which ought to be swept away from our system. That may or may not be so; but it is a question of politics, and, while some think it a barbarism, others think it is not; and, for my part, I cannot say that I agree with him. But there seems but little ground in this case for such a complaint of hardship, for before any charge was made against the prisoners of any sort there was a preliminary investigation before the coroner, at which they appeared, and at which they were represented by counsel. So much for that. Now, the first matter which you must direct your attention to is, was the death of this woman caused by the culpable conduct of the prisoners, or of any of them, or was it not? I am not now dealing with the question of whether they are guilty of murder or manslaughter; but it is urged by one of my learned friends that they are guilty of neither, and that the death was not caused by any culpable conduct at all. The evidence divides itself into two parts— that which relates to the circumstances before 12th April and that which relates to the removal from Cudham to Penge and afterwards. We have evidence which seems to me pretty satisfactory as to the condition of Harriet Staunton on 12th April, when she was removed from the Woodlands. We have that not only from Clara Brown, but also from the medical evidence. There can be no doubt about this, as the post-mortem shows it, what the state of Harriet Staunton must have been the day before she died. Now, what was her condition? She was in a condition of extreme emaciation. She was insensible, incapable of walking, and she presented the appearance of a woman of forty-five years of age instead of only about thirty-six. She was certainly in a filthy condition, and she had vermin on her. Now, how did she come into this state? Did she get in that condition in consequence of natural causes, and natural causes only? Did she become so in consequence of disease, or in consequence of ill-treatment, or of ill-treatment and disease combined? If she was in that condition from disease no one is responsible, but if from ill-treatment and neglect alone, or from ill-treatment and disease combined, then some one is responsible and some one is culpable. On that question we have to deal with the testimony of the medical men, and that is a task of some difficulty. The prosecution say the case is one of starvation, and starvation alone, and death arose from exhaustion consequent on the want of sufficient food; we say that she was subjected to confinement, and not allowed reasonable air and exercise. On the other hand, it is said it is not a case of starvation, but of something else. On the part of the prosecution we have called, in the first place,

Staunton Trial.

Attorney-General Dr. Longrigg, the gentleman at Penge who attended this lady and saw her symptoms while still alive, and who was present at the post-mortem. In addition to Dr. Longrigg we have several other medical men who took part in the post-mortem— Dr. Bright and Dr. Wilkinson. Then we have Professor Rodgers, who examined the contents of the stomach and some of the organs, and we have also Dr. Bond. These men had ample opportunity of ascertaining what was the cause of death if it could be ascertained, and I must remind you that Mr. Harman, another medical man, was there on behalf of the prisoners, and he had every opportunity of examining the body with the others. He consulted with them and agreed with the rest. Dr. Longrigg told you what he saw when the lady was at Forbes Road. She was perfectly insensible, and all he heard her utter was a low groan. She lay there in that state until she died, and he told you the appearance at the post-mortem. He said he took some notes and afterwards amplified them, but he is attacked because he did not take more voluminous notes. So be it; but what of that? Dr. Bright did take the notes, and a copy of them long ago was handed over to the counsel for the prisoners. Dr. Longrigg took notes, Dr. Bright took complete notes, and Dr. Longrigg amplified his afterwards; but Mr. Clarke says the examination was incomplete and inaccurate. But in what way? It is very easy to call medical men to tell you about some obscure diseases, and that possibly, if such-and-such things had been done, some slight indications of an obscure and rare disease might have been found. But take a reasonable view of the matter. In what way was the post-mortem incomplete? Mr. Clarke says they did not weigh the brain; but would the weighing of the brain show the cause of death? If it would, we should have heard it from Dr. Payne and Dr. Bristowe. Then one of the gentlemen Mr. Clarke called said that, if a tubercular deposit on the brain was not visible to the naked eye, it ought to have been examined with a microscope. It is stretching matters rather far, if you find ample symptoms to account for death, to say it was to be required or necessary that you have recourse to microscopical examination. The doctors for the prosecution tell you this, "We investigated as closely and carefully as we could, and we came to the conclusion it was a case of exhaustion from starvation, and we came to the conclusion it was so because we found this extreme emaciation." This woman, in all human probability, had been a woman of about 9 or 10 stones in weight. The body was, I think, 5 stones 4½ lbs. only—about half its usual weight. But not only was there this great wasting away, this exceeding emaciation which is spoken of, but every organ of the body was diminished in weight, and there was not a particle of fat in any portion of the

The Attorney-General's Reply.

body. When they find those appearances and discover this extreme emaciation—because it is admitted to be extreme—and that the organs of the body are in a healthy condition, and nothing upon them which can account for death, and when they see the appearances which are known to follow upon a case of starvation, that is to say, the congestion of the outlets, then they come to the conclusion that it is a case of starvation.

How is that combated? When the medical witnesses appeared in the box they were subjected to a severe and able cross-examination by my learned friends, and it was suggested to them this was a case, or might be a case, in the first place, of Addison's disease, and then it might be a case of diabetes; and, again, it might be a case of what is called tubercular meningitis. It was said, why did not you examine for diabetes? Why should they? There was not a symptom of diabetes during life, nothing to suggest diabetes; and it is clear from the evidence called by the defence that it was not alleged that this was a case of diabetes. So with regard to Addison's disease. Why did you not examine the super-renal capsules? They did not do so because Addison's disease did not suggest itself; and this disease does not suggest itself to Dr. Payne or Dr. Bristowe, who are called to lay their theories on this matter before you. But what is said upon the matter is this—that this was a case not of starvation alone, but where death occurred in consequence of a disease which is called tubercular meningitis. Now, about the investigation which took place for poison. There was, you will remember, at the time of death some appearance of a fit, and there were indications that some narcotic poison had been administered, and on the post-mortem was found irritation and congestion, leading to the supposition that some irritant poison had been given. The stomach and organs of the body were therefore submitted for analysis to Professor Rodgers, but no poison was found. The doctors, consequently, became united in their opinion that it was a case of starvation. But it was put to them, "May not this be a case of meningitis, and may not that have caused her death?" These words are mostly derived from the Greek, and puzzle most people, and they are apt to say the doctors must settle the matter among themselves. But when they cannot, gentlemen, we must do it for ourselves. The coatings of the brain—the membranes around the brain by which the brain is encompassed—are called meninges, and when there is inflammation of these coatings of the brain that is a disease called meningitis. This inflammation may be caused by a variety of circumstances, but among other things the deposit of tubercles may cause it. So that when there is a deposit of tubercles on the brain, which causes inflamma-

tion of the brain, that is meningitis or tuberculosis, and it is
a disease which destroys the patient in a short time, less than
a month—in fact, a few days.

Now, in the course of the examination, having dealt with
diabetes and Addison's disease, my friend came to this disease,
tuberculosis, and he asks the doctors called for the prosecution
a variety of questions to get from them evidence to support
that theory. What do the doctors say? Dr. Bright gave
very clear and satisfactory evidence on this point, and he was
confirmed by the other medical men who followed him. He
says, " I do not think there is any case of meningitis. If
there had been there would have been flattening and bulging
of the sides and lobes of the brain—there would be effusion
in the chambers of the brain." The complete absence of that
effusion is all-important. Then, there would have been
tubercular deposits, or, at all events, in all probability there
would have been tubercular deposits at the base of the brain.
Congestion of the outlets is a symptom of starvation, and
that appearance was presented in the body. Nothing has
been kept back by the medical men, and I believe this country
can furnish medical men of greater skill than, perhaps, any
other country. You have heard Dr. Payne, but Dr. Bristowe,
as you will remember, admitted that he had not heard the
evidence for the prosecution, that he had had no papers submitted to him, that he had not even consulted Dr. Payne,
and that he knew nothing of the case except what he had seen
in the newspapers. Such evidence, gentlemen, cannot be
regarded as satisfactory. Take Dr. Bristowe's evidence in
its fullest sense, and he agrees with Dr. Payne, and what does
it amount to? He says that, in his opinion, this was not a
case of starvation, and starvation alone, but of acute tubercular meningitis. He gives you his reason, and says, looking
at the notes, there was congestion of the vessels of the brain,
and he says that was inconsistent with starvation. He says
there was congestion of the stomach, which was inconsistent
with starvation ; that there was inflammation of the peritoneum
or coatings which cover the stomach and intestines, and that,
in his opinion, is inconsistent with starvation. Can these
reasons really and truly prevail? He was asked if there was
delirium whether he would not expect congestion of the brain,
and he answered in the affirmative. Consider the state of this
poor lady as she lay upon the bed, the dilation of one eye
and the contraction of the other. When asked whether
exhaustion caused by starvation would be likely to produce
delirium and convulsions, he says he should not expect to find
it. I put it to him whether, if a person was starved for a
considerable time, and then was allowed to take food, or had
food administered in considerable quantity, there might be

The Attorney-General's Reply.

congestion of the stomach, and he admitted it. He spoke about inflammation of the peritoneum, but that is not distinctly marked in the evidence. All that Mr. Longrigg and Dr. Bright say is that there was slight inflammation of the peritoneum. I also asked Dr. Payne if food came into connection with the interior coating of the stomach, that might cause redness, which is all that is meant by inflammation of the peritoneum. He says the appearances were inconsistent with starvation, but when you take the reasons one by one they disappear until they are all got rid of. When further examined he says he should expect to find tubercles in the base of the brain in meningitis. Dr. Bristowe seems to say that meningitis is due to the presence of tubercles beginning near the base of the brain, and is generally most intense there. When you hear that the tubercles are found in greatest quantity at the base of the brain, is not that a piece of very important testimony in favour of the prosecution after the evidence of Dr. Payne? It is sometimes difficult to understand scientific subjects and scientific language; but let us look at the case in the light of common sense. What causes the discharge of serum except inflammation? What causes softening of the brain except the discharge of serum on the brain? What conclusion can you come to but that Dr. Payne was mistaken in these views? You have a case presented to you—one of starvation—and you have the appearances consistent with starvation. Yet you have an obscure denial, in which there are certain appearances; but they are obliged to say that these appearances are consistent with starvation. I have dealt with this part of the subject as fully and completely as I can, because a great deal depends on the medical evidence. Suppose, for a moment, that this was a case of acute meningitis—I use the word " acute " advisedly—did the acute meningitis account for the emaciation that took place? I said to Dr. Payne, " This woman was probably 9 stones in weight at the beginning of August. She is now only 5 stones 4¼ lbs. It is a case of extreme emaciation, is it not? " " Yes," he replied, " there is not a particle of fat in the body." I said, " Does not that lead you to the inference that it is a case of exceeding emaciation? " " Yes, it does," he answered. " Then," I said, " how do you account for it? " and his answer was that he could not account for it unless he knew the history of the case. Of course not. It is said that meningitis, when it does not assume an acute form, may endure for a considerable number of years. Consequently, the emaciation might be the gradual result of meningitis, or it might be the result of starvation. Supposing this emaciation had been going on for several months, and this woman had been wasting away in consequence of this disease, that

Staunton Trial.

she had been kept practically in confinement without the necessaries of life, without food and air, without necessary exercise, and without medical assistance or advice—don't you think that that would be ill-treatment, and that such neglect would expedite the operation of the disease which was upon her, and so lead to her death? It has been proved beyond doubt that deceased was a woman of weak intellect, but physically she was in a good and perfect condition of life as late as October, 1876. After her confinement, however, at the Woodlands, it was in evidence that her strength had gone, as we say by ill-treatment, or it might be ill-treatment combined with disease. But, gentlemen, the case does not rest there. It is nothing to the Treasury whether the prisoners are condemned or not. The Treasury desires only to get at the truth, and thus it was that Clara Brown, after the statements she had made, was removed, in order that no outside influence might be exerted upon her. My learned friends have called her an accomplice, and I call her an accomplice, too, in fairness to the prisoners and in the interests of justice; but there are some portions of her evidence, corroborated as they are by circumstances and facts, which I think you must regard as being consistent with the truth. Her testimony as to the deceased getting thinner and thinner, or to her condition just previous to her removal. is corroborated, I think, by the facts that have transpired. The story of the lost letter from Louis to Alice, and the black eye, are confirmed to my mind satisfactorily.

Mr. Justice Hawkins—She said that she found the letter, but did not mention it, because she was afraid they might be angry with her, and she burnt it because she did not wish them to know that she had seen it.

The Attorney-General—That is so, gentlemen, and you will recollect the passage, " There will be a time when Harriet is out of the way, and we shall be happy together. You must know, dear Alice, how I love you, for we have been together two years." I say that the girl is corroborated in her testimony as to that letter by what was found in the cottage afterwards by the police. In a letter then discovered Alice writes, " I have searched high and low for the lost letter, but cannot find it. I am sure Harriet has not got it, but where it can be I cannot judge at all. Come down to see me as soon as you can, if only for a few hours, for you cannot think how happy it makes me to see your old face again.—With kindest love," &c. These letters, at all events, show that an intercourse was being carried on between Louis Staunton and Alice Rhodes, which ought not to have existed at all. The rest of the letter, as Clara Brown told you, related to the death of Louis Staunton's father in the hospital. Now, even if the girl had

The Attorney-General's Reply.

invented the first part of the letter, which I say she did not, what motive could she have had for inventing that portion of the letter which she said had reference to the father? The Treasury have investigated into the matter, and it has been found that Mr. Staunton, the elder, was taken to the hospital in June, and that he died there soon afterwards. The letter of Alice speaking of having lost the letter sent to her by Louis confirms, I say, the girl's statement in a marvellous and extraordinary manner.

Taking, then, the statement of the girl as being worthy of belief, can you doubt that the condition in which the poor woman was, just prior to her removal, was not the result of some culpable neglect on the part of somebody? If you want confirmation of that you have it, I submit, in the statements of the prisoners themselves—false though those statements may be. Gentlemen, you will have to ask yourselves whether the condition in which this woman was was not due to culpable conduct, and whether it was not such culpable conduct as makes all the prisoners, or some of them, responsible to the law. Can you think that Louis Staunton ever had any affection for the deceased, or do you not rather think that, to use a vulgar phrase, he " married her for her money "? Though there may have been some adulterous intercourse between Louis and Alice Rhodes before his marriage, you are not here to investigate any offence against morality ; still it may be an element for your consideration in dealing with the question of murder. We hear that all the money was absorbed, and that Louis and Alice Rhodes were anxious to live together as man and wife. You have Alice going down to him after he had taken the Little Grays farm. We find her then at the head of the household, whilst the wife was practically a prisoner at Cudham. Why was Alice there but for her own purpose? And what was to become of the wife? I do not think she was to be murdered ; but why was she to be kept in confinement at the house of the brother? We have been told that it was in order that she should know nothing of the adulterous intercourse that was going on between Alice and her husband. There is no doubt that Alice was in the position of the wife, that she sat in her seat, and that she possessed the affection of the husband. But how long was the confinement of the wife to last? Was it to last for a month or two, or for years? And did all the prisoners aid in the concealment? Was it that she should be deprived of all the necessaries of life and reduced to such a state that she would not be likely to live? It was obvious that it would never do, if such a design was entertained by anybody, that this woman and her child should remain and die at the Woodlands ; nor must she be attended there by any

Staunton Trial.

medical man, for the whole secret would have become known. If she died, the death would have to be registered, and possibly, in the absence of a medical man, a coroner's inquest might be held. If at any time such a design was entertained by anybody, by Louis, by Patrick, or by any of these prisoners, and that design was carried into execution, and the others aided and abetted, knowing all the circumstances, knowing that death was intended, or that acts were intended to be accomplished, the necessary consequences, or the probable consequences of which would be death, I submit to you that that would be murder. You will ask yourselves, no doubt, as to the motive. Of adequate motive there can be none. Consider the case of the husband. He had got all the money he could from his wife. She had evidently become distasteful to him. It was said that she drank, and undoubtedly she was an imbecile. He loved another woman with a strong and overwhelming love, and it might be that he thought, if he could get rid of his wife, he could marry Alice, and they could live happy and comfortable together.

With regard to Patrick no such motive as that existed. Evidently he had a very strong affection for Louis, and the affection was mutual; in fact, there was an extraordinary affection one for the other. Between Patrick and his brother there was a motive which had its origin in affection and love, and a desire to serve him in any way that he could. Alice Rhodes was the sister of Patrick's wife, and one knows the influence of a wife over her husband in cases of that kind. Now, with respect to Mrs. Patrick Staunton, Alice Rhodes, as I have said, was her sister; and although she may have disapproved of her conduct with Louis, yet her reputation was dear to her, and she would naturally desire to conceal her shame as best she could. It may be said, what do you mean by this woman being deprived of the necessaries of life? I answer that a woman is entitled to have all that is necessary to sustain her life. I do not mean that she should have been loaded with food; but if she was stinted, if she was kept practically in confinement, if she was prevented obtaining health and exercise, if she was subjected to cold, if she was kept in a room without fire and warmth, if she could not get medical aid when she was in a condition that it was absolutely necessary, then I say that this woman was deprived of the necessaries of life. Well, gentlemen, the next point to which I wish to draw your attention is the removal of the deceased from Cudham to Penge. It is evident that some time before that occurred this lady must have been extremely ill, requiring medical attendance, requiring judicious treatment, and, in all respects, she appears to have been in a lamentable condition. I cannot abstain from saying that the conduct of Louis

The Attorney-General's Reply.

with regard to her child at this time showed how careless, indifferent, and hard-hearted he was. That, too, was removed from the Woodlands to the hospital, because its removal was an act that was absolutely necessary if the secret was not to be known. A few days later Harriet is removed. You have heard the story of her removal. I must confess that I did not attach so much importance to that part of the case as I do now, and you know what Clara Brown says of her condition. You remember the false statements that were made to Dr. Longrigg, and how he was persuaded by the prisoners that there was nothing improper, but that the lady had had an apoplectic fit; and how he was induced to give a certificate that the cause of death arose from some cerebral mischief. Their conduct is such, in fact, as to disarm suspicion; and I do not think you will come to the conclusion that much can be said in their favour on account of anything that happened at Penge. The doctor's certificate was transmitted to the proper authorities, and the funeral was appointed to take place, when the whole evidence against the prisoners would be removed. If the lady had been interred there would have been no possibility of a post-mortem examination, no opportunity of ascertaining how she came by her death, for the organs would in time have been destroyed, and the greatest medical science would have been unable to elucidate the truth. Suspicion, however, was created in the minds of one or two persons, and, the gossip reaching the ears of the registrar, an investigation was set on foot, and that which was intended as a secret became known. Did I not know there are many murders that are never discovered, I should say there was an interposition of destiny in this case.

Well, gentlemen, I will deal with another question—the question as to who was responsible for the condition of the lady when she was removed. If she had been removed in a lamentable condition, and somebody had struck her a blow which caused her death, the prisoners would not, of course, be responsible for that. If it was murder, then all who took part would be responsible. Now, what was the part taken by these several prisoners? Louis must have known the condition in which his wife was—it was his duty to give her all the assistance she required. It was Louis who assisted to remove her—it was Louis who made the arrangements at Penge, he was a party to what happened there. If there was any design to take life, did he take part in carrying that into accomplishment? Then there was Patrick. He was the man who made the arrangement with his brother to take Harriet under his roof. It was he who gave instructions that she should not be allowed to go out of the house—he was receiving £1 a week, one would assume, for the purpose of providing

Staunton Trial.

her with necessaries, and he must have known that she did not have them.   Then, with respect to Mrs. Patrick Staunton, it has been urged that she is not to blame, for she acted under the coercion of her husband ; that there was nothing to show that she took any part in the design.   Gentlemen, I must remind you here that in law there is no presumption that in the crime of murder a wife acts under the coercion of her husband, although there may be such a presumption in crimes of a lesser magnitude.   I do not, and never did, understand why a doctrine such as that should be laid down in the case of a wife when it does not exist in the case of a young child.   But the law is so, and the coercion of a wife does not prevail in the case of murder.   It is true that she was heard to say, " Don't hit the woman," but, if we are to believe Clara Brown, it was she who told Mrs. Harriet not to leave her room—not to come downstairs.   If there was a design, and if they were carrying it out by means of confining this woman to her room, here is Mrs. Patrick giving orders at the same time that her husband does.   She had many opportunities to aid the woman if she was desirous of doing so.   There must have been times out of number when Harriet was under her control. She tells the girl she must keep her in the house, and that she must wait for food.   Does all this not show that she was endeavouring to deceive and to assist in the concealment of the woman ?   With regard to Alice Rhodes, if there was this design to kill, originating at any time before the death, Alice was constantly with Louis, and occasionally she must have seen the condition in which Harriet was ; or, at all events, she must have known that she was kept a prisoner there, and what was intended to be done with her.   Alice, in fact, took part in endeavouring to conceal the whereabouts of the wife, because it is in evidence that when she was asked by Mrs Butterfield where she was, she replied at Brighton.   Then, again, Alice was one of those who removed her, and that is a material fact against her.

As to the removal itself, you must consider whether the woman was in such a state, to the knowledge of the prisoners, as that the change would accelerate her death.   If they knew that the probable consequences of removing the woman would be that she would die, it is murder.   I care not how she had been brought into the condition in which she was—either by disease, for which the prisoners were not to blame, or by disease and neglect combined, it matters not— if the people removed her, knowing that the probable effects of the removal would be that she would die, that, I say, is murder.   According to the evidence she had not been seen for a long time ; she was seriously ill when brought downstairs ; she was in a sort of drowsy stupor ; food was obtained for

The Attorney-General's Reply.

her, but she declined it; she was apparently almost insensible, moaning, and in a weak, lamentable state. She remains in that state until the evening of 12th April, when, for reasons of their own, the prisoners resolve to remove her. What were they going to do? They were going to take the woman in her then condition in an open vehicle, drive her 8 miles to Bromley station, then to take her by train to Penge, there to place her in another vehicle and convey her to her lodgings in Forbes Road. Was she in a fit state for the journey? I say, gentlemen, that she was in a condition that no reasonable being would have thought of removing her. What has Clara Brown told us? Patrick was heard to say that he should like to have kept her a little later, for fear the people at Portlands should see her; whereupon Mrs. Patrick said, "You had better take her at once, or she will not last the journey." If that was said, does it not go a long way to convince you that these people knew that she was in a very precarious condition? The girl further states that Mrs. Harriet was sitting in a chair propped up by pillows, and that Patrick tried to rouse her several times, when Mrs. Patrick observed that she had better not go to sleep, and Patrick added that if she does she will never wake again. The poor woman, it seems, never spoke when she got to the railway station. She was carried out between the two men, or rather dragged along, with her slippers coming off, and she was put into the carriage. She was heard to moan, and nothing more. She was got out again at Penge, where she drew her hand away from the person who was supporting her, and that was the only movement that was seen. One of the women was heard to say, "Never mind, dear, you will have your supper presently." That would lead you to suppose that the woman had been praying for food. When she got to the lodging she was put to bed. It was found that all the sound proceeding from her was a low moaning noise, and she dies. Well, now, gentlemen, ask yourselves whether this woman was in a fit condition to be removed and exposed to the cold. Must the prisoners not have known of her condition when they resolved to take her to Penge? If so, they are answerable to the law. Suppose you take a lenient view of the case, and say that it is not a case of ill-treatment, of design, or neglect, but simply a case of gross culpability, then all who took part in it would be guilty of manslaughter. It may be that some of the prisoners may be guilty of murder and others of manslaughter. That is for you to determine. If Mrs. Patrick Staunton went before the coroner for the purpose of screening Louis and enabling him to escape from justice by telling a falsehood, she must be an accessory after the fact—that is, if she knew that the offence of culpable misdemeanour had been committed. The

R

Staunton Trial.

Attorney-General same would apply to Alice Rhodes as to the rest. Now, gentlemen, in conclusion, I can only say that I have discharged my duty to the best of my ability. You will hear the summing up of my lord; it will then be your duty to discharge the most serious responsibility that the law imposes upon a subject; but, I think, considering the intelligence you have exhibited during this trial, and the extraordinary patience you have shown, that your verdict will be the result of an earnest and careful and unimpassioned deliberation, and that therefore there will be found in it the voice of reason, and of reason only.

Seventh Day—Wednesday, 26th September, 1877.

The Court sat at half-past ten o'clock, and Mr. JUSTICE
HAWKINS at once proceeded to sum up the evidence in the case.
He said—Gentlemen of the jury, we have arrived, after six
days of most anxious investigation in this all-important case,
to the last stage but one of it, and ere this day closes you
will be called upon to give your verdict and pronounce your
opinion upon the culpability or the innocence of the persons
who now stand charged before you. I am quite sure, from
what I have observed, and anxiously observed, during this
inquiry, of your conduct and demeanour in that box, that you
will give your verdict and pass your opinion in this momentous
issue without any feeling of sympathy or prejudice, and without
regard to the consequences which may attach to your verdict—
that you will decide this momentous issue, I know, according
to your honest and conscientious opinions, according to your
honest belief, and your verdict will be that of truth. Momentous
indeed the issue is, not only to the prisoners at the bar, who,
if innocent of this crime, deserve the deepest sympathy, for
the accusation made against them is indeed a terrible one—
momentous to the public and to society at large. The interests
of society demand that, if this hideous crime which is charged
against these persons is made out to your satisfaction, they
should receive the punishment the law awards. It is a source
of great comfort to me to know that each of these prisoners
has been most ably defended by the learned counsel. It is a
source of equal comfort to me to know that those learned
counsel have but done common justice to the Attorney-General
when they acknowledge the fair, the temperate, and the humane
way in which he has discharged his stern, imperative, but
painful duty. Gentlemen, before I proceed to call your attention to the circumstances of this case and to the facts upon
which you are to determine the issues before you, it may be
well, and proper, and convenient that I should first of all state
to you the general propositions of law by which you will be
guided throughout this inquiry. Generally, I may state the
law to be this, that every person who is under a legal duty,
whether such duty be imposed by the law or imposed by contract, or by the act of taking charge, wrongfully or otherwise,
of another person, to provide the necessaries of life for such

Staunton Trial.

other person—every person who takes charge and has that legal duty imposed on him is criminally responsible for the culpable neglect of that duty if, by reason of that neglect, death ensues to the person so neglected. If the person so neglected, and to whom that duty is owing, is from age, health, insanity, or any other cause unable to take care of himself, and death ensues, the crime will be murder, and the interests of society demand that justice should be meted out to the perpetrator. For the person who has such a charge has a legal obligation cast upon him to take charge and provide the necessaries of life; or, if he contracts to provide the necessaries of life for another person, he takes charge of that person, and if he neglects culpably the duty so imposed upon him, and if by reason of that neglect of duty the death ensues of the person so neglected, he is criminally responsible to the charge of murder if that neglect of duty has arisen from an intention or with a design to bring about the death or grievous bodily injury to the person so neglected. But if the neglect of duty is the result of mere carelessness, without any such intent as I have mentioned, then the crime is manslaughter, provided that you should come to the conclusion that there has been culpable neglect of the duty which is cast upon the individual. There is another alternative. Supposing the neglect of duty be such that those who neglect it must be aware that the consequences of that neglect will result in death, in that case it will be murder if death does result from such neglect. Now, that being the general proposition of law, I shall have to advert to it again hereafter when I come to deal with the case as it affects the various prisoners before you.

Let me now proceed to call your attention to the facts of the case in chronological order. Gentlemen, the deceased lady, Harriet Staunton, was a daughter of a lady named Butterfield, who has been a witness before you. Mrs. Butterfield had been married previously to a gentleman named Richardson, by whom she had issue a daughter, Miss Richardson, who ultimately became Mrs. Louis Staunton Now, Harriet Staunton, at the time of her death, was thirty-six years of age, and she had lived until about the year 1874, as far as we know, with her mother; but in that year she was paying a visit to a Mrs. Hincksman, who lived in Heygate Street, Walworth Road. Mr. Hincksman was a son of a sister of Mrs. Richardson, and, consequently, Mr. Hincksman was the nephew of Mrs. Butterfield or Richardson, and would be the cousin of Harriet Richardson. Mr. Hincksman had married the widow of a person named Rhodes, and Mrs. Hincksman, by her first husband, had had two daughters—the two prisoners at the bar. One of them had been for some time married to Patrick Staunton, artist, who seems to have been living at 9 Lough-

The Judge's Summing Up.

borough Park; the other daughter, Alice Rhodes, was still unmarried. Although we have no direct evidence upon the subject, we find that in the course of the years 1874 and 1875 Miss Harriet Richardson was staying with Mrs. Hincksman, and, in all probability, it was there that she first became acquainted with the prisoner Louis Staunton, who afterwards became her husband. She was entitled, according to the evidence, to a fortune of somewhere about £4000, about £1600 or £1800 of which—it is not very material which—she was entitled to in possession. The rest of the £4000 consisted of a reversionary interest which had been bequeathed to her under the will of the late Lady Rivers. There is no evidence as to what Louis Staunton's occupation was or what his means were when he first made the acquaintance of Miss Richardson. Certainly we have no evidence at all that he was personally possessed of any independent property. Shortly after we find him following the profession of an auctioneer in the Lough-borough Road, because it was not until some time after his marriage that he took offices at Gipsy Hill.

Now, Mrs. Butterfield had, after the death of her first husband, married the Rev. Mr. Butterfield, of Burstead, in Essex, and she had before the period to which I am about to refer thought that her daughter was not quite in a condition to be able to take care of herself or to manage her own affairs. Louis Staunton, however, had met Miss Richardson and made overtures of marriage to her, and she had consented to become his wife. This appears to be in the year 1874, and some time in that year Mrs. Butterfield did all she could to oppose the union. She filed a petition in the Court of Chancery for the purpose of making her daughter a ward in Chancery. She made an affidavit of the weak state of intellect of her daughter. She spoke in that affidavit of having remonstrated with her daughter against her contemplated marriage, and there is no doubt that the daughter had herself exhibited acts of violence to her mother in consequence of the opposition which she had offered to the marriage. In the result, however, the Court of Chancery declined to interfere with the personal liberty of Miss Richardson, she being then thirty-five years of age; and on 16th June, 1875, she was married to Louis Staunton, at Clapham, against the will of her mother, and not having lived under her mother's roof certainly for many months before that period. There was no settlement made on the marriage, so that all the property which she had in possession, about £1800, of course became the absolute property of Louis Staunton. That was the condition of things when the marriage took place in 1875. Although her mother had been estranged from her daughter for many months before the marriage took place, nevertheless two or three weeks after that event she thought

245

Staunton Trial.

it right and proper to pay her daughter a visit. Her daughter
had then gone to live at the house No. 8 Loughborough Road,
opposite to the house occupied by Patrick Staunton, Louis
Staunton having taken and furnished No. 8. The deceased
was residing there in the early part of July with her husband,
and there it was that Mrs. Butterfield paid her daughter that
first and last visit. You had better hear from Mrs. Butterfield's own lips the account of that visit, because a great deal
has been said about it and about her impropriety of conduct—
a great deal has been said about a quarrel, or of bad feeling
exhibited on her part, about her daughter's household. I
will therefore read from her evidence what really did take
place. You must be the judges of all matters of fact, and,
without discussing now whether or not this point is material,
I leave it to you to say if there was in Mrs. Butterfield's
conduct anything beyond the natural solicitude of a mother
who, having been opposed to her daughter's marriage, was
anxious, after that marriage had taken place, to make
matters up and resume friendly relations. She says—
"Three weeks after the marriage I paid her a visit at
8 Loughborough Park. I knocked at the door, and my
daughter opened it. She asked me in. She called her husband,
saying, 'Louis, mamma is here.' He came, and I went into
the dining-room, and he was present. I asked my daughter
if she was happy, and she said, 'Pretty well, mamma—
middling.' Louis said he was sorry he could not ask me to
take something, as he had nothing but spirits in the house. I
asked him why he did not keep a servant, and he said he had
advertised for one. He then said, 'Take your mamma upstairs,
my dear, and show her the house.' I went upstairs, and saw
only one of the rooms was furnished, and I said something
about it. I did not stay more than ten minutes or a quarter
of an hour, and when I left they both accompanied me to the
station. We waited there ten minutes for the train, and when
I left Louis bade me good-bye and lifted his hat. There was
no quarrel and no angry words of any kind or sort passed
between us, and nothing to show we were on any other than
friendly terms." That is the account Mrs. Butterfield gives
of this interview, and she never saw her daughter again alive.
She next saw her dead at Penge on 15th April, 1877.

Upon the following day—certainly within forty-eight hours
after that visit—Mrs. Butterfield received two letters—the one
was stated to be from her daughter, the other from Louis
Staunton. It is said, on behalf of the prisoners, that Harriet
wilfully abstained from permitting her mother to come into
her presence. But for the prosecution it is asserted that,
whatsoever was done to keep Mrs. Butterfield away from June,
1875, till the death of her poor daughter in April, 1877, was

The Judge's Summing Up.

done by Louis Staunton, and that the daughter would have been quite willing to see her mother if she had been so permitted to do. The suggestion is that the mother was prevented from having access to her by the influence of Louis Staunton. She says—that is, Mrs. Butterfield—that she received the next day, or the day following, a letter from Louis, enclosing one from her daughter—" In my daughter's letter she told me that her husband objected to my calling upon her, and she thought I had better not come again for fear of causing a disturbance. His letter was very rude, telling me that he would not have me go to the house again, and in consequence of that I did not go." In consequence she heard nothing of her daughter until she heard of her confinement on 23rd March, 1876. There is no evidence of the terms on which Louis Staunton was living with his wife from that time, July, 1875, to March, 1876. I have looked in vain for any particle of evidence to show how or upon what terms Louis Staunton and his wife were living during that period. Patrick Staunton lived opposite till November, 1875, when he left and took a small house at Cudham, called the Woodlands, of which we have heard so much in this trial, and there he resided until the melancholy tragedy occurred into which we are now inquiring. When he left Louis Staunton was still at 8 Loughborough Park. Some little time before the confinement of Mrs. Louis Staunton Clara Brown—on whose evidence I shall have a great deal to say—came up to town for the purpose of attending her during her confinement. Alice Rhodes was also present during the period of confinement, and the residents at Louis Staunton's house for a month were Mr. and Mrs. Louis Staunton, Alice Rhodes, Clara Brown, and a child of Mrs. Patrick's.[1] During that month Clara Brown says she noticed that there was a great deal more affection between Louis and Alice Rhodes than was proper. Mrs. Louis Staunton, of course, was in her room, and could not see all that was going on, but she knew, or suspected something, for, according to Clara Brown, she made some complaint. Then Clara Brown on one occasion found in a drawer in Louis Staunton's room the nightdress of Alice Rhodes. Of course, this depends on the credit which you may ultimately give to the evidence of Clara Brown, and I should point out that she made the statement in answer to a question put by the Solicitor-General. It is said, on the part of the prisoners, that this does not prove anything material, or that there was any undue familiarity at that time between these two; they say also that there was no chest of drawers in Alice's room, and that, therefore, it may be taken as a matter of no importance that the nightdress was

---

[1] There was also the nurse Emma Denton, but she was not called at the trial.

found in a chest of drawers in Louis' room. Mr. Gye, in his very able address to you yesterday, dwelt upon that, and asked you to dismiss that from your minds. The question for you is whether you can so summarily dismiss the matter. Where—if Alice Rhodes slept in a different room—where do you suppose that during the daytime, when it was not worn, would her nightdress be found? I leave it to you to consider whether it would be left on or under the pillow of her own bed, or whether it would be taken into another room, where Louis Staunton slept, and placed in a chest of drawers. Dr. Russell attended Mrs. Louis Staunton in her confinement, and it is well that we should know her state at that time. She had been described by her mother as a lady about 5 feet 4½ inches or 5 feet 5½ inches in height, and about 9 or 10 stones in weight. You have had a photograph handed to you, produced by the mother, who says it is a fair representation of her at the time it was taken—about a year before her marriage. Dr. Russell, in the spring of 1876, describes her as being in good health. Nothing is more important than to keep in your mind the condition of this lady at different periods. She was before her marriage healthy, temperate, cleanly in her person, and particular in her dress, and, as her mother says, knew how to dress. The mother saw her after marriage, and observed nothing particular in her appearance. Dr. Russell describes her as having got over her confinement well, and in three weeks he ceased to attend her. He was shown her photograph, and says it was a fair representation of what she was at the time of her confinement. In his evidence he says—"I attended her three weeks. She was in a healthy condition; her body was well nourished. She was, I should say, from 9 stones to 10 stones in weight." Then, upon cross-examination, with a view of testing the opportunity he had of observing her, he said— "I saw the lady not only while she was in bed during her confinement, but I saw her up both before and afterwards." Now, here is a gentleman who had three weeks' opportunity of observing the state of this lady in March, 1876. He gave a description of her, and there is no doubt that this gentleman was quite capable of forming an opinion. It is not suggested that he is forgetful about the matter. He is a trustworthy witness, according to everybody's account. He says—"She got well through her confinement. I look at the photograph. I say that is like the lady I attended. I saw her during her confinement, whilst she was in bed, and for three weeks I was constantly attending upon her, and when I ceased my attendance she was a healthy woman." That is his account of her in the month of March, 1876. "In a healthy condition," is his expression, "and the body was well nourished." If you

The Judge's Summing Up.

desire to look at this photograph you can. It is the one shown to Dr. Russell, and it is the one Mrs. Butterfield recognises. (The photograph was handed to the jury.)

Gentlemen, that closes the end of the month of March. After the confinement, about the latter end of April, Clara Brown and Mrs. Patrick Staunton's child returned to Cudham, leaving Alice Rhodes still a resident in the house of Louis Staunton. Within three weeks, according to Clara Brown's evidence, Louis Staunton, with his wife and Alice Rhodes, came down to pay a first visit at the Woodlands from Saturday till Monday. When they returned to town on the Monday morning they did not take the child back with them, but they left it in the care of Mr. and Mrs. Patrick Staunton; at all events, they left it at the Woodlands, and, as far as we know, the child never left the Woodlands again until 8th April in the present year, when it was taken to the hospital and died. On three or four other occasions Mr. and Mrs. Louis Staunton came down to pay a short visit—some forty-eight hours or so—between that time and the month of August; and upon one occasion Mrs. Harriet Staunton paid a visit, and remained there a week. She seems, further, having paid these visits some time early in the month of August, to have gone down again to stay at the Woodlands, and from that period until her death she never left the Woodlands again except on two occasions, to which I shall have to advert more particularly, when she came up to see Mr. Keene, who was to take her acknowledgment of a deed which was finally to dispose of the whole property which she was entitled in reversion. From the early part of the month of August until her death, with the exception of those two occasions, you may take it that, according to all the evidence, she never left the Woodlands.

Now, it seems to me to be just as well at this period that one should, by reference to letters, see the condition and state of things at Loughborough Park. As to the exact date at which the house in Loughborough Park was left, and the residence in Norwood, Gipsy Hill, was taken, we have no very precise evidence. It was clear it was some time before the month of August—I think it was in June—because in the month of June we have some letters that will show that in that month the house had been taken; but, at all events, in the summer of 1876 Louis Staunton had removed to Gipsy Hill, and he remained there until the latter end of the month of October, when he went to reside at Little Grays farm. I am speaking of the period now between the month of March and the month of August, for the purpose of showing you what the condition of things was at that period. There are several letters, one of June, 1876, two in August, 1876, and one in September, which show what Louis' relations were at that time with his

249

Staunton Trial.

wife. Writing from Gipsy Hill under date 28th June, 1876, Louis Staunton says to his brother—

> My dear Bay,—Many, many thanks for your kind letter. I am glad to say my hand is better; but no one knows, dear Bay, what I have had to put up with from Harriet the last six months. Her temper has been something frightful. I have talked to her for hours together, and tried to reason with her, but it is all of no use. From the time she gets up in the morning until she goes to bed at night, she does nothing but try to aggravate, and make me as miserable as she possibly can. Although I say it, I have been quite disheartened and cried for hours to think I should have laid out money to have things nice, and no one to take any interest in the place. I am, indeed, truly unhappy; but oh, dear Bay, I can never thank you and dear Lizzie enough for all your kindness to me, but rest assured I shall not forget it. I would have been glad to have been with you a few days, but am now afraid I shall not be able to, having had a few words with Bradford, which I will tell you about when I see you on Friday. I shall be at the hospital about three o'clock. Your ever affectionate brother,
>
> LOUIS STAUNTON.
>
> P.S. 1 have not heard how dear papa is yet. Am going over to Brixton to-day.

One of the learned counsel says that Mrs. Harriet Staunton was violent in her habits, and it has been said she was addicted to intemperance. That is one of the questions you will have to determine. But there may have been good reason for the excitability and the irritability of Mrs. Harriet Staunton if she had discovered, as Clara Brown suggests she had done, that, soon after her marriage with Louis Staunton, he had proved unfaithful to her, and had formed an illicit connection with Alice Rhodes. It becomes, therefore, material for you to remember for yourselves, as nearly as you can, the events attendant upon this illicit connection. In the early part of August Alice Rhodes was staying at the Woodlands, and on 1st August we have a letter, written in pencil, shown to be in her handwriting, addressed to Louis Staunton at Gipsy Hill. I will read this letter, inviting you to form an opinion as to the terms on which Louis and Alice were on when it was written—

> The Woodlands, Cudham. Tuesday.
>
> My dear Louis,—I was very sorry to see it rain so soon after you left here yesterday morning. I am afraid you got very wet. It rained here incessantly until about 5 o'clock, and then I went as far as Roberts's to try and get some jam pots, but I could not get them anywhere. I had a good walk with Florie this morning to get Tommy's milk. You cannot tell how I missed my dear old sweety, and I hope he was not in mischief last night. Not that I think you would do it intentionally, but feeling dull, might call on ——, and take strawberries and cream. I think myself it might be tempting. Come down as soon as you can, and then I shall have a great deal to tell you. Come down without Harriet if you can when you take me home. The men have just come to make the hay

The Judge's Summing Up.

here. Hoping I shall see my own darling soon, I remain his truly
affectionate wife, Alice. I am not bad yet.

"Tommy" was the name of the child. "Come down without
Harriet if you can when you take me home." You must
draw your own inference from that letter, written unquestionably by Alice Rhodes to Louis Staunton on 1st August. Then
there is the postscript, "I am not bad yet." Is that the
language of a girl who is innocently writing to a man who was
her friend, or does it show that an illicit intercourse had commenced not immediately before, for the language was such as
to show that there had been a considerable amount of freedom
going on for a considerable time? It is an important letter
for your consideration when you come to look at the relations
which existed between Louis Staunton and his wife Harriet
during the summer and autumn of 1876. Couple this letter
with the statement of Clara Brown, if you believe her, and
then ask yourselves whether, during the whole of that summer
and autumn, there had been an illicit intercourse existing
between Louis Staunton and Alice Rhodes? It is clear that
somewhere between 1st August and the 19th of the same
month—although the date is not exactly fixed—Alice Rhodes
went down and paid a visit to the Woodlands. Harriet
Staunton had also gone there, and her name is mentioned in
the letter. That is proved by a letter dated 19th August, which
has been proved in evidence; so that you may take it that
these two women—Alice Rhodes and Mrs. Harriet Staunton—were
staying at the Woodlands together at that time; and, if you
believe, it will be equally clear that during that time Louis
Staunton came down, but whether to visit Alice Rhodes or to
visit his wife is a question for you but not for me to judge.

Now, Clara Brown is introduced to you by the learned
Attorney-General as a person on whom you ought not implicitly
to rely, unless you find her in material points of her statement
corroborated by independent witnesses. According to the
argument of the learned counsel for the prisoners in this case,
if Clara Brown is speaking the truth, she was an accomplice
in the crime which, by her evidence, it is sought to fix upon
the persons before you. I may tell you that in law it is
not necessary that an accomplice should be corroborated. A
jury may—I say may—in law, if they think fit, act upon the
uncorroborated testimony of an accomplice. But it has been
the practice of learned judges for many and many a year,
in dealing with the evidence of accomplices, to recommend
you—not to take for granted such evidence as that which
Clara Brown has given, unless you find that there is so much
corroboration of her testimony in some respects as induces
you to believe that now at last she is telling the truth. The
observations made to you as to Clara Brown are well deserv-

Staunton Trial.

ing of your attention; but I must call your attention to the
fact that there are many crimes which would go absolutely
and altogether unpunished unless the evidence of accomplices
were admitted in Courts of justice. If an accomplice were
to require corroboration in every respect—that is to say, if
you were to take no part of an accomplice's statement without
it were corroborated with unimpeachable testimony—you
would have no necessity to have the testimony of an accomplice at all. It is the duty of a jury to regard the evidence
of an accomplice with a considerable amount of suspicion.
If you see a man as an accomplice come into the witness-
box for the purpose of giving evidence against his comrade—
if you hear him confess that he was there, and you feel that
he is endeavouring to implicate another for the purpose of
extricating himself from the difficulty in which he is placed,
by evidence which beyond all question might implicate himself, you naturally say, " How can I place reliance upon a
man who is implicating another, unless, indeed, I have reason
to believe that, great as his interest is in endeavouring to
implicate the other, nevertheless he is speaking the truth?"
And for that reason it is, gentlemen, that, in dealing with
the testimony of an accomplice, you must see how far in
material respects it is corroborated by independent and unimpeachable proof, and, if you are satisfied upon that point,
there is no reason why the evidence should not be acted
upon. In taking Clara Brown's account it is infinitely
better, with a witness of this description, that you should have
it in the words which fell from her own lips. She says she
went into the service of Mrs. Patrick Staunton in September,
1873. She remembered Louis being married. She went to
Cudham in 1875, when the family consisted of Mr. and Mrs.
Patrick, their two children, and herself. " When Mrs. Louis
was confined," she says, " I went up to London to help the
nurse. Dr. Russell attended Mrs. Louis, and I remained till
after the month. During the month there were in the house
Louis, Alice Rhodes, the nurse, myself, and Mrs. Harriet and
her baby. I thought that during that time Louis and Alice
Rhodes were too affectionate towards each other. I am not
sure that she always slept in her own bed." It is but fair
to the witness to remark on that, that she did not volunteer
that statement, but in answer to a question from the Attorney-
General, " Did they sleep together?" Then she goes on, " I
found a nightdress of Alice's in a drawer in Mr. Louis's
room." I have already commented on that. " I heard Mrs.
Harriet complain of the behaviour of Alice Rhodes and her
husband. I have seen notes sent down to her husband, and I
have seen Mr. Staunton read them. When, after the month I
went to Cudham, I left Alice Rhodes at No. 8. All four came

The Judge's Summing Up.

down to Cudham from Saturday to Monday, and they did not take the baby back. They left it with Mrs. Patrick to be fed with the bottle. Harriet afterwards came twice with Louis. I remember Alice Rhodes staying at Woodlands. I heard something pass between the two sisters about Harriet. I think Alice wanted Mrs. Patrick to allow Harriet to come down for a week. I did not hear the answer."

Now comes the first important statement about Mrs. Harriet's stay at the Woodlands. "I heard Louis speak to Patrick about his wife's hat and jacket. He said, ' You had better put her hat and jacket away, or else she will come after me.' " That certainly shows a desire to leave her. " I saw Mrs. Patrick put the hat and jacket in a box and lock it up. I heard Mrs. Harriet ask for them, and Mrs. Patrick say that Louis had taken them away with him. Except on two occasions, Mrs. Harriet never again left the Woodlands, and on those she came back the same night."

I will now refer to the lost letter. Clara Brown says, " I found one day a letter. I remember taking it up and reading it. I burned it. It was in Louis's handwriting, addressed to Alice Rhodes. I found it in Mrs. Patrick's bedroom. Alice had been there, but was gone. It began—

" My own Darling—I was very sorry to see you cry so when I left you. It seems as though it never would be; but there will be a time when Harriet will be out of the way, and we shall be happy together. Dear Alice, you must know how much I love you by this time. We have been together two years now."

The Attorney-General says, taking that letter as a fact, it shows that the intimacy was of a very questionable character, which had existed for a considerable period of time between them—it may be before the marriage of Louis. The letter was clearly picked up in August, if picked up at all. It says, " We have been together two years now." That would go back to 1874, months before the marriage took place. The question is ay or no, did this girl correctly repeat to you that which was a fact? In the first place, did she find a letter? The fact of the letter being lost depends not on her testimony, but upon a letter about which there can be no possible doubt—Alice's letter of 19th August, which I have already read to you. It is said that she invented the story after the inquest, when she heard that a letter had been lost. If you believe that she invented that letter for the purpose of giving strong evidence against her relatives—persons nearly related to her—with whom she never seems to have had one single word of anger, who had never, as far as we know, behaved otherwise than with kindness to her, if you believe she invented the letter, she must be the vilest person that

253

Staunton Trial.

ever entered a witness-box, and you could not place reliance
on her testimony.   If capable of inventing a story like this,
without a particle of foundation, it shows her to be a person
on whom no reliance could be placed.   You would then have
to discard her testimony altogether, and fall back upon that
of others entirely.   Now, is she inventing this story or not?
I have looked through this evidence—you have heard Clara
Brown   cross-examined—you   have   heard   Police   Sergeant
Bateman cross-examined on the subject of the communications
he has had with Clara Brown.   I don't think it was suggested
—certainly it was not proved—that when this story of finding
the letter was first of all mentioned by Clara Brown, that
she was then aware of the existence of the letter of 19th
August.   If she had not heard of that letter in which a lost
letter is missing—if she had not heard of it, do you not
accept it as a   remarkable corroboration?   Now, as regards
the finding of that letter.   Let me call your attention to the
letter of 19th August.   It is signed " Alice," and dated from
Woodlands during the time she and Harriet Staunton were
there together.   It is dated " Woodlands, Saturday morning,
19th August."   If anything like the letter Clara Brown tells
us she found had been lost—a letter addressed by the husband
of Harriet Staunton to Alice Rhodes—it is natural that Alice
Rhodes should be most anxious that it should not get into
the hands of any other person.   And it is quite clear that
such a letter, missed from Alice Rhodes' possession, would be
very anxiously looked after.   This is the letter—

Dear Louis—I was extremely thankful to have a letter from you
yesterday.   You must know that it is dreadfully dull down here.
I have searched high and low for the lost letter, but cannot find it.
I am sure that Harriet has not got it.   Where it can be I cannot
tell.   Come down to me as soon as you can, if only for a few hours,
for I cannot tell you how happy it would make me to see your
dear old face again.   With fondest love, and trusting to see you
soon, I remain your affectionate   ALICE.

She adds these lines—

> Though absence parts us for a while,
>   And distance rolls between,
> Believe, whoever may revile,
>   I'm still what I have been.

In this letter express reference is made to the lost letter.
And more than that, old Mr. Staunton, the father of Louis,
was in Guy's Hospital in June, and he remained there until
15th August, when he died.   Clara Brown, with a view to
testing her, was asked this question, which was suddenly put
to her in cross-examination—not a question put and answered
before the coroner—and requiring, without any prompting,
an immediate answer.   It is this—" You say you read this

254

The Judge's Summing Up.

letter; how long was it?" She replied that it filled four pages of notepaper. She was then asked what else was in the letter, and she said, "I do not remember, but there was something in it about Mr. Staunton's father." The letter referred to could not have been lost more than a day or two before this letter dated 19th August. On 15th August old Mr. Staunton died in the hospital, and you must ask yourself if there is a probability that Louis, writing about that time to the girl with whom he had formed an illicit connection, would make a reference to his father's death. Clara Brown says the letter did contain such a reference, and I think you will consider that a corroboration of her statement. An observation has been made that, supposing this letter was found, it did not contain the words Clara Brown says it did, but look at the probabilities. Do you think it probable that a girl of Clara Brown's age—sixteen years—would, having found a letter of this description addressed to her own first cousin—having read it, and having seen the character of its contents—is it or is it not likely that she would read that letter over more than twice? It related to her own cousin upon a matter which had been called to her attention so long before as the confinement of Harriet Staunton. Do you think it probable her story is true, and that having got it in her possession she would naturally read it more than once?

Mr. WILLIAMS—There is no mention in the letter of 19th August, or any reference to, the death of the father.

Mr. JUSTICE HAWKINS—I have not said so.

Mr. WILLIAMS—Is it not an extraordinary thing that if a mention of the father's death is made in one letter there should be no mention of it in the reply of Alice Rhodes?

Mr. JUSTICE HAWKINS—I do not know at all why she should. We do not know what was said of the father's death. If you ask me to reason off the probabilities, I would rather not. I must leave it to the jury to say whether Louis would write to her without mentioning the death of his father in the hospital. It is one of those circumstances which the learned Attorney-General relied upon as affording a test of the probability of her story; whether you think so or not is for you, gentlemen, to say. There is the remarkable circumstance that the father's death did occur on 15th August. It is an event which you may come to the conclusion would probably be mentioned in Louis Staunton's letter to Alice Rhodes. It remains for you to say whether you think that Clara Brown has related accurately to you the contents of the letter she found. I will read to you now two or three more letters, which were written at the close of the month of August, 1876, for the purpose of showing you the state of feeling there was between Louis Staunton and his wife, having previously stated to you

Staunton Trial.

what was the state of feeling between Louis Staunton and Alice Rhodes.

Dear Bay—I was indeed glad to get your letter this morning, but grieved to hear the two dear children are still so ill, but trust they may soon get better. It makes me quite miserable to think you and dear Lizzie are in such trouble and I cannot help you. I want you to send Harriet up to-morrow, for I am sure you cannot be bothered with her just now, and I will then send Alice down to help dear Lizzie. Give my love to her and say I hope to see her soon, and if I can possibly run down I will do so. With fondest love, your ever affectionate brother, Louis.

On 31st August he writes again—

My dear Bay—I find your train will arrive at London Bridge at about five o'clock, and there is one for Gypsy-hill at 5.15, so I shall expect you about six o'clock unless you come up in the morning. I have now got a girl, so dear Lizzie cannot have any excuse for not bringing up the two children. I feel so sorry Harriet should have given you so much trouble; what to do with her I do not know. I told them down home Harriet came back last Saturday, so if you go down to the terrace first you will know what to say.
Your ever affectionate brother, Louis.

We know from the evidence before us that at that time Harriet had been staying since the early part of August in the house of Patrick. We know now as a matter of fact that she never did return to her home at Gipsy Hill. We know she never left the Woodlands, if you take the account of Clara Brown, except on the two occasions of the visits to Mr. Keene. It is clear she did not come up, because the letter of the 31st says—" I do not know what to do with her." Why should there be a mystery about her coming up or going down is a matter I cannot say anything about. I cannot withdraw it from you, because this is a case a decision on which cannot be formed upon one isolated fact or so, but upon a combination of the whole of the circumstances. This is the last letter—

Sept. 1, 1876.

My dear Bay—I have received your letter and am sorry I said anything, but the fact is I was very annoyed at the time to think Harriet had been giving you any trouble, for I know you have enough already with the two children ill, but I hope you will not say or think anything more about it. I had hoped to have seen you all to-day, but suppose it will now be Monday.
With fondest love to all, your ever affectionate brother, Louis.

These are the letters written by Louis to his brother. Upon those letters I will make one observation, and you will take it for what it is worth. You will find when you come to look at the statements to which I shall have to refer at some length, that there is no reference made to the intemperate habits of Harriet Staunton. There was a long examination of the

The Judge's Summing Up.

doctor upon that. You will not find in either of these letters a suggestion of intemperate habits.[2] They had had words and he had complained of her irritating him, whether with or without reason I do not stop to inquire, but here no reference is made to intemperance.

In August Louis had secured the last remnant of Harriet Staunton's property. The money she was in possession of at her marriage had become his absolute property, but she was also entitled to a reversionary interest which would be of the value of £2200, according to Mrs. Butterfield, who said that the whole of the property of the deceased would be of the value of about £4000. We have no evidence of the age of the person on whose death the reversion would fall in ; but instructions were given to sell the reversion about August, 1876, and this circumstance is not altogether undeserving of your consideration. There may have been reasons for it. If there were I know them not. It is quite clear from the evidence before us that, in August, 1876, Harriet Staunton was not in immediate want of money. Of this there is no suggestion. She had gone to stay at Woodlands, and was now living with the wife of Patrick Staunton. There was no pressure for money upon her. Why, then, was this reversion sold, instead of waiting for the death of the person, when it would fall in ; for we know reversions must be sold at a sacrifice? Mr. Keene tells us it was sold in August, and realised not £2200, but £1100. The transaction, however, was not then completed, and therefore I presume the money was not paid till October of the same year. Louis Staunton, upon leaving Loughborough Park, had taken up his abode at Gipsy Hill, Norwood. The letters which from time to time he wrote were addressed from an estate office facing the railway station at that place. The precise date of his going does not appear, but it was probably between May and June, because Mrs. Harriet Staunton was confined on 23rd March, and would be there for a month, which would bring it up to 23rd April. We may take it that about the end of April or the beginning of May he went to Gipsy Hill and opened his estate office. At the end of September, at Michaelmas, 1876, there was a little farm called Little Grays farm, containing about 20 acres of grass land, and let at the rent of £70 a year, and Louis Staunton agreed to take it. He was entitled to enter into the possession of it at Michaelmas, and he was to take it for three years, with the option of continuing on it for seven years. One of the learned counsel stated that the business at Gipsy Hill was abandoned, and certainly we have no proof that the business

---

2 See the Attorney-General's opening speech, pp. 38, 39.

Staunton Trial.

at Gipsy Hill was carried on at any period after September,
1876.

I now desire to call your attention to the position of Little
Grays farm, and also to the Woodlands. The Woodlands
was a small cottage containing only four rooms, two of which
were bedrooms. One of these bedrooms was occupied by Mr.
and Mrs. Patrick Staunton and one of their children, while the
other bedroom was occupied by Clara Brown and another of
the children of Mr. and Mrs. Patrick Staunton and by Mrs.
Harriet Staunton and her child. The house was a mile from
the little village of Cudham. The house opposite to it was
called the Portlands, and between the Woodlands and the
Portlands there was another house, the name of the occupier
of which we do not know. Therefore, the Woodlands would
appear to have been a house inconveniently crowded, having
regard to the number of rooms and the occupants of them.
Now, Little Grays farm was about a quarter or twenty minutes'
walk from the Woodlands. This house had four bedrooms,
two of which were furnished and two were not. For whom was
that home taken? It is admitted by all the counsel for the
prisoners that it was taken for Alice Rhodes, and for Alice
Rhodes alone. The reason is given. It was to enable Alice
Rhodes to pass as the wife of Louis Staunton while the child
of their connection was born. Although taken in September,
the farm was not occupied until the end of the month of
October, and that is a date deserving of consideration, because
it was on 23rd October that the last remnant of property
belonging to Mrs. Harriet Staunton was disposed of. Mrs.
Harriet Staunton had gone to live at the Woodlands under
the notion that she was a visitor there. She went in August,
and remained during the months of September and October,
evidently devotedly attached to her husband. Whatever her
suspicions may have been, and whatever jealousy may have
been caused, there can be no doubt at all that towards her
husband at that time Mrs. Harriet Staunton did feel most
affectionately. I will tell you why I say so. She wrote a
letter which has been produced. It was found by Sergeant
Bateman, and it is as follows:—

Friday.

My own darling. I write these few lines hopeing they will find you
well. Will you be down on, Sunday if not I shall be disapointed
hope to see you on Monday if not will let me know which day you
will be down by Pursey. it has been raining all day. Will you
bring me down peace ribon and frilling for my colour and sleves.
I hope to return to town with you soon Persy is coming back
to-morrow night so I beleve. Tomie is quite well so good night
my dear God bless you will you let me know I have not had clean
flanel for a month I have here month on Saturday it is time I shall
be a home my boots has worn out from yours ever affectionate wife
HARRIET.[3]

---

[3] See p. 50 *supra*.

258

The Judge's Summing Up.

Now, in this letter she entreats to be taken home, but at that
moment, if you believe the evidence, preparations must have
been in contemplation to dispose of the only home she had,
for that at Gipsy Hill was disposed of when Little Grays farm
was taken, and Little Grays was never intended to be a home
for her.   I say that is a striking letter, and one to which
I direct your most serious observation.   Whether there was
a reply to this letter or not I cannot say, but here we have
the letter of the wife writing to her husband in the most
affectionate of terms, and writing at a time when he was
carrying on beyond all doubt the most illicit intercourse with
that girl who was to pass as his wife at Little Grays farm
while his own wife was occupying half a bedroom at the
Woodlands.   If the letter speaks the genuine feelings of Mrs.
Harriet Staunton, it is quite clear at that time she was ignorant
of any such arrangement as that which is spoken to by Louis
Staunton in his deposition before the coroner.   It is there
said that Louis Staunton had made an arrangement with his
brother Patrick Staunton to take charge of Mrs. Harriet
Staunton for 20s. a week.   In one of the depositions you
will find it also stated that the reason that there was a mutual
separation by agreement was on account of the intemperance
of Mrs. Harriet Staunton, but there is no mention of intemperance in the letters, and the medical evidence says there were
no traces of intemperance in the body of the deceased.   If
that arrangement be true it speaks of a very strange state of
things.   Here is a lady who, according to all the evidence,
was possessed of property which, when realised, fetched a sum
of £3000, which would give an interest at 5 per cent. of £150,
and within eighteen months, or less than that, of the marriage
her home is abandoned, and she is placed with Patrick
Staunton, where she is to be maintained upon 20s. a week.
It is avowed that Mrs. Harriet Staunton was to know nothing
of the home at Little Grays, and, according to the evidence
not a trace of her has ever been seen in the neighbourhood of
that house.   Now, it was suggested before the coroner that
all this was done with the sanction and approval of Mrs. Harriet
Staunton, but there is no evidence before us that such was
the case.   On 17th October it was arranged that the sale
of the reversionary interest should be completed.   I may tell
you, very shortly, gentlemen, if you do not already know it,
when a married woman is about to dispose of her property,
before effect can be given to the deed of transfer which is
executed by her, it is necessary she should appear before
commissioners, who are appointed to examine her and see that
what she does is done of her own free will, and if, before the
commissioner, a woman, though she had executed the deed,
and signed, sealed, and delivered it with all solemnity, were

Staunton Trial.

then to say, " I refuse to acknowledge this deed, because I
was coerced into the making of it by my husband; I have sold my
property and assigned it so far as it goes, but not by my free
will," the commissioner would refuse to give his sanction, and
he would not acknowledge the deed. Now, on 17th October,
when Mrs. Harriet Staunton first went to the commissioner,
she was suffering from a nervous trepidation, and she was told
she had better go away for a week and come back again. She
accordingly went away, and returned on 23rd October, when
she completed the assignment which was to divest her of every
portion of what she possessed in this world. I should be
doing wrong, perhaps, if I did not here call attention to a
matter which may not have a direct bearing upon the issue,
but which is of some importance. You will remember that
Clara Brown says that on one occasion Patrick Staunton struck
Mrs. Harriet Staunton, and gave her a black eye, and she says
this was just before Mrs. Harriet Staunton went to Mr. Keene's,
the solicitor. Mr. Keene is called, and he says that he did
notice when Mrs. Harriet Staunton called upon him to go before
the commissioner, on one of the occasions she had a
discoloration under the eye.

I have now, gentlemen, taken you down to the end of the
month of October. Let me next call your attention to a body
of evidence which was given on the second or third day of this
inquiry, which may possibly be deemed of more importance
than it appeared at first sight—I mean the evidence called to
show the state of things at the Woodlands during the late
autumn and early spring of 1876-7. There called at the
Woodlands the butcher, the baker, the fishmonger, the man
who served hay and straw to the pony belonging to Mr. Patrick
Staunton, and other tradespeople. These witnesses have been
examined before you, and I will call your attention to their
evidence. The first of these witnesses is a man named
Marchant, a gamekeeper. He was cross-examined as to whether
he had not had any difference with Mr. Patrick Staunton, and
he says he had a difference with him as to the fencing in of
some pond. It will be for you to say whether that difference
is of such a character as to have an interest in it which would
induce him to come here and tell that which is a deliberate
falsehood. That is the only thing I know that might be said
against him. Marchant says he lived at the adjoining farm,
about three-quarters of a mile from the house. " I have seen
the lady in this photograph in August, 1876. I have seen
her in the wood and round the house. I saw her often up to
the end of October or the beginning of November. About the
19th I saw her leaving in a wagonette belonging to Louis
Staunton." He does not fix the date more accurately at the
time, but we know what happened on the 17th and 23rd, and

The Judge's Summing Up.

that would fix the date. "Patrick was with her. I tucked
her dress up to keep it off the wheel. I afterwards saw her
in the stable. I was in the stable looking at the pony. The
lady was without her bonnet, and Patrick said, ' If you are
not off, I have a policeman here, and I will run you in.' "
Marchant says he never saw her afterwards. "I heard
inquiries made for her by Mrs. Butterfield. I watched the
woods to see if I could see the lady, but I never saw her
again."

According to his statement, the last he saw of her was in
the end of October or beginning of November, and he speaks
of that which, standing alone, would be, as he treated it, a
joke—only she came out at Patrick's bidding, and went back
to the house. He is cross-examined, and says, " I have seen
her hanging out clothes. I said before the magistrate that
the expression made use of by Mr. Patrick was put down by
me as a joke." If that matter stood alone it might be so
treated, but we have reason to think it was said seriously.
She was doing nothing to justify her being given into custody ;
but it is used by the prosecution to show the system of
terrorism that was practised, and they say it could not have
been a joke, because Patrick Staunton was not in the habit
of joking with her, and we must take it in connection with the
evidence of Clara Brown. "I remember," he goes on to
say, " seeing the lady with a baby. I swear she did not say
it was her sister-in-law's child. That was before November.
There was a little difference between me and Patrick." Now,
subject to those observations I have made, you are asked what
weight this evidence has. But it does not stop here. On
the part of the prosecution they say, " We will call everybody
we know of for the purpose of seeing whether this woman really
was out and about the grounds and seen by anybody," and
accordingly they proceed to call them. George Dewsbury, who
served them with straw for the pony, was called, and he says,
" I never saw the deceased. I did not know she was living
there. I was always about the place. I was in the wood,
and I heard a female scream in the direction of the Woodlands.
It was about October, on a Sunday afternoon. It seemed as
if a woman was being roughly knocked about." The
Attorney-General says he does not place much reliance upon
that ; it is a circumstance standing alone. But Clara Brown
spoke of Harriet having a black eye, and Mr. Keene says there
was a discoloration on the 23rd.

Mr. CLARKE—Clara Brown says the giving of the black eye
occurred the last thing at night. The scream was in the
afternoon.

Mr. JUSTICE HAWKINS—So much has been said about it that
I will not trust myself to give you, gentlemen, a summary of

Staunton Trial.

this evidence, but I will read it. John Staples, a labourer, says he is a fishmonger on his own account, and used to call at the Woodlands with fish. He saw the deceased lady, and he says, " She looked as if she had been very ill or half-starved. I only saw her once." Alfred Nicholls, who worked with his father as a baker, seems to have gone there three times a week, and he never saw the deceased at the house. Owen Davis, the butcher, says he called four times a week, and continued to do so until April, 1877, at nine, ten, and one in the day, so that he went at various hours, but he never saw the deceased, nor did he know that such a person was living in the house. Another witness, Henry West, speaks of going to the Woodlands from March to November, but he never heard of the deceased. Two other witnesses speak of having watched the house sometimes for hours together, but they could not hear or see anything of the deceased. From the latter end of October, when the property of deceased had been conveyed away, and when Louis Staunton and Alice Rhodes came down, Mrs. Harriet Staunton was seen no more. There is also the evidence of the girls Longridge and Weatherley, who refer to a person, supposed to be Mrs. Harriet Staunton, being heard moving about, and it would seem that she was almost in fear of the servant girls.

I come now to the evidence of Clara Brown. With regard to Clara Brown they say, " Before the coroner you gave evidence directly at variance with the story you are telling to-day." Says the girl, " Indeed, I avow it, and my reason for doing so was this : at that time I was influenced by the two female prisoners, who were my own near relatives. The deceased lady had died under circumstances which raised, rightly or wrongly, suspicion against them. An inquiry was going on, and what I said to the coroner was untrue so far as it went to shield my relatives, and my statement was made at their request and subject to their dictation." Well, she is cross-examined—and cross-examined most properly—on the statement she did make to the coroner. She says, " Before I was called upon to subscribe my hand to the depositions which I had made I told the coroner that I had told an untruth." Now, gentlemen, that she did tell the coroner so is placed beyond all doubt, because Mr. Carttar, the coroner, who took her depositions, says the girl made that statement to him. But Mr. Carttar told her that, having already made the deposition after having been sworn, true or false, she must sign it, and, accordingly, she did sign it. Now, nobody will suppose Mr. Carttar wished or intended Clara Brown to subscribe her name to an untrue statement with a view to influence the mind of that jury. Mr. Carttar viewed her as having been sworn, and, as she had made that statement, he must insist upon her sub-

The Judge's Summing Up.

scribing her name to it. If he had adopted the other course, and had torn up the depositions, then it would have been said what Clara Brown said in favour of the prisoners was not forthcoming. Well, gentlemen, it is for you to next ask yourselves whether Sergeant Bateman induced Clara Brown to make a false statement. Clara Brown says Sergeant Bateman said to her that, if she had been falsely swearing, she was to mind what she was about, or she might get herself into trouble. Gentlemen, I attach no blame to Sergeant Bateman for saying that. It is an observation that any one of you would have made in order to preserve the girl from making, any further false statements. Clara Brown was further asked where she had been living since the coroner's inquiry, and she said at Penge. She was taken there to be out of the influence of those who had caused her to make her first false statement. The learned counsel for the prisoners, in their addresses to you, have stated that they could not cast any blame upon the Treasury for their way of conducting this prosecution, inasmuch as the Treasury has only the interests of society and the safety of the public at heart in the matter. You must ask yourselves whether you can suppose that this girl, Clara Brown, has been influenced by the Treasury officials. Is there anything to lead you to suppose that she has been prompted to say that which is untrue? It is a question entirely for your decision as to whether you can believe her story. I have the right to form an opinion on the matter, but I have no right to express it to you with the view of dictating to you as to what you should believe. You must judge for yourselves as to whether or not you believe the girl's story. If you do not believe it, then, of course, you will disregard it; but that would not prevent you from forming an opinion upon other evidence in the case which has been submitted to you, and with reference to which no such observations as have been made about Clara Brown can apply. I will now take up her evidence at a later stage. She says—" I have heard Mr. Patrick speak to his wife about having Mrs. Harriet Staunton out of the house. This was after the visits to London, when she went to see Mr. Keene. I have heard him say to her, ' You must not go outside the house so that any one can see you.' He has spoken to me on the same subject. He has said, ' Do not let Mrs. Staunton go out so that any one can see her.' When she first came to us she took her meals with the rest of the family, but just before Christmas there was an alteration, and her meals were sent upstairs. She had the same as the rest, but not always. Sometimes pudding was sent and no meat, which the others had. On several occasions she has complained of not having enough food, and Mr. Patrick was very angry, and struck her once, which left a bruise on her

Staunton Trial.

arm. On another occasion Mrs. Harriet Staunton shut the
door in Mr. Patrick's face, and he struck her and pushed her
down." This was in the back bedroom. There was a bed,
a chair, and two boxes in that room, but no basin, or jug, or any
means for her to cleanse herself. You will remember that the
two policemen examined the room, and they described the room
as being without any washing apparatus. She says that after
Mr. Patrick Staunton gave Mrs. Harriet Staunton a black eye
she went up to London to Mr. Keene's office. Well, there is
evidence that she came to London twice to Mr. Keene's office
in reference to the settlement of the sale of the reversionary
interests; and Mr. Keene says that on one of these occasions
he saw a discoloration on the eye of Mrs. Harriet Staunton.

At this point the Court adjourned for luncheon. On
reassembling,

Mr. JUSTICE HAWKINS proceeded—I had got to that part of the
evidence of Clara Brown in which she goes on to give a description of the state of the bedroom, after which she says—
"Patrick Staunton has struck Mrs. Harriet Staunton, and Mrs.
Patrick Staunton has seen him, and I have heard her ask him
to leave her alone. She had only one pair of boots while she
was there. She had no boots when she was removed. She had
then a pair of Mrs. Patrick's slippers. She had no boots on for
three weeks. The room she occupied was rather dirty. I remember his saying, ' Get out, you damned cat, or I shall break
your back.' I have heard this more than once. I have heard
Mrs. Patrick say, ' Don't come downstairs, Harriet; we do not
want you down '; and after that I don't remember her coming
down. When she has complained of not having had sufficient
food, I have known her to be without food for a day. I have
asked Mrs. Patrick whether I should take it up to her, and she
has said, ' No, let her wait.' She got gradually worse." She
goes on—"At the latter part of 1876, from November until
Mrs. Harriet Staunton was removed, Louis was living at Little
Grays, twenty minutes' walk from the Woodlands. When he
came he always saw his wife. I do not remember hearing
him speaking of her, but I have heard him speak to her.
Louis and Alice Rhodes were living at Little Grays." She
next gave us an account of having picked up that letter about
which I have already made some observations, which I will not
repeat, but she is asked this question about it, " Alice Rhodes
made inquiries about it a week after she lost it. She asked
me if I had seen a letter addressed to her, and I said, ' No.'
In fact, I had then burnt it."

Then she says this about her examination before the coroner—
" I was examined as a witness before the coroner, and made
certain statements there. Before I was examined all the

The Judge's Summing Up.

prisoners had spoken to me about my being a witness. They
told me to say everything I did before the coroner. Between
the death of Mrs. Staunton and the examination before the
coroner I had been to Mr. Bradford's. I think I was examined two days. What I said before the coroner was not
true." The name of Mr. Bradford is a name that I shall have
to revert to hereafter, because in the statement of the prisoners it
would appear that Bradford was a friend. I don't know whether
it is stated that Bradford was in the habit of visiting, but I
think he was—the girl had been to Bradford's, and, if he was
in the habit of visiting at that period, it is a matter which
cannot escape your observation that Bradford has not been
called. The importance of this part of the case is that, if it
was true, as this girl states, and as the doctors say must have
been the case, that this poor woman was gradually wasting
away until she arrived at the state of emaciation in which she
was when she died—the object of this evidence is to show
that those who were about her and saw her from week to
week had an opportunity of seeing the condition to which she
was being reduced, and must have known of it. One of those
persons was her husband. Another was Alice Rhodes, who
was living, we know, unseen by Mrs. Harriet Staunton,
with Louis Staunton, and keeping their whereabouts a secret
from her. Now then, Clara Brown is examined by Mr. Williams
on the part of Louis Staunton. " In August, 1876, Harriet came
to Cudham. I was the only servant at Patrick's. I was in
the habit of going frequently out. On the 29th (of May) I made
another statement. I think before the coroner I spoke about a
hat and jacket being taken away, but I am not sure. I cannot
say if I mentioned it before the 23rd (of June). I do not
remember if I told the coroner of Patrick Staunton telling Mrs.
Harriet Staunton not to go out. I do not believe I told the
coroner she was kept without food for a day." If her statements were true—that in what she said before the coroner she
was influenced by feelings, as I have already mentioned to you,
for her relatives, and if what she said was dictated by her relatives, it is quite likely she may have said it to the coroner, for
it was not likely that it would have advanced their interests
if it were known that Patrick Staunton had kept Mrs. Harriet
without food for a day. She goes on—" I do not remember
saying anything about Patrick striking her before 23rd June.
I think I did say I did not consider her very ill till three or
four on the Thursday evening, when she sat drowsily over the
fire." Then she speaks of the child, and said her mistress said
the child was going to the hospital, and that Mrs. Harriet
Staunton hoped she would be able to get in. That was not
true. She thinks she said that the deceased was aware that
Alice Rhodes was passing as Mrs. Staunton, but that if she

Staunton Trial.

said she heard Mrs. Harriet make that statement it was false. After the statements of the learned counsel, we cannot hesitate to accept the statement that Mrs. Harriet Staunton did not know of their living at Little Grays, and, if the witness did say that the witness was aware that Alice Rhodes was passing as Mrs. Staunton, it must have been false.

Clara Brown goes on to state that she never said that Harriet Staunton came home the worse for liquor, though she believed she once saw her the worse for liquor, and that she went more by what she heard, but that she believed she had seen Harriet Staunton a little intoxicated. The witness proceeds to state that Patrick Staunton used to be away, and that when Mrs. Patrick went to Little Grays farm the deceased and witness used to be left at home together. There is strong evidence that Mrs. Patrick knew who was at Little Grays farm, and approved, by her presence, the connection existing between Alice Rhodes and the husband of the lady who was living in her little back bedroom. When I come to deal with Mrs. Butterfield's evidence you will find she saw Mrs. Patrick actually in the house. In cross-examination Clara Brown says she thinks Patrick Staunton had been examined on the same day, but before her, and the foreman said, " Fear no one." That seems to convey an impression on his part that the witness was under some fear. Then she is cross-examined by Mr. Poland, and she stated that Patrick Staunton was an artist, and used to paint in the larger of the parlours at Cudham. She also described the size of the house and the way in which the inmates slept, to which I have already alluded. Then, with reference to the connection which existed between Louis Staunton and Alice Rhodes, she said in reply to the learned counsel, Mr. Williams, " There were no drawers in Alice Rhodes's room when I found the nightdress, and I don't remember any other article of dress being found in the same room." The girl further said that after she left the Woodlands she went to live with Mrs. Hincksman, who is the mother of these two women, but latterly she had lived with Mrs. Judd, Wakeley Road, Penge, and she thought that the Treasury had paid for her lodgings. She added that she was staying with her aunt while the inquiry before the magistrates was going on. She described how the butcher and the baker from the adjacent villages used to call for orders, how she used to go into Cudham for golden syrup for the deceased lady, and gave other details of the matters connected with the domestic management of the household. She said, " I have heard quarrels between Mrs. Patrick Staunton and the deceased about her not doing her hair. Mrs. Patrick used to remonstrate with her." Other evidence was also given by Clara Brown, and I call your attention to the fact that during the time she was in residence with

The Judge's Summing Up.

over to the care of Sister Mary, Mrs. Patrick saying that the mother was unable to take care of it, and that she and her husband had brought it, out of kindness, to the hospital. It is idle to suppose that in a house like Patrick's, where Clara Brown was acting as a servant, there was a necessity for removing the child to the hospital. If there had been, it proved beyond all question that in the estimation of Mrs. Patrick, Mrs. Harriet Staunton was then in such a condition that she was unable to attend to her little baby. The name and address were asked. The name was given with a slight variation, but the spelling is immaterial. They gave the true address, Frith Cottage, which is another name for Woodlands. That was much dwelt upon by the learned counsel who addressed you, and who argued that if mischief had been intended they would not have given the correct name and address of the little child that died on the evening of 8th April. Sister Mary continued, " I told her that the child was gradually sinking. I asked its age, and she said about twelve months. It was not dressed as a child of that age should be. It was dressed like a child one month old. It died the same night. It gradually sank. It was unable to take any nourishment. There was a mark upon its left cheek." You will remember that Clara Brown gave evidence as to Patrick Staunton striking the child, and the evidence of Sister Mary corroborates it to some extent. The fact of the blow would show the sort of feeling which prevailed in the mind of Patrick Staunton with regard to the child's mother, for if he had much feeling for her he would hardly think of striking her child. We now come to the burial of the child, from which it appears that in connection with that matter Louis appeared on the scene as " John Harris," representing that the father was away in the country, and that he was the representative of the firm in which the father was employed. I recall your attention to this evidence for the purpose of directing your consideration to the fact that on 10th April Louis Staunton wrote to Mr. Butterfield,[4] two days after the baby died, and after he had arranged and paid for its burial, and never said one word of its death. As to the condition of this unfortunate lady at that time you must form your own judgment; but the statements made by Mrs. Patrick and by Louis with regard to the child as to its mother having been long ill are worthy of consideration.

I now come to that most eventful day in the history of this case, Thursday, 12th April, when Louis and Mrs. Patrick Staunton went together from Cudham to Penge. I invite your attention to the conversation held on that morning by them with the landlady at 34 Forbes Road, and with Dr. Longrigg, because it affects not merely Louis Staunton, but Mrs. Patrick

---

4 See p. 157.

Staunton Trial.

Mr. Justice Hawkins also, firstly, because the case on the part of the prisoners now is that the lady was in perfect health up to the 9th or 10th of April—and certainly there was no apprehension of any fatality up to that period—and, secondly, it is material to see whether or not the view taken by the learned counsel for the prosecution, namely, that Louis and Mrs. Patrick joined in a falsehood about this poor lady being attended by a medical man is correct; or whether the suggestion of the prisoners that they did not say so, but that the medical man named was their general family attendant, should be adopted. It certainly is an important circumstance, although not conclusive in any way. We have the evidence of Mrs. Chalklin, who says that in April she had lodgings to let, and at twelve o'clock at noon on 12th April Louis and Mrs. Patrick Staunton came to her house. They said they wanted lodgings for an invalid lady, and they would be wanted for three weeks or a month. Mrs. Chalklin positively swears that Louis said the deceased was attended at Cudham by a doctor who did not understand her case. If he made that statement there is overwhelming evidence that it is false. Then it becomes a serious question, why was that falsehood uttered? Mrs. Patrick Staunton added that they wanted to get nearer London to get better advice. Louis said he understood there were good doctors in that neighbourhood, and asked to have one recommended to him, which Mrs. Chalklin did. She was further told that the deceased lady could eat, but had refused to eat, and was inclined to be paralytic, especially about the feet. They went to see Dr. Longrigg, who is in practice in Penge, and told him they wished to place this lady under his charge, and to him Louis said she had been under the care of a doctor who lived a good distance from their place, and could not attend properly to her. It was suggested by counsel for the defence that Dr. Longrigg asked who was their general medical attendant, but the witness denied this, and the natural inference was that he had no concern with who was the medical attendant of the family, but would be concerned to know whether the invalid had been attended. Mrs. Patrick Staunton said Dr. Creasey, of Brastead, attended her. The statement as to the refusal of the invalid to eat was evidently aimed at accounting for her emaciated condition. To Dr. Longrigg they represented that the patient whom they desired him to see was a lady of weak intellect, that she was paralysed, and in reply to his question, were her habits cleanly, they said they were. So also said Clara Brown, speaking of what she knew of her up to the beginning of the year 1877, and so said Mrs. Butterfield.

It is not, continued the learned judge (after going minutely over further evidence showing the condition in which the deceased was when she was driven in an open wagonette to Penge), contended that there was absolute deprivation of all

276

The Judge's Summing Up.

food so as to bring about rapid starvation. If so, it would have been impossible to have avoided immediate detection. The patient of necessity would sink so rapidly that inquiry would at once be challenged. A patient kept without all food would probably not survive more than eight or ten days. It is not suggested that that was the state of things. But it is suggested that, systematically, and with motive and intent, the deceased had been kept without a sufficient supply of the necessaries of life, so that little by little she might be reduced in health and strength until at last Nature could no longer support the deprivation, but would probably yield and waste away so gradually as to awaken no exceptional notice. And so in this case it is said the process went on from October to November or Christmas. It is important to see whether there is ground for that theory. To the evidence that food was administered and medical assistance obtained, counsel for the prosecution says, " It was then too late; you had done your work—Nature was exhausted, and could not be revived." For the prosecution more is urged—that this was wilfully done, and that the poor lady was removed for this, among other reasons, that inquiry might not be instigated, and it is further urged that her removal accelerated her death. Immediately before her removal you have her carried downstairs by Patrick, and propped up in a chair in the kitchen. She was drowsy, and Patrick tried to rouse her. Mrs. Patrick Staunton said it would be better to let her go to sleep, to which Patrick replied, "If she goes to sleep she won't wake up again, in my opinion." Gentlemen, these are distressing matters to deal with; they are harrowing to the feelings, and as feeling men you cannot help, whatever may be the conclusion at which you may arrive, the deepest commiseration for this poor woman. I would pause here to entreat you, though I know you will not allow feeling to sway your judgment, to discard all sympathy from your minds in applying yourselves to the evidence. If this is true, it is most cogent and grave evidence, and it becomes you to consider closely whether this part of Clara Brown's evidence is corroborated by those who saw the deceased on the journey to Penge. So far as the evidence goes, no further clothing was sent with Mrs. Harriet to the lodgings taken for her than that which the poor woman wore on her back.

Mr. CLARKE—There was a basket of whose contents there was no list made.

Mr. JUSTICE HAWKINS—There was a basket brought with provisions. Point me any particle of evidence to show that any change of clothing was provided for the lady. I am dealing with the evidence; if I were to speculate I might do injustice.

Mr. CLARKE—It is in evidence that there was a basket.

Staunton Trial.

Mr. JUSTICE HAWKINS (it being now twenty minutes to six o'clock) suggested that it might be convenient to adjourn for a short time.

The FOREMAN—We should like a quarter of an hour.

The Court then adjourned, and upon reassembling after a brief interval, his lordship resumed reading the evidence of Mrs. Chalklin and of Dr. Longrigg. It was noticeable, he continued, that Louis did not remain in the house during the night when his wife was so seriously ill. It may be said there was not a bed for him, but could he make that a *sine qua non* under the circumstances? However, the fact is that he left her, returning the next morning. The doctor saw the poor woman that morning, and, again being sent for, he went and found her dying. The nurse, finding her dying, went to Louis and asked him if he wished to see the last of the lady; but Mrs. Patrick Staunton interposed, saying, " Don't ask him; it will worry him "— worry him to see the last moments of his wife—and he did not go to see her. Nobody complains of the conduct of Alice Rhodes or of Mrs. Patrick Staunton that morning, but, as the learned Attorney-General said, it was too late then. The question is not whether there was any humanity shown on the afternoon of the death; if guilty business there was, it was done before, and it is for the consequence of those previous acts, and not for the acts of that morning, that they are now arraigned. But, no sooner was the breath out of the body than they left the poor dead creature in the hands of a strange nurse, in a strange house, and they came no more near the place till the undertaker came to put it in a coffin to convey it to its last home. We come to the certificate of Dr. Longrigg, that the deceased died from a cerebral disease; but he explains to you now that he gave it upon the statements of the prisoners, and that he necessarily knew exceedingly little of the deceased at the time. The funeral was deferred, the undertaker being apprised by Mr. Casabianca that there were circumstances calling for inquiry. In due course an inquest was held, and a post-mortem examination held. At that post-mortem examination Mr. Harman, a surgeon, was present on behalf of the prisoners, and I take it for granted that he is a gentleman of skill and honour. He has not been called to say what his opinion was, or what view he took. It was not the duty of the prosecution to call him, and no excuse is offered on the part of the defence.[5]

Mr. CLARKE—As to the appearances at the post-mortem examination, they have never been challenged.

Mr. JUSTICE HAWKINS—Never challenged!

---

[5] See Appendix vii., p. 306.

Appendix I.

APPENDIX I.

MEDICAL CERTIFICATE OF CAUSE OF DEATH.

I hereby certify that I attended Harriet Staunton, whose age was stated to be thirty-six years, that I last saw her on the 13th day of April, 1877, that she died on the 13th day of April, 1877, at 34 Forbes Road, and that to the best of my knowledge and belief the cause of her death was as hereunder written—

(a) Primary, cerebral disease.
(b) Secondary, apoplexy.

Witness my hand this 14th day of April, 1877.

Signature— DEAN LONGRIGG.
Registered Qualification—M.R.C.S.
Residence—Penge, S.E.

Staunton Trial.

APPENDIX II.

TELEGRAM DATED APRIL 15, 1877.

Handed in at Bromley Street Office at 8.45 p.m.
Received here 8.30 a.m.

From

    Uridge,

        Bromley, Kent.

To

    Mrs. Butterfield,

        Vicarage,

           Burstead, Brentwood.

Harriet Staunton died yesterday at Thirty Four Forbes Road, Beckenham, Kent. Will be buried to-day Sunday.

Appendix III.

APPENDIX III.

SIR JAMES STEPHEN'S CHARGE TO THE GRAND JURY.

[*The Times*, Wednesday, July 11, 1877.]

SUMMER ASSIZES—SOUTH-EASTERN CIRCUIT—Maidstone, July 10.

Crown Court.

Sir James Stephen, who sat in the Crown Court and charged the Grand Jury, dwelt particularly on the Penge case, the prisoners charged in which having been committed for trial at these Assizes, the case had necessarily come before the Grand Jury here, though in the event of an indictment being found, there is an order of the Queen's Bench, under Palmer's Act, to remove it to the Central Criminal Court for trial. He referred to the charge against four persons—Louis Staunton, Patrick Staunton, and Elizabeth Staunton (his wife), and Alice Rhodes (her sister)—for the murder of Harriet Staunton, wife of Louis Staunton. The case, he said, was one of the deepest gravity, involving as it did the capital charge against these four persons, closely connected by relationship or affinity. He would first state the outline of the facts, and then the different hypotheses arising out of them, and the law applicable thereto. The deceased woman was the wife of Louis Staunton, and she was thirty-six years of age, and the daughter of a Mrs. Butterfield. Her mother stated that she had always been of weak mind, and this would be found to be of some importance in the case. In 1874, indeed, her mother took proceedings in lunacy for the purpose of having her declared a lunatic, and having a committee of her person appointed, but these proceedings failed, and subsequently her daughter made the acquaintance of Louis Staunton, and became engaged to him. The engagement lasted some months, and ultimately they were married without the mother's approval. They were married on the 16th June, 1875, and went to live at Loughborough Road, Brixton. The wife was entitled to £2500, which her husband received. Some weeks after the marriage Mrs. Butterfield went to see them, and it did not appear to have been a happy marriage. Some days afterwards she received two letters, one from Louis Staunton, the other from her daughter. The letter from Louis Staunton forbade the mother the house, telling her that, in consequence of her past conduct, he would not permit any intercourse between her and her daughter, and the letter from her daughter was to the effect that, as her husband took a strong view on the subject of her mother's conduct, it was as well that she should not come to see her. Towards the end of 1875 Alice Rhodes came to live at Louis Staunton's, apparently as a friend or companion. In March, 1876, a child was born of the marriage, and the nurse and medical attendant stated circumstances which seemed to show neglect of Mrs. Staunton at the time. It also appeared that at this time she showed jealousy as to Alice Rhodes' relations with her husband—a jealousy which, as subsequent events showed, was amply justified. In May, 1876, they removed from Brixton to Gipsy Hill, Norwood, but during the summer—in August

Staunton Trial.

and September—Louis Staunton sent his wife for some time to stay at the house of his brother Patrick, at a place called Woodlands, in this county, a remarkably lonely part of the country. After the removal of the prisoners there had been found at this house four letters from Louis Staunton to his brother, dated in August and September, and relating to his wife, speaking of her as having a violent temper; but it is remarkable that, though complaining of her, he does not in these letters hint at her indulging in drink, and this is to be borne in mind. During this visit the wife was seen by a witness about the place engaged as she naturally might be, and this is remarkable with reference to what subsequently occurred. She was there, it seems, until October, but in November, 1876, Louis Staunton left Gipsy Hill and came to live at a place only twenty minutes' walk from Woodlands, the house of his brother Patrick, and when he came to live there with Alice Rhodes he sent his wife again to Woodlands—a singular arrangement, but which he accounted for before the coroner by saying that it was to prevent her from drinking. In the meantime he lived with Alice Rhodes, who passed as his wife, so that while his real wife was at Woodlands, under the care of his brother, Alice Rhodes was living with him as his wife in the neighbourhood. From that time forward (with one or two slight exceptions) no one seems to have seen Mrs. Staunton. Louis Staunton before the coroner stated that she was perfectly free, and lived as one of the family, he allowing £1 a week for her support, and that he went several times a week to see her. That was his own account of the way in which they passed the period between November, 1876, and April, 1877 (when she died). But evidence will be adduced to suggest a very different state of things. At the end of October or beginning of November a witness saw Mrs. Staunton come to the door and heard Patrick say to her, " I've a policeman here, and if you don't go, he will run you in "; and upon that she went in, and the witness says that though he constantly (having communicated with her mother) looked for her, he never saw her again. When the house was searched a letter of hers was found to her husband, which throws some light on the case—

" My own darling,—I write these few lines hoping this will find you well. Will you be down on Sunday? If not, I shall be disappointed. I hope to see you on Monday. If not, will you let me know when you will be down? Will you bring me a piece of riband, &c.? I have not had clean flannel for a month. I have been here a month on Saturday. It is time I should be at home; my boots is worn out.—Your ever affectionate wife."

Now, here it appears that she had been there a month; that she had not had clean flannel for a month, and that she wanted to be at home, where she had an undoubted right to be. But nothing appears to have been seen of her again until the Wednesday before Christmas, when a tradesman, calling at the house, heard some one walking through the kitchen, and heard the servant say, " Go back, ma'am," and then heard a door locked. Now, of course, it is practically impossible to hear or know what is going on in a lonely house, but it appears that Mrs. Staunton was seen by no one. Tradesmen went from time to time to the house and saw every one else there, but never saw her. On the 20th of January, 1877, Mrs. Butterfield, her mother, received a letter from Louis Staunton in these terms—" I hear from my sister that you called and wished to see your daughter. I only wish I had been there at the time. I will tell you once for all that for your unnatural conduct she never wishes

Appendix IV.

The prisoners pleaded " Not Guilty." Mrs. Patrick Staunton wept bitterly when placed in the dock, but the three other prisoners were self-possessed, if somewhat dejected in demeanour.

Mr. Montagu Williams said that he was instructed on behalf of the prisoner, Louis Staunton, to apply for a postponement of his trial, and the grounds upon which the application was based was that they had been unable to prepare the necessary evidence for the defence. He was in a position to say that if the application were granted, the necessary evidence would, on a future occasion, be forthcoming. He hoped that his lordship, in the interest of the accused, would not ask him to state the details of the evidence he proposed to adduce, and that it would be sufficient if he stated what medical evidence would be produced at the trial. They had endeavoured to obtain that evidence, and had succeeded in obtaining the deposition of one eminent medical gentleman—a deposition which justified an opinion already formed. It was not the fault of those who instructed counsel for the prisoners that they now had to make the application. The matter came into the hands of the solicitors who were instructed to defend the whole of the prisoners at the end of June, and they set to work at once to get other evidence to endorse that which they had already procured. Owing to the pressure of work and the season of the year, it was found difficult to obtain that evidence.

The Lord Chief-Justice—Between the month of June and the present date of August, surely medical evidence might have been obtained? I do not think that this is sufficient ground for the postponement of the trial. If you have been unable to obtain medical evidence up to the present time, how can I assume that you will be able to get it between this and the next session?

Mr. Montagu Williams said that, owing to the pressure of business or for some other cause, the papers sent had been returned without the necessary opinion. He could satisfy the Attorney-General that the gentlemen by whom they were instructed were acting with perfect *bona fides.*

The Lord Chief-Justice—It is but a few days since the prisoners, without reserve, stated their desire to have the case tried as soon as possible. With the abundance of medical men to be found, and bearing in mind the readiness with which medical men lend their assistance to that which they consider right, I cannot understand the difficulty.

Mr. Montagu Williams said he was in a position to place before his lordship the names of the gentlemen who had been consulted.

The Lord Chief-Justice—But who have not given evidence?

Mr. Montagu Williams—Only on the ground that they have been too much occupied with other engagements.

Mr. Clarke said that he should like to add a word or two to those that had fallen from his learned friend, Mr. Williams. He represented Patrick Staunton, who, individually, was anxious that the trial should proceed, and did express a wish that that course should be pursued. It was only after careful consideration of this matter that the learned counsel felt he could, in the exercise of his duty, concur in this application, and he therefore hoped his lordship would grant it. It was not that they were without medical evidence—there had been time to obtain certain evidence—but it was because they had certain material which was of vital importance to corroborate. If the result of their inquiries had been that they found they had no reasonable expectation of obtaining evidence on the difficult medical question, they would not have made the application.

The Lord Chief-Justice said the only facts on which medical testimony could be obtained were simple. There was the state in which

299

Staunton Trial.

the deceased was found, the appearances after death and at the post-mortem examination. It all lay in a narrow compass, and any medical man who was asked to give evidence could probably do so in the course of the trial.

Mr. Clarke said there was a large mass of evidence in the depositions.

The Lord Chief-Justice said that the medical evidence was not very long.

Mr. Clarke said that, in inferences drawn as to the cause of death, the medical opinion was that it was a most difficult question to deal with.

The Lord Chief-Justice—It is not a difficult question, but a matter of fact about the appearances. It all lies in a narrow compass.

Mr. Clarke—Facts that lie within a small compass frequently cover large issues.

The Lord Chief-Justice—True; but a medical man would be able to form an opinion easily.

Mr. Clarke said that, as his learned friend had already stated, various medical men had declined to entertain the question at the present moment. They were in possession of evidence which, if supported by others, would materially affect the result of the trial, and it would be impossible to educe it at present.

Mr. Douglas Straight, who represents Mrs. Patrick Staunton, concurred in the application, as he felt that in his best judgment the prisoners were not at present able to give a full and complete defence.

Mr. Gye, on behalf of Alice Rhodes, supported the same view, as he thought this not only affected his client, but the whole of the prisoners. It was a most material matter, and he respectfully urged that the evidence could not be produced at this trial.

The Attorney-General said his learned friends had informed the Court that medical evidence could be obtained which would be of advantage to the prisoners at the bar. If that were so, he could not, on behalf of the Crown, considering the awful nature of the charge made against the accused, offer any opposition to the application. At the same time it seemed to him to be almost inconceivable that evidence of the character which had been referred to should not have been procured before now. The appearances after death were all described at the coroner's inquest, and before medical men who appeared on behalf of the prisoners. There could be no controversy as to those appearances, and the only question with which any medical gentleman would have to deal was as to how those appearances were produced. The prisoners had been permitted in the middle of June to furnish themselves with such testimony, and he could not imagine why it had not been forthcoming. However, after what his learned friends had said, he would not resist the application.

The Lord Chief-Justice said the application which had been made appeared to him to be a most unreasonable one, and he had very much doubt as to whether he would be justified in acceding to it. It was perfectly monstrous to say that, if medical evidence was capable of being obtained in a particular direction, there had not been abundant time and opportunity for having it procured. The application implied gross negligence on the part of those whose duty it was to have such testimony forthcoming, if they deemed it necessary, but who did not seem to have taken the necessary steps for that purpose within the time which had been allowed, and which had been abundantly sufficient. This being so, he had no hesitation in saying that if there had been any opposition to the application on the part of the Crown, he should have felt it his duty to refuse to allow a postponement of the trial. Indeed, even after what had been said, he had some doubt as to whether, in the interest of public justice and the

Appendix V.

maintenance of the regular course of the administration of justice, those who represented the Crown were not doing wrong in acceding to the application, and as to whether he himself was not doing wrong in allowing it to prevail. However, as the Attorney-General had stated that he did not object on the part of the prosecution to the application being granted, he would not stand in the way, but would allow the case to stand over until next session.

The prisoners were about to be removed from the bar when The Lord Chief-Justice added that he understood a still further difficulty existed in connection with the case. It was quite certain, he believed, that the charge could not be tried even next session, the condition of one of the female prisoners being such that the case would have to be again adjourned. It was possible that might have something to do with the present application.

The Attorney-General asked his lordship whether, after what he had just said, he would not postpone the trial until the session after next.

The Lord Chief-Justice said he would not. The case must be allowed to take its course. He did not resist a postponement until next session, but at present he would grant nothing further.

The prisoners were then removed from the bar.

During the day the Grand Jury returned a true bill against Louis Adolphus Staunton, Patrick Staunton, and Elizabeth Staunton, for the manslaughter of the child of the first-named prisoner.

APPENDIX V.

Evidence of EMMA DENTON, of Pound Road, Church Street, Camberwell, wife of James Denton, labourer. This witness was not called at the trial.

Before the Coroner—

I nursed Mrs. Louis Staunton in her confinement in March and April, 1876. Mr. Louis Staunton, Mr. and Mrs. Patrick Staunton, Alice Rhodes, and Clara Brown were in the house.

Mrs. Staunton was only allowed ordinary food. Alice Rhodes was mistress of the house. Mrs. Staunton did not suckle the child. I asked Mr. Staunton about it. He said he did not wish it to suck. He had a motive of his own and forbade her. She was always fretting. She was not strong-minded. The Stauntons are Roman Catholics. When I left Mr. Staunton invited me to call and see his wife. I called once. The baby was removed to Norwood. She was always clean, and acted like a lady. She did not drink. I told Mr. Staunton that the doctor had ordered meat and stout, and it was not supplied her, Mr. Staunton saying it was not the doctor's business to give such orders. She was not properly treated.

Before the magistrates—

Witness repeated to counsel the same story, with the following addition—" I considered she was very much kept down and was afraid to say anything. She seemed to be continually crying from morning to night. Crying to see her husband repeatedly."

Staunton Trial.

Recalled by the bench—

She swore—" The husband I did not consider attentive to his wife. He went out in the morning without seeing his wife, and sometimes at night. She cried because she was continually hearing them laughing and playing together, and she repeatedly rang the bell. I mean Louis Staunton and Alice Rhodes."

APPENDIX VI.

FINAL STATEMENT BY CLARA BROWN.

[From *The Daily Telegraph*, Monday, October 1, 1877.]

A correspondent forwards the following statement as having been made by the witness, Clara Brown, since the condemnation of the Stauntons. It contains a number of allegations against the accused that were not made by the witness in any of her previous depositions, the only reason given for making them now being to reply to the grave censure that has been passed upon her in various quarters for the discrepancies in her evidence, and still more for not having made known while Harriet Staunton was alive the shocking treatment to which she was subjected. We publish the extraordinary narrative simply as we receive it—

"She says that before any one can understand or form any idea of the case, they must take into consideration the tempers and failings of all the parties, and then they would see how acts of aggravation have been resented by acts of cruelty. Of course Louis and Alice were so strongly attached to each other that no one could ever keep them apart. Though Harriet patiently and quietly bore a good deal at first, yet afterwards, when she found them together, or when she thought he had been in her company, she took to screaming and grinning at him in rage, till the whole neighbourhood was frequently raised. When the screaming was heard by Farmer Dubery (*sic*), it was because deceased found him and Alice lying by the side of each other on the lawn at Patrick's. Harriet set up screaming without being touched. She told him that she would not go into the house and help me to lay the cloth for him, and then he got up and struck her, and pushed her indoors. Her habit of grinning and screaming was the cause of many of the first blows she had. Though from the very first she was always very badly treated, yet it was not until last Christmas week that the cruelties began. In that week Percy (that is Patrick) went upstairs and strongly nailed the window of the back bedroom down, and so darkened the window that no one could either see in or out. He then ordered her upstairs, took away from her all her clothing but a dirty old nightgown and an old petticoat body which she had round her legs, and dared her to come down ever again on any account whatever. At first she was obstinate and daring, and used to come to the top of the stairs and shout out, ' I will come down; I'll come down in spite of you.' Then every time she did that he would run upstairs, knock her down, and treat her dreadfully. After some of these beatings I have seen her face puffed,

302

Appendix VI.

her eyes swollen round as big as my two hands, so that you could not see a bit of her eyes at all, and she herself could not see a single thing. Her screams used to be frightful. At such times as these, when he had been so savagely beating her, Mrs. Patrick would run upstairs, and, getting between them, would call on him to stop before he killed her, till at last many a time she has been knocked down by his blows herself. He took to keeping her so long without anything to eat that she became desperate for food. Her cries and moans were very sad, and the beatings to make her be quiet went on day and night, so that the place was not like any place on earth. Many a time I have jumped out of bed with fright at the scenes, and gone out of the house into the wood, sometimes taking their little baby that was with me in the bed, wrapped up in the blanket, at all hours of the night. After he took to reducing her to one meal a day, he would not let that go up till supper time, as, after she began to get weak, she generally went to sleep a bit after a meal, and I was then able to get some rest. So, in order to keep her quiet all day, they used to promise her she should have some supper, but if she made any noise that then she should not have that. One night, after she had had nothing all day, and nothing was put for her supper, I said, ' Shall I take Harriet some supper up? ' He flew into a rage and said, ' No; let her go to bed without.' When Harriet saw I had no supper for her she began to cry dreadfully. She was very hungry and cold, for there never was any fire allowed her in the room but once all through the winter. She kept moaning and begging of me to fetch her a bit of food. As soon as I thought he had gone to sleep, I went downstairs to the pantry and cut her what I could without it being missed. It was always difficult to take her anything, for he could somehow always tell when the loaf was cut. We had not used to have much meat, but we used to have chiefly boiled rice, sweetened with condensed milk, which Harriet used to be very fond of, ate ravenously, and was her chief food. One thing I used to think very cruel of him, and that was the delight he seemed to take in jeering her and seeing her suffer. He used to mock her, and ridicule the faces she used to pull in her sufferings. When he was keeping her a very long time without food he would go upstairs and laugh at her, and say, ' Well, Harriet, are you hungry yet? '

" Whenever he had kept her without food the previous day and night he would invariably come into the room as soon as he was up in the morning, and say, with a sneer and jeer, ' Well, Harriet, do you want your supper yet? ' One morning, after he had given no supper for her, he came in and said, ' Well, Harriet, did you get any supper last night? ' As she lay in bed she very foolishly grinned at him and said, ' Yes, I got my supper for all you, for Clara went and fetched me some.' With that he flew into a rage, and threatened us all, and always after that locked up the pantry, and I had very little chance to give her anything again. What followed after that I cannot bear to think of. For three days and nights after that Harriet never had a taste of anything either to eat or drink. She cried all day and moaned all that night, begging me to fetch her some food, but I could not. Next morning he came in and said, ' Well, Harriet, do you want your supper? ' She did not grin at him then, and he went downstairs, but during the day he went up several times and said, ' Well, Harriet, ain't you hungry yet? ' When I went upstairs the second night, and she saw I had no supper for her, it was pitiable to see her. Throughout the night she cried, and besought me to fetch her food, even if only a bit of bread; but I could not, for it was all locked up. I had no sleep till five in the morning, when I just dropped off. He came into the room and waked me

303

again at half-past seven, and then, turning to Harriet, in his usual way said, ' Well, Harriet, don't you want your supper yet?' On the third day it was dreadful to see her. She entreated him to give her food, and she promised to be always quiet if he would only give her a bit of bread. The third night I had to go upstairs without any supper for her again. I thought that was cruel, and I was afraid then that he really meant starving her to death. I shall never forget that night. When she saw I had no supper for her the third night she seemed completely to give way. She cried and sobbed, and begged me to fetch her something—anything—even if it was only a drop of water. I could not help crying myself; but I was afraid he would come and beat her again, and I had to keep her as quiet as I could by telling her if she did not keep quiet Percy would come and beat her again. After a bit she seemed to go almost mad. She grinned at me, made the most hideous noises, and said I should get her food. While she was on in this way Tommy was often crying as well. Next morning Percy came into the room at seven o'clock, and said, laughing, ' Well, Harriet, have you had any supper yet? Ain't you hungry? Don't you want your supper?' She had been sitting up and down on the iron chair bedstead, but was then trying to stand, but was too weak. She managed to pull herself up by holding on to the mantelpiece, and then, holding on by one hand, she shook her fist at him and grinned, saying, ' Yes, I do want my supper. I am famishing.' I shall never get the sight of her as she then stood out of my mind. She seemed going quite mad. She had scarcely anything round her, and when she shook her fist at him she looked like a mad skeleton. He laughed and mocked the faces she was making, till at last she called him names he did not like, and he then ran at her, struck her in the face, and knocked her down in the fireplace. Mrs. Patrick ran in and stopped him striking her again, but Harriet then, I think, was insensible. They then picked her up and put her on her bed, but after that she was so weak she was never able even to raise herself up again. Patrick was always a very bad-tempered man, and would strike anybody—man, woman, or child—if they said anything to him. After this her sufferings seemed to get a great deal more dreadful. She struggled to get up, but could not. During the last five weeks no one could describe the agony she seemed to be in. The lice got all over her body by thousands, and were eating her all over. She appeared to be nearly tearing herself to pieces with scratching. She lingered in this manner, with sometimes one bit of food a day and sometimes none, till just one week before she died. Then it was that she got quite insensible, and they got frightened. They did all they could to try and bring her round a bit with pouring chicken broth down her throat, but she was never conscious again, and was perfectly helpless when she was moved.

" As it regards poor little Tommy, his sufferings were frightful. They treated him, if possible, worse than his mother. They starved him at the same time in the same way. He had scarcely any clothes on, and had to lie in the bassinet by the side of his mother, with no bed, nothing during all that cold weather but a bit of old carpet under him and a bit of an old shawl to cover him. He got so thin, only like the skeleton of a child, and at last, not being able to bear his own weight, his back grew so round that it seemed as though his backbone was coming through the skin. Percy used to say it would not do to let his bones come through his skin, and he knew how to keep his back straight; so every day he used to strap him down flat on his back on a large board he had used sometimes as an extra easel. In this way the poor little thing was left crying piteously,

Appendix VI.

with one strap tight round its body and another round its knees, for four and five hours every day at least. When it had been a long time in this position, unable to move a limb, it would roll its eyes round and round in the sockets as if in the intensest agony. It had not used to cry like other children, but shriek and make a kind of hideous noise. He would frequently beat it dreadfully, and once when it was so strapped on the board, and was crying, he struck it a violent blow in the face, making bruises on its forehead and face, which never went off, but lasted till death, and which were afterwards spoken to by Sister Mary and the hospital doctor. Many a time I have cried at the dreadful scenes that were going on, and wondered what I could do to save them. When Mrs. Harriet was strong enough to walk downstairs I could help her a little then. When I was sure that they had gone across to the farm, or any distance, I used to get her down into the back kitchen, and have washed her many a time when they have been out; but the lice were so thick on her that I could not use a towel. I had to wipe them off with wet rags, and at last I burnt so many that they began to miss them. Towards the last I used to wipe off what I could, and burn the rags, for the vermin of different kinds were getting all over the room. I thought sometimes that I would tell the neighbours, but I was afraid lest things should take a wrong course, and that it would make matters worse. I thought if I told, perhaps the neighbours would only talk without doing anything, and that I should be found out, perhaps get something done to me, and very likely Harriet be put out of the road at once. Several times I have gone to Mrs. Weatherley's crying, and said what dreadful scenes were going on between Patrick and his wife, but she used to say that she did not want to hear anything about rows between men and their wives, and though I wanted to tell her about Harriet, when I saw how Mrs. Weatherley used to take things I was afraid to begin. Then I thought that if I tried to run away I should only starve, or be caught and brought back, and treated I don't know how. I thought no one would have me in that way in service, for I had scarcely anything but an old frock on. I had neither shoes nor stockings, and not one penny piece, for they never gave me a shilling all the time I was there. I had neither father nor mother. If I had got up to London as I was, I had no one to go to but my aunt Rhodes, Mrs. Patrick's mother's, and I thought the best thing was to wait in the hope that some of Mrs. Harriet's friends would come. I had no chance to do anything in that lonely place, for they would not, if they knew it, allow me to speak to a single soul. Even my own brother came to see me one day. We had not seen each other for a long time, but when he came to the door they sent me upstairs and him away, and would not let me see him. Everybody that approached the house they were afraid of, lest they were sent to look for Harriet, or lest her groans should be heard. I very much regret now that I did not have more courage, and risk everything; but Percy was always watching me, and threatening what he would do if ever he caught me mentioning Harriet's name out of the house. When I went before the coroner they used to tell me when we were at home that if I did not stick to what they told me that it would all be found out, and that I should be locked up as well as them. If I had only known where to have found some kind friends I could have trusted, none of them would have come to the end they have.

"Mrs. Weatherley and other persons state that the girl frequently came to them crying, but they would not hear her, as they thought she only wanted to begin on family matters. The girl adds that she does not know that either Alice or Louis knew of the beatings, and that Mrs. Patrick seemed powerless to prevent them."

Staunton Trial.

APPENDIX VII.

LETTER OF DR. HARMAN.

[From *The Daily Telegraph*, Thursday, October 4, 1877.]

The following letter is addressed to us by the medical practitioner who was present at the post-mortem examination of Harriet Staunton, on behalf of the convicts, but who was not called upon the trial:—

To the Editor of *The Daily Telegraph.*

Sir,—I am unable to resist the conviction that it is my duty to make known the opinion I formed after witnessing the post-mortem examination of the body of Mrs. Harriet Staunton, and chiefly for this reason—because the learned judge drew from the fact that my evidence was withheld, an inference which was natural, which was inevitable, and, I think, an inference of grave import, but, as it happened, an entirely mistaken one.[1]   I shall note the important points as concisely as I am able.

After the post-mortem examination the gentlemen who were present, with myself, held a consultation. At that consultation *we all agreed* that we had found no evidence sufficient to account either for death or for the emaciation. *The sole reference* made within my hearing at that consultation to the subject of starvation was the following:—I had observed to Dr. Bright that the marked redness of the stomach had no bearing upon starvation, and he replied, " he believed all authorities were agreed that post-mortem appearances as to starvation were very unreliable."

At the inquest I was asked only two questions, and my answers to those questions were both cut short in the midst. In answer to the first (as to cause of death) I endeavoured to say—what I take to be of essential importance, as the sole foundation for any safe opinion in this case—that there was no positive evidence sufficient to warrant a positive opinion either as to cause of death or of the emaciation. But I was stopped at the third or fourth word. To the second question, Did I agree with the others doctors? I replied, " I agree with Professor Rodgers."   At this point I was again stopped, or I should have added that I agreed with him because, in his *first* answer, he said nothing about starvation. On signing my depositions I noticed the statement that I agreed " with the other medical men." Of course I protested strongly that I had not made that statement.   The coroner still urged me to sign. I considered, and did so, for this reason: I did not wish to deny that starvation was *one* hypothesis in the case; and I had full warrant, from the result of our consultation and from the manner in which those gentlemen came eventually to mention starvation at the inquest, for believing that the opinion was with them, as with me, a purely hypothetical one.

At the trial the opinion of those gentlemen as to starvation first assumed (in their expression of it) a decided and positive form. At the trial, therefore, I should have felt it my duty to separate myself entirely from any agreement with them. I will now state, as concisely as I can, precisely what I was prepared to express at the trial.

1. That the opinion that death, in this case, was the result of

---

[1] See *supra*, p. 278.

Appendix VII.

starvation alone, can by no possibility, from a purely medical point of view, be more than mere hypothesis.

2. That the symptoms immediately preceding death, and the post-mortem appearances in the membranes of the brain, are inexplicable by *starvation alone*. I have searched all the records I can find of post-mortem appearances in cases of death by starvation, and in not one are those appearances or those symptoms mentioned. On the other hand, taken together, those symptoms and appearances agree precisely, so far as they go, with tubercular meningitis.

3. The emaciation might be fully accounted for by the assumption of general tuberculosis with the tubercular diathesis preceding. I have seen emaciation at least as extreme—I think more extreme, in my deliberate judgment—from those conditions, than existed in this case. And it is well known that this emaciation is sometimes fearfully rapid in its progress.

4. The meningitis was in an incipient stage. This agrees with the brief duration of the attack on the brain; and with probable hastening of the fatal result, both by the journey, and, especially, by the low general condition which must previously have existed. If we assume the existence of tubercular meningitis, even if only in an incipient stage, we assume at once the existence of an inevitably fatal disease.

The opinion I have here expressed I have held firmly from the first until now. Moreover, I formed that opinion on a review of the whole case, without asking the opinion or advice of *any one;* and committed myself wholly to it in writing, without knowing that there would be found anywhere even one who would endorse that opinion. I have not, either in public or in private, uttered one word inconsistent with that opinion. I was fully prepared to declare it at the trial, on oath. I am still ready to substantiate it by my oath, as being in accordance with my deliberate conviction.

I received the usual notices to give evidence for the defence; and I waited four days in Court fully expecting to be called. I know of one reason only in explanation of the course pursued. Dr. Payne founded his opinion, I believe, as to meningitis partly on the deposit, "probably tubercular," removed by Dr. Longrigge. My opinion was, and is, that those so-called deposits were probably not tubercular, and I declined to found my opinion upon anything doubtful. Of course Dr. Payne rightly gave his opinion on the assumption that Dr. Longrigge's opinion was correct. I could not; and the learned counsel probably feared—I think needlessly—that I should weaken Dr. Payne's and Dr. Bristowe's evidence. For I judge, on the whole, that one would hardly have expected in this case to find tubercles visible to the naked eye. The learned judge observed that I did not suggest a microscopic examination. No; and for a very good reason. Dr. Longrigge conducted the post-mortem examination, and, after noticing the congestion of the pia-mater, he examined the brain substance (naturally expecting to find the explanation of congestion there), and so thoroughly that the membranes were necessarily completely destroyed; or, at least, further examination of any kind was rendered impossible.

Lastly, there were other morbid appearances. These may have indicated that there probably were other diseased conditions. I limit myself to this: That the assumption of starvation alone does not, from a purely medical point of view, any more than the assumption of diabetes alone, account for the *manner of death*, as well as for the emaciation; and that the assumption of tubercular disease alone does fairly account for both, and is not inconsistent with any facts of the case that are within my knowledge.—I am, yours faithfully,

25 Gresham Road, Brixton, Oct. 3, 1877.   J. HARMAN.

P.S.—I have forwarded a copy of this letter to the Home Secretary.

Staunton Trial.

LETTERS OF CHARLES READE.

———

[*The Daily Telegraph*, Wednesday, October 10, 1877.]

———

HANG IN HASTE, REPENT AT LEISURE.

To the Editor of *The Daily Telegraph*.

Sir,—When a woman of property is half starved by people who are eating her bread, and her husband, with his paramour, lives but one mile distant, on the money of their injured benefactress, and the victim dies covered with vermin and weighing about 5 stone, the wildfire of indignation will, I hope, always run through every vein of the country, and the judges share the just wrath of the gentry and of the millions who work so hard to feed their own helpless charges.

But great wrath, even when just, is still a fever of the mind, and cannot discriminate. Whilst the heart is yet hot with that ire which has been so truly called "a passing phrenzy" (*ira furor brevis*), the culpable ones seem criminal, the criminal ones seem monsters, and "our great revenge has stomach for them all."

I, who write these lines, am but a man recovering fast from a fever in a nation which is recovering slowly but surely. I recover fast because from my youth I have been trained in a great school to reason closely and discriminate keenly, and armed with Oxford steel against the tricks and sophistries of rhetoric, against the derangement of dates (which single artifice will turn true facts into lies), against those fatal traps, equivoques in language, and against all gaps in evidence, however small they may appear to the unwary. I grieve to say that I receive shoals of insulting letters telling me I am a Whalleyite and a novelist, and so disqualified. This draws a few unwilling words from me to disarm prejudice. I declared against Orton, in the *Daily News*, before ever the Crown tried him. I then laid down the scientific principle which governs his case, the doctrine of multiplied coincidences; and though I write novels at one time, I can write logic at another, and when I write a novel I give the public my lowest gifts, but I give them my highest when I write in a great journal upon life and death and justice. But the best thing the public, and those who govern it, can do will be to go by things, not names, to sift my arguments as closely as I shall analyse the evidence and the hasty inferences in the greatest judicial error of modern times.

The verdict against the Stauntons and Rhodes is a hodge-podge, in which the legally criminal and the legally culpable are confounded, and both sets of legal culprits are confounded with the moral culprits, who are clear of the case by the law of England and the rules of evidence that bind the Central Criminal Court.

Few observers of mankind will deny me this, which, indeed, reads like a truism—

Where A, B, and C confound four things, and D, on the same evidence, distinguishes them, it is a thousand to one that D is right and A, B, and C are wrong.

This position becomes even stronger when we find that A, B, and C have been subject to several confusing influences. It may

Appendix VIII.

be worth while to point out the confusing processes that muddled the jury, of which processes some rise from the habitual malpractices of this particular Court, and others from faults that have been imported into it for this single occasion.

Processes of Confusion.

1. The Court, for its convenience, tried four dissimilar cases in the lump, and the four prisoners stood together at the bar.

2. Being near and dear to each other, and involved in one danger, they suffered and sympathised openly.

3. Twelve unguarded men looked on, and, deluded by the senses, which are always stronger than the judgment in untrained minds, said to themselves, " They are all in one boat." So they were—in one family boat. But the family boat being in a legal dock, these good souls took it for a legal boat directly.

4. The four separate indictments, with their various counts, would have tended to cure this. But here the malpractices of the Court came in with another process of confusion.

By the law of England the arraignment of a prisoner consists of three parts—

(a) He is called to the bar by his name; (b) the indictment is read to him; (c) he is invited to plead to the indictment, and no other form of words, and he has a right to plead guilty to one count and not guilty to another count; and, if he is legally culpable, but not criminal, it is the wisest thing he can do.

This being done by the Clerk of Arraigns, the paper that clerk has read from becomes, by the universal practice of all our Courts, the property of the jury so long as that trial lasts.

But the Clerk of Arraigns, by a modern malpractice, broke this just and necessary law, and the judge let him. So each prisoner was grossly robbed of his right to admit one count and deny another, and the jury were grossly robbed of a copy of the indictment, though the mere preliminary jury, whose responsibility is so much less, had one to study and find a true bill on; and though it is not merely the right but the duty of the jury, as laid down by Blackstone himself very clearly, to study the indictment very closely, and to find " guilty " on one count, and " not guilty " on another, and to carry discrimination even further, for they can find guilty on one half of a divisible count and acquit upon the other.

5. Law, justice, and common sense having thus been defied by the Central Criminal Court, and the great written instrument of discrimination withheld from them contrary to law, they were manipulated and confused by a rhetorician on the bench, who picked out the highest count and ignored the others, and with gentle hand extinguished their one faint gleam of incipient discrimination, and left no doubt to the jury in a case crammed with doubts; which was unprecedented.

The result corresponded with all these co-operating processes.

The judge laid down the law that whoever has by law or takes upon himself the charge of a helpless person, and does not give her enough to live upon, is guilty of murder by omission. He did not say one-fourth of the charge, for that is not the law.

Staunton Trial.

The Charge.

Under this ruling, on which I have something to say hereafter, the jury, on the evidence, contrived to see four persons, all of whom had, either by law or their own act, " the charge " of Harriet Staunton, and all saw her pine to death, and let her pine to death.

Now, let all men in whose minds the very landmarks of truth are not obliterated, look on that picture conjured up by a jury under several processes of confusion along with this picture which the evidence reveals to a discriminating eye.

Patrick Staunton, a committer of a crime responsible for Harriet Staunton's life by a pecuniary contract with Louis. He docks her food, strikes her, terrifies and strikes his wife for interfering, &c. The evidence suggests that if the man had died in 1876 Harriet Staunton might be alive now. He comes under the judge's ruling. He had " the charge." This is the only committer of them all. Yet the jury can see nothing exceptional in his position. We now step down in law to a much lower grade of crime.

The Mere Omitters.

At the head is Mrs. Patrick Staunton, a grown up woman, experienced, and no fool. Her neglect of Harriet is *prima facie* barbarous; but it transpires that there was conjugal influence and coercion. The woman encountered blows in defence of the victim. The deterring effect of those blows, and her pregnancy, cannot be exactly estimated; nor is it necessary. The law, always disposed to assume conjugal influence, is amply satisfied with the admissions made on this head, and she is not a criminal, but a culpable offender. Two years' imprisonment. The next omitter is Clara Brown. She slept in the same room with the victim, allowed the vermin to accumulate, saw her sufferings more than Mrs. P. Staunton; filled her own belly and let her perish; nor did she show any positive goodness of heart, as the elder woman did once or twice. I mean she never faced a blow, nor got an angry word, and she never told a soul till the Crown Solicitor inspired her with higher sentiments. On the other hand, she was young, inexperienced, and stupid; and, though she saw most of the victim, never anticipated her death, which blindness in her rouses a suspicion that the whole set were much greater fools and smaller villains than they look. We now take a step in law which is as wide as the step down from the one committer to the four omitters. We go out of the house. We don't even go next door, but to another house a mile distant, where two self-indulgent adulterers were hiding themselves from Harriet Staunton, and absorbed in adultery, which was made smooth by Patrick's control of the injured wife. I never knew how low the human understanding could sink till I saw a jury who could confound this situation with that of Mrs. Patrick Staunton and Clara Brown, two people living in the house where Harriet Staunton pined on the first floor. That first floor Louis Staunton and Alice Rhodes avoided from self-indulgent motives that are out of the case. Of these two persons the law never had any hold on Rhodes. A mistress living in one house is not bound to provide food for the wife who lives in another. Rhodes is out of the case. Louis Staunton, until some day in August, 1876, was deep in the case. But the judge, in order to make hostile comments on his niggardliness, let in as evidence that he made a contract with Patrick Staunton of this kind. Patrick was to keep Harriet in his own house, and receive 20s. per week. Louis was a mean scoundrel to offer so small a sum, but a rustic labourer and

Appendix VIII.

eight children live on less. It crushes the charge of murder as completely as £20 a week would. It is a contract in which both contracting parties distinctly contemplated, not the death, but the indefinite life of Harriet Staunton. Its very niggardliness proves that on behalf of Louis Staunton. A man can transfer his legal responsibility. It is done daily. The legal responsibility of Louis passed by that pecuniary contract to Patrick as much as did the responsibility of that mother who handed her child for 5s. a week to a baby farmer, which baby farmer neglected the child till it died, a bag of bones, and was tried by Sir *James* [*sic*] Hawkins two days after the Stauntons (see *The Daily Telegraph*, October 1). The attempts made to drag Rhodes into the case at all, and to drag Louis back into it after admission of that contract, are pure sophistry and equivocation, as I shall show in the proper place. Meantime, here is the true picture—

1. Committer and criminal omitter.

2. Culpable omitters; one condemned to die, one walking about London.

3 and 4. Two vile moral omitters clear of the crime, but relieved by the lawyers of all their ill-gotten money, defended with admirable speeches, but worse defended on the evidence than they could have defended themselves, and condemned to die.

The blunder has been brought about partly by the recent malpractices and the inherent defects of the Central Criminal Court, whose system is so faulty that it never gets below the surface of a case, and is the worst instrument for the discovery of truth in Europe; and partly from special vices and errors that found their way into this case, and surprise the whole legal profession, so opposed are they to precedent and to the best traditions and most sober habits of the Court. These it will be my next duty to analyse closely, but I think I can hit upon a briefer method than I have been able to pursue in this letter.—Yours faithfully,

CHARLES READE.

2 Albert Terrace, Knightsbridge.

[*The Daily Telegraph*, Saturday, October 13, 1877.]

To the Editor of *The Daily Telegraph*.

Sir,—In reply to reasonable comments, let me say I have not dealt with that branch of law which concerns the aiding and abetting any kind of murder, whether by commission or omission, because the judge did not lay that down to the jury, and he was bound to do so if that was the law he relied on.

He never treated Louis Staunton as an " accessory before the fact," which, under this head of law, was the only cap that could be made to fit him. He never told the jury what precise evidence the law demands against a man who has made a niggardly contract, contemplating, by its very niggardliness, the indefinite life of the victim ere a jury is to pronounce that he did " procure, counsel, command and abet " the murder of that person.

Of course no lawyer will pretend that a man living out of the

311

Staunton Trial.

house of murder can be accessory *at* the fact, or what the text-books call "a principal in the first degree"; nor will any lawyer deny that if he lives out of the house, but procures, counsels, commands, or abets the murder, *beyond doubt* he can be an accessory *before* the fact, or a principal in the second degree. But there must be high evidence, and direct evidence, and if spoken or written words are relied on, they should be addressed to the very person who does the murder, and must be unequivocal. A doubtful phrase addressed to Rhodes, who took no part in the murder, is not at all the kind of evidence required by all the books and all the cases. See the word "accessory" in any text-book or report whatever.

The Facts.

In our Criminal Court, where the prisoners, the only people who really know the ins and outs of the case, are not allowed to open their lips and correct any of the shallow guesswork that is going on about them in their astonished ears, one great abuse like that I denounced in my last letter is sure to let in many more. Clara Brown, the one witness on whom the case for the Crown really depends, was allowed by the judge to swear she had destroyed a letter, and yet to cite so much of it, correctly or incorrectly, as fitted the two horns of the prosecution. That abuse led at once to another. This model witness was allowed another privilege the rules of evidence do not grant, viz., to argue the case. For this the defendants are indebted to their counsel.

He asked whether she understood the sentence about Harriet being "out of the way" to refer to her death. To this question she replied, "Yes." (Note, see p—.)

French counsel surprised by a prosecution would have immediately had a personal conference with the prisoners, and would have asked the girl questions that would have greatly benefited the prisoners. The jury, hearing a witness swear to an interpretation of a doubtful phrase, were not aware this was not evidence, and ought severely to be rejected from their minds. So one abuse led to another, and it is not too much to say that this imaginary letter, with the witness's interpretation, was the rope that is to hang Louis Staunton.

Well, such a rope of sand has never hung an Englishman in my day. It is pitiable to see how little, if anything, that can even by courtesy be called mental power was brought to bear by twelve men of the world on this quotation of a letter without its contents, one of the stalest frauds in the world, and also in literature of every kind, especially controversial theology.

Permit me to test this imaginary extract from what was proved, I think, to be a real letter, by one or two sure methods of which I am not the inventor.

Have those twelve gentlemen counted the number of words a young servant girl swore she had remembered in their exact order for nine months and more, though she had burned the letter, and the subject had never been recalled to her mind till she fell into the hands of the prosecution?

The words are 64 in number.

"My own darling,—I was sorry to see you cry so when I left you. It seems as though it never must be; but there will be a time when Harriet will be out of the way, and we shall be happy together. Dear Alice, you must know how——"

Now, sir, even if those fatal words about a time when Harriet will be out of the way were ever written without some explanatory context, I think the jury ought to have been throughout reminded of

Appendix VIII.

them and guarded against the illogical interpretation of them. The just rule of interpretation is that you should always prefer a literal to a vague or metaphorical interpretation. The words "out of the way" mean out of the way; they don't mean dead. A man can say "dead," and if Rhodes was projecting murder with him, why should he not?

The next rule is that you prefer the interpretation which the writer himself confesses by his own act, and the next is that you prefer the interpretation that is first fulfilled in order of time. Now, it was Louis, the writer of the words, who took a farm soon after, settled Harriet with Patrick, and lived in smooth adultery with Rhodes; whereas it was other people who killed Harriet Staunton, and nine months afterwards. But I shall now show the extract as sworn to was never written.

1st Objection. It is too long, and too short, which two traits can never meet in a genuine extract.

(a) Too long for a servant girl to remember, word for word, nine months after hearing it.

(b) Too short. Louis Staunton was not preparing his own prosecution. It was not on the cards of mere accident that he should furnish in 64 words *two equivocal* expressions—one establishing a long adulterous intercourse of which there is no corroborative proof, but the reverse, and another quibble projecting distant murder, of which there is no corroborative proof, since Harriet was well used for months after.

2. The line reminding her she had been his mistress for two years is worded by a woman, and not by Staunton or any other man. Decent women like Clara Brown have a delicate vocabulary unknown to men. "We have been together," which means everything the prosecution wanted, but says nothing at all, is a woman's word.

3. The statement itself is not true, and from that you must argue backward against the genuineness of the quotation, since he would not say this to a girl who knew better.

4. The witness could remember nothing but her lesson: sixty-four consecutive words, all neat and telling, and meeting the two great views of the prosecution; but, that done, a blank—a total blank; not six consecutive words. This is barefaced. Daniel Defoe would have managed better. He would have armed the witness with ten consecutive words on some matter quite foreign to the objects of the prosecution. The quotation is fabricated, though not maliciously.

The process has nothing exceptional in it, nor is there any one to blame except the Court for letting in parole evidence about a written document destroyed by the witness herself.

Allow ten thousand such witnesses, and, if the case is ably prepared, you must, in the very nature of things, have ten thousand inaccurate quotations all leaning towards the side of that calling the witness.

The people who get up a prosecution have but one way of dealing with such a witness. She comes to them remembering a word or two here and there. She is advised to speak the truth, and take time. But, as the conference proceeds, she is asked whether she happens to remember anything of such a kind. She is very ductile, and forces her memory a bit in the direction she instinctively sees is desired.

Staunton Trial.

The very person who is examining her with an *ex parte* view does not see that she is so waxlike as she is.

Add a small grain of self-deception on both sides, and a mixture of truth and falsehood comes into the unwary and most inconsistent Court, which stops Louis Staunton's mouth, yet lets in a worse kind of evidence than the prisoner's own, because this horrible melange of memory and imagination, and prompting, which, *in the very nature of things, and by the mere infirmity of the human mind, must be a lie.*

That a man should die only because he is tried in England! Bring your minds to bear on this, my countrymen. If an ignorant man like this Staunton is defendant in a suit for £51, he can go into the witness-box and explain all the errors of the plaintiff, if any; but if he is tried for his life, which is dearer to every man than all the money in the world, he is not allowed to say one word to the jury, if he has counsel. He is allowed, indeed, to speak after his counsel have done muddling with his case, but with truly heartless mockery. When ignorance all round has hanged him he is allowed to speak. To whom? To the judge. On what? On nice quibbles of the law, but not on facts nor motives—this being the one thing he can never do, and the other being the thing he could generally do, and flood the groping Court with light, especially as to his true motives and the extenuating circumstances of his case. By this system the bloodthirsty murderer, who chooses his time, and slays swiftly in the dark, gains an advantage he cannot have in the wiser Courts of Europe.

But God keep the malefactor who is not an habitual criminal, or one of the deepest dye, but a mixed sinner who has glided from folly into sin, and from sin into his first crime, and who has been fool as well as villain. His mouth is closed, and all the extenuating circumstances that mouth could always reveal are hidden with it, or, as in this case, grossly and foully perverted into aggravating circumstances.

This is very unfair. The nation will see that one day.

At present what is to be done? After all, thank God, it is a free country, and one in which bad law is sometimes corrected by just men.

To all such I appeal against the rope of sand I have had to untwist in this letter.

The post enables me to do something more.

Resolved to resist foul play and garbled quotations, and those most dangerous of all lies, equivoques in language, such as " Harriet out of the way," the very kind of lies Holy Writ ascribes to Satan, and the great poets of every age have described as hellish, which they are—

> And damned be those equivocating fiends
> That palter with us in a double sense—

So, to give him one little chance of untwisting that rope of sand, although he has the misfortune not to be a Frenchman, I conveyed a short letter to Mr. Louis Staunton, through the proper authorities, requesting him to try and remember the entire matter of a certain letter he had unquestionably written to Alice Rhodes in August, 1876, and to send it to me verbatim. Some delay took place while my letter was submitted to authorities outside the gaol, but fair play prevailed, and I now append the letter to my own. which is of less value. I send it all the same, because I have looked narrowly into Staunton's, and I don't see any of that self-evident mendacity I have felt it my duty to point out in the garbled quotation, the rope of sand. This letter, at all events, may be true. For I see youth, with its selfish vices, not looking months and months ahead,

Appendix VIII.

either for good or bad, but getting Harriet out of the way without a metaphor, to enjoy the sweet vice his self-indulgent soul was filled with, and not with long, cold-blooded schemes of murder such as belong to more hardened natures than his, who, we learn from the Crown itself, and on oath, sat down and cried because his wife upset the house.

The following is

LOUIS STAUNTON'S LETTER.

Maidstone Gaol, Oct. 11, 1877.

Sir,—I duly received your letter of the 9th inst., and now beg to reply to it. The letter in question I wrote to Alice Rhodes on or about Aug. 17, 1876. The facts are these: I had several times promised to take Alice Rhodes down to Brighton for a week, but had been prevented from doing so; but on Saturday, Aug. 14, Mrs. Staunton, Alice Rhodes, and myself, went down to Cudham for the purpose of leaving Mrs. Staunton there, that we might go to Brighton on the Tuesday, but on the Monday I received a telegram to say my father was worse. My brother and myself immediately came up to London, leaving Alice Rhodes and Mrs. Staunton at Cudham. I then wrote her this letter—

" My own Darling,

" I know you will be sorry to hear that my poor dear father passed away yesterday. This is a sad blow to me, but we all have our troubles. Our trip must now be put off again. It seems as if it is not to be; but I will arrange another time to get Harriet out of the way, so you must not be disappointed. I shall have to remain down home for a few days, so Harriet had better stop down with you."

I believe I have now given you word for word what I said in this letter. I have thought well over it, and cannot remember saying anything more. What I meant by " it seems as if it is not to be " was our going to Brighton, and of getting Harriet out of the way that she might not know anything about it.

This is the whole truth of the letter.—I am, Sir, yours obediently,

LOUIS STAUNTON.

Charles Reade, Esq.

The public is to understand that I deal fairly with the powerful journal which has done me the honour to allow me to express boldly my unalterable convictions. I do not write letters and say, " Thus saith Staunton." I tender you his handwriting, begging you to do me the honour to keep it and show it to few or many, as you think proper. I do not lead witnesses as I think Clara Brown was led—unconsciously, no doubt. My short letter, to which this is a reply, lies in Maidstone Gaol. I can't remember what I write, like this young sinner, nor imagine what other people write, like Miss Brown *plus* an attorney's clerk. But I am sure it is a short line, just asking the man to send the truth. He looks on himself as a dying man; has no hope of saving himself; and I think he has come pretty near the truth in his letter. Yours faithfully,

CHARLES READE.

Staunton Trial.

APPENDIX IX.

SOME REMARKS ON THE MEDICAL EVIDENCE IN THE STAUNTON CASE.

By W. S. Greenfield, M.D.,
Assistant Physician to, and Lecturer on Morbid Anatomy at,
St. Thomas's Hospital.

[*Lancet*, October 6, 1877.]

The recent trial of four persons for the murder of one of them by starvation and neglect has attracted so much public attention, and the points of interest to the medical profession are so numerous, that no apology is needed for some remarks on the medico-legal questions raised by it.

To my own position with regard to the case I may make a brief reference. Having been consulted for the defence, such medical evidence as came before the committing magistrate, and the post-mortem notes, were submitted to me for an opinion. I gave that opinion only reluctantly, and under a sense of duty, knowing that the papers had already been sent to several distinguished pathologists who were out of town or about to leave. Nor did I know of any one on whom I could devolve the task. The evidence which was laid before me was, in my opinion, of a very incomplete nature, and such as to warrant no definite opinion as to the cause of death. But at the same time it contained sufficient evidence to warrant very grave doubt as to whether death resulted from starvation alone. I gave my opinion then fully and impartially, and not concealing my great doubts as to the nature of the case.

Subpœnaed as a witness, I received also the information that notice would be given as to when my appearance in Court would be necessary. Owing, however, to the error of a clerk, no notice was sent to me until after the medical evidence for the prosecution had been given; and as I was not aware it was coming on, I missed the opportunity of hearing it. Owing to a misunderstanding on the part of the learned counsel for the defence, questions were put to me to which no definite answer could be returned; and as the judge made a strong objection to my testimony on the ground that I had not been in Court during the evidence for the prosecution, it was thought best, seeing his evident bias, to withdraw me as a witness.[2]

I have made this explanation solely because I hold that it is the duty of every medical witness, when placed in the unsatisfactory position of an expert, to be ready to state precisely the grounds on which his evidence is based and the motives by which he is guided. No method could be less adapted for the elucidation of truth than that in practice in courts of law. But for my own part I could not consent to abate any portion of the truth to serve one or other side. The case, so far as I am concerned, has a purely scientific interest.

To the various points raised by the case I have of necessity given anxious consideration. The difficulty in forming any definite opinion as to the cause of death from the post-mortem notes alone resided in the fact that no definite statement was made of the tubercular nature of the bodies in the piamater. But now that it has been definitely stated that miliary tubercle existed in the piamater, and that statement is concurred in by all the witnesses of the post-mortem, and is corroborated by the presence of tubercle in the lungs, it must be

---

[2] See p. 188 *supra*.

Appendix IX.

accepted as a fact that there was tuberculosis of the meninge. I shall therefore assume this as being for the purpose an undoubted fact, and shall not further question it.

In examining the medical evidence adduced by the prosecution, I can only indicate the chief points under each head. I shall not attempt to detail the evidence on which my opinions are grounded. In the course of a paper like the present, extended quotations from authorities or detail of cases would be impossible. My statements as to tubercular meningitis are chiefly grounded on cases which have come under my own observation, of thirty-five of which I have more or less complete notes. I hope on a future occasion to give more fully the details of the more important, and fuller references to authorities.

The evidence consisted (1) of symptoms observed by Mr. Longrigg; (2) of some statements by Clara Brown and the nurse, Gooding; and (3) short account of the post-mortem examination by Mr. Longrigg, Dr. Bright, and Dr. Wilkinson, in which Mr. Harman concurred.

The post-mortem notes have already been published in the *Lancet;* they agree in the main with the evidence, though in some points the latter was fuller and more explicit.

Mr. Longrigg's evidence described the state four hours before death, consisting in (1) coma, with stertorous breathing; (2) rigidity of one arm; and (3) minute contraction of one pupil, with dilatation of the other.

The evidence of the nurse was that there was diarrhœa in the night preceding death, and that the patient "lay as if in a fit," of what nature is not stated. That of the girl Clara Brown is very unreliable; all that can be accepted as probably true is that the first acute symptoms were difficulty in understanding when spoken to, then drowsiness, and that there was no fit.

The more definite statements on the subject of tubercle are found in Mr. Longrigg's evidence, in which the other witnesses concurred. "There were old adhesions between the internal and external membranes, with a deposit of tubercular substances in the lining membranes. . . . There were other minute tubercles on the brain, and although there were symptoms of inflammation and tubercles in the lungs, I did not think it necessary to follow up the discovery of tubercles on the brain by microscopic examination. . . . There is a disease called granular tubercle, and it is indicated by tubercles such as I have mentioned on the brain. It produces emaciation, but it is rapid in its progress, and is sometimes fatal in forty-eight hours. . . . That disease is not sufficiently advanced to produce the symptoms." He was also asked, "If she had had acute tuberculosis, what effect would that have had upon the brain?" and replied, "It would have produced softening of the brain." Mr. Longrigg is probably not responsible for the form of the words, but they may be taken as conveying generally his meaning.

Before considering the conclusions which must inevitably follow if the account of the post-mortem is correct, a word may be said as to the value of the post-mortem notes in determining the cause of death. Their value is vitiated by the fact (1) that the examination was not made till one hundred and forty-three hours after death; (2) that it was very incomplete, and the notes still more so, whilst the way in which they were made and recorded reduce their value to a minimum; (3) that no due allowance was made for the changes in the body which must ensue in such weather in six days, and of the presence of some of which there is distinct evidence; (4) that certain statements are made of appearances which, though regarded as normal, would be remarkable indications of disease.

Two or three points deserve special mention. It is stated that "*all*

317

Staunton Trial.

the cavities of the heart were contracted and empty." Such a fact, even as regards the left ventricle, so long after death in ordinary temperatures, would be very remarkable, and is inconsistent with the statement, " coronary vessels much congested, giving the appearance of being injected," which can only refer to the colour of the lining of the membrane either of the coronary veins or arteries (which is not stated), evidently the result of post-mortem dissolution of the blood, and consequent staining.

On the subject of " congestion," a term which seems to be used to include fulness of vessels as well as abnormal redness of whatever kind, I shall comment later. Only on the appearances of the brain I may remark (1) that if it was " very firm " six days after death, with adhesions of the opposed surfaces of the arnachroid, I should regard it as presumptive evidence of old disease, probably diffuse sclerotic change; and (2) that whilst a general reddening, especially on the surface, occurs as a post-mortem change, a distension and engagement of the sinuses and veins and marked excess of puncta cruenta, do not result from that cause, but would indicate a condition produced in life. If any importance attaches to the extreme general redness of the membranes of the brain, which, if there was really a healthy, firm condition of the brain, must be assumed to be the case, it would be a sign, not merely of congestion, but of commencing encephalitis.

I shall now briefly summarise the grounds which lead me to consider that death was due to tubercular meningitis, if the statement of the medical witnesses as to facts are accepted.

The symptoms observed in life—drowsiness, passing rather rapidly into coma, with stertorous breathing, rigidity of one arm, and extreme inequality of pupils—are consistent with cerebral disease, and in my experience inconsistent with starvation *alone*.

The presence of miliary tubercle in the piamater, even if in small amount as seen with the naked eye, is of itself a sign of very serious cerebral disease, and, so far as my own experience goes, or that of pathologists of large experience of whom I have inquired, or whose works I have read, it is never found after death in cases which have not presented cerebral symptoms during life (Bristowe, Murchison, Payne, Wilks, and Moxon).

In the rarer form of tubercular meningitis, in which the tubercle exists *only* on the convexity of the brain, there is an absence of lymph, exudation at the base, and of hydrocephalus; and there may be an absence of exudation on the convexity and of softening of the brain substance, a condition of extreme engorgement of the superficial veins, of general intense reddening of the piamater, and a very vascular condition of the subjacent cortex, with more or less of the white matter being the only sign of real inflammation visible with the naked eye. This also rests on my own observation and the statements of authorities (Huguenin and Gee).

In this form (tubercular meningitis of the convexity) death is usually much more rapid; in some cases only from twenty-four to thirty-six hours elapse between the definition of the disease and death.

The symptoms of tubercular meningitis, protean even in the child, are far more so in the adult, in whom they may simulate almost any form of cerebral disease. Drowsiness, passing into coma, may be the only symptom observed (Bristowe). Precise distinction between the symptoms of meningitis of the convexity and of the base is not possible in all cases. In some cases of the former the symptoms closely resemble these of meningeal hemorrhage.

Convulsions, the rule in children, both in the basic and convexity forms, and more marked in the latter, are far rarer in adults, usually indeed absent unless in certain cases of the convexity form.

318

Appendix IX.

Rigidity of one or more limbs is observed in a certain number of cases. It may be a constant tonic contraction, or a resistance of one limb to movement, attempts to move it being made by resistance of the muscles, the limb usually lying quiet as if paralysed; or there may be a rigidity, simulating cataleptic rigidity, of the limbs, trunk, and neck. In cases of meningitis of the convexity in children this condition often persists till death, alternating with slight convulsive movements. In the adult the rigidity is often of more passive form, visible convulsive movements hardly occurring. But the variations of this frequent symptom in meningitis constitute too wide a subject to be discussed here.

Inequality of the pupils may or may not be present in tubercular meningitis of the base. In many cases the pupils are equal, or nearly so, throughout, so far as my observations go. So far as I have been able to judge by observation during life, and minute research after death, this inequality of pupils does not depend, as usually stated, upon implications of the nerves at the base, but upon central irritation. My observations upon this point in convexity meningitis are not sufficiently extensive to be of any decisive value, but in one case of meningitis of the convexity, the tubercular nature of which was not decided, but which I now believe to have been tubercular, from analogy with other cases, and on the authority of a dictum of Hillier, there was, about two hours before death, minute contraction of one pupil, whilst the other was dilated and of irregular outline (the *Lancet*, 20th September, 1873). I have no similar note as regards any case of basic meningitis in which I have frequently noted equality or nearly equality of the pupils shortly before death. There is, of course, no doubt that great inequality of the pupils may occur in basic meningitis.

Diarrhœa persisting up to the time of death does not negative the presence of tubercular meningitis. I have noted its presence in two cases in very marked degree. It is usually, but by no means necessarily, associated with tubercular ulceration of the bowels.

I may add to these that at the onset of tubercular meningitis in the adult it is almost invariably mistaken for some other disease, often, I believe, for hysteria in females; or the patient becomes stupid, drowsy, and torpid, says and does odd things, and is supposed to be going out of his or her mind. In females the catamenia may be absent or may cease suddenly, and the slight head symptoms be supposed to be due to this cause. Headache is not a necessary, though a very common symptom of onset.

Emaciation does not *necessarily* accompany or precede tubercular meningitis. But it is an error to say that where it does exist it is of necessity dependent upon associated general tuberculosis. For example, in two recent cases of young women (aged twenty-one and twenty-four) both were well nourished, one had abundant subcutaneous fat, yet both had general tuberculosis of some standing. On the other hand, in a male aged thirty-four, he had only tubercular meningitis of very acute and rapid form, and no tubercle discoverable elsewhere in the body, there was great emaciation, and the liver weighed only 34 ounces. There were no other discoverable antecedent causes to account for the emaciation. And other cases might be brought to show that in the adult, as in the child, great emaciation without obvious causes may precede the onset of the acute disease, and no amount of extended tuberculosis or lung disease being found to account for it.

Here I may mention a patient now under my care, a young woman, twenty years old, 5 feet 4½ inches high, not of particularly slender build, who for some few months has been losing flesh, who has no discoverable disease beyond a small patch of dulness at one apex, with no active signs. All the other causes of emaciation have been

Staunton Trial.

most carefully sought and never found. She weighs, with her boots and most of her clothes on, only 80 lbs. (the weight of the body of Harriet Staunton was 75 lbs.); yet she has no acute symptoms, no suffering, can walk about well, and in a sense enjoys life. A year ago she was robust, stout, and hearty.

The *weights* of organs in persons dying of this disease naturally vary within wide limits. But a striking fact may be mentioned, viz., that in two cases of tubercular meningitis, mentioned above, in which there was absolutely *no* emaciation, the weight of the healthy livers was respectively 32½ ounces and 34 ounces, and in marked disproportion to the other organs. The subject of weights of organs is too wide a one to be treated here in detail; as a general statement derived from a careful analysis of their weights in the notes of 800 post-mortems, I may state that 7¾ ounces for the heart is rather a high than a low average weight for an emaciated female thirty-four years of age, and that it is quite consistent with health and no emaciation; that 4½ ounces for the spleen is considerably in excess of a number of cases of men and women, younger and of the same age, in perfect health; that 7¾ ounces for the kidneys is also perfectly compatible with health, and that the weight of the kidneys is, perhaps, the least valuable criterion of emaciation.

One or two words in conclusion as to post-mortem evidence of *starvation*. I have myself made and noted nearly 900 post-mortems, and I have seen, perhaps, 400 more. I can honestly state that I know of no criterion by which the emaciation due to want of food, from inability to ingest it, or from deficient supply, can be distinguished from that resulting from chronic wasting disease, or even from acute febrile disease or diarrhœa. The exact number of cases in which there was inability to ingest food, owing to stricture of the œsophagus, or disease about the mouth or throat, I cannot precisely state, and perhaps the number is not large. But to state that a congested appearance of the stomach or of the brain, or of the outlets of the body, is a sign (?) of starvation, and, moreover, of chronic starvation, is, to my mind, an outrage upon medical science.

I have already remarked that the appearances derived from " congestion " in a body six days after death are utterly fallacious. But even if they had been seen soon after death, what would they have proved?

Of the *vulva* and *vagina* in a woman with leucorrhœa they would prove absolutely nothing.

It is said to have been " much congested, and presented a striking contrast to the bowels above the sigmoid flexure, the membrane of which was pale and exsanguine." Now, this candid description is that of a very common post-mortem phenomenon. The simple explanation is that the distribution of the vascular supply of the lower 4 inches of the rectum is different from that of the upper part (see Quain's Anatomy, article Rectum). Any one who has examined the rectum frequently will often have noticed this marked difference. Moreover, when diarrhœa is present it would be especially liable to occur.

Of the *stomach* " very marked and intense congestion of the internal lining, especially along the upper curvature," more or less congestion of the mucous membrane of the stomach, and even ecchymoses are very common, and the ordinary rule is not to attach much importance to it. " This congestion was remarkable, and quite unlike ordinary post-mortem congestion." " Post-mortem congestion " is one of two things, a subsidence of the blood in the veins to the most dependent part, or a staining of the coats due to dissolution and transudation of the blood colouring. But in persons who die during the process of digestion the mucous membrane is often of deep red colour dependent on active hyperæmia. It is well known that when fluids are taken they pass

320

Appendix IX.

first along the lesser curvature, and, if of irritant character, set up irritation there; but brandy and water or sal volatile would be quite sufficient to set up congestion of the character and position described. That it is evidence of starvation is pure hypothesis. *Total* deprivation of food for some time, and then the ingestion of food, *might* cause it, and therefore it is held to be evidence of *chronic* starvation.

As to the *brain*, the statement that congestion of the brain is one mark of chronic starvation is not only not true, but is the exact reverse of truth. That it may occur in acute starvation no one would deny; but one of the most essential results of chronic deficiency of food, whether experimental or from disease, is to cause an anæmic condition of the brain. In fact, it has been shown by the experiment of Panum and others that, whilst in acute complete starvation the blood corpuscles do not notably diminish before death, in slower starvation there is a very great decrease, so that the blood becomes thin, pale, and watery. All organs show the effect of this, but notably the brain, since it is the last organ in the body to waste. If there was in reality, as stated, an extreme congestion of all the blood vessels and of the brain, and the blood was of normal colour, it would be one of the strongest evidences that death was not due to chronic starvation. The theory adopted was, " Convulsions may occur in acute starvation, congestion may be supposed to be the cause of convulsions—*ergo*, congestion may occur in, therefore is a sign of starvation." Such logic, though well enough for legal argument, will not serve even for a formal hypothesis in science. I do not for one moment deny that congestion of the vessels of the brain may occur in the course of, and be found post-mortem after, the various cerebral accidents which sometimes complicate anæmia and exhaustion. I have, in fact, myself given instances (in a paper on " Insanity as a Sequel of Acute Disease and Hæmorrhage," St. Thomas's Hospital Reports, 1873); but on a careful search into the literature of the subject I could find but few examples of such a condition, nor does my own experience furnish any. In all the cases that I have seen, even after convulsions and delirium, the brain was pale and anæmic. And, be it added, in nearly all these rare cases of acute cerebral symptoms in conditions of exhaustion there was an immediate determining cause, *i.e.*, the cause was acute, the symptoms rapidly following. Minute contraction of one pupil, with dilatation of the other, would, so far as my knowledge goes, if the eyes were perfectly healthy, be absolutely inconsistent with such a case as starvation or anæmia.

The condition which alone, apart from emaciation, would point to death from starvation—namely, a wasted and contracted condition of the stomach and atrophy of the intestines—is not even mentioned in the post-mortem notes.

So far, then, there seems to be in the medical statements as to facts no particle of evidence that the emaciation was due to want of food, and still less to wilful starvation. On the other hand there is evidence that the immediate cause of death was an acute disease, nor is there anything to show that it was induced or increased by starvation or neglect. Undoubtedly its fatal issue may have been accelerated by incautious removal. But to a similar indictment a very large number of those who bring patients to hospitals must also plead guilty. I have not here entered fully into the question—which is of necessity raised by the general evidence given on the trial and facts which have since come to light—how far the mental disease which is proved to have existed might in part account for the emaciation and acuter symptoms. and to what extent the condition of the brain which was found after death indicates chronic brain disease. In my original report, given before there was positive evidence as to tubercle, I pointed out the possibility that the greater part of the morbid conditions and of the

Staunton Trial.

symptoms might have been associated with paralytic dementia. At that time I knew nothing of the history of the deceased, but the further evidence has strongly confirmed my view. I quote therefore entire the portion of my report bearing upon this subject.

" Thus far it has been assumed that the bodies found in the piamater were tubercular, or that there is at least reasonable ground for the belief that they were so. But it is possible that this belief may not be maintained, or that further and more complete statements as to the nature, position, and appearance of these bodies may lead to great doubt as to whether they were such. That they were indicative of some disease there can be no doubt. Is there any alternative view which may be offered as to their nature which is consistent with other appear ances, symptoms, and mode of death?

" The appearances described in the brain and its membranes in-dicative of some diseases were (1) undue adhesion of the dura to the piamater attributed by the medical men to old inflammation, which they believed to have resulted from a blow or fall. The extent and character of these adhesions are not stated. (2) The presence of small millet-seed-like bodies in the piamater above described. (3) A *firm condition* of the brain *six days after death*, with marked distinction of the grey and white matter. If this condition is accurately de-scribed, it is very remarkable. (4) General and well-marked congestion of the vessels and membranes of the brain and of the brain substance.

" It seems not improbable that the first three of these conditions may have been the result of some old chronic changes such as are found in some forms of insanity, for (*a*) the hypothesis of injury to account for (1) unless there were other signs of such injury, would, I think, be inconsistent with experience; (*b*) these may have been small fibrous nodules, such as are found under similar conditions to (1). This must remain uncertain; (*c*) a firm condition of the brain so long after death in such weather would, in my experience, be inconsistent with health, and would very probably indicate a similar indurated or fibrous condition which may be associated with (1) and (2).

" If any value attaches to (4) it would probably indicate that death occurred in an attack of acute congestion supervening on the chronic brain disease. . . . At present, as the tubercular nature of these bodies in the piamater is maintained, the further questions arising out of the other possible view need not be discussed; *but it is important that this alternative be not lost sight of*."

It is only right to add that, as I have said before, the tubercular nature of the nodules seems now to be pretty certainly established. Of the " acute congestive attack " in paralytic dementia, I do not think I have had any post-mortem experience; the statement rests on the authority of Griesinger. But by the combination of paralytic dementia with tubercle, all the facts of the case would be fully explained. Rapid wasting is not infrequent in some cases of general paralysis and other forms of insanity, even where food is taken in fair quantity.

In view of the importance of the issues, not only in the present case but in future cases of a similar kind, it has seemed only right to state the grounds on which the view of starvation alone appears to me to be untenable. And if food was supplied in insufficient quantity, the proof of that fact must, in my opinion, rest entirely upon positive evidence as to the food actually given.

Appendix X.

APPENDIX X.

"The Lancet" on the Verdict and Evidence.

[*Lancet*, October 6, 1877, Leading Article.]

Viewed from the politico-social standpoint, the conclusion at which the jury in the Penge case arrived may appear just and the sentence pronounced expedient. It is not for us to question the abstract justice of the verdict returned, and in the face of such a verdict no discretion rested with the judge as minister of the law. We have already expressed our belief that the evidence of criminal neglect was overwhelming. It has long been a painful duty devolving on the organs of medical opinion to protest that the law should be brought to bear against the practice of compassing by neglect the death of persons who are unable, by reason of mental or bodily incapacity, to protect their own lives. We have persistently and urgently pleaded that the young, the weak, the sick have an especial claim on the humanity of those about them, which it is the solemn duty of humanity to maintain and enforce. No feeling of sympathy with criminals convicted of neglect can be allowed to stultify the judgment that the righteous punishment of the cruel indifference shown towards the sufferings of the deceased woman, Harriet Staunton, is indispensable to the safety of the subject and the honour of the State.

Nevertheless there are, as we pointed out immediately upon the close of the trial, momentous and conclusive reasons why the sentence of death should not be carried into effect. The objection does not arise out of consideration for either of the prisoners. If any are worthy of punishment all share the guilt. We are not concerned with degrees of culpability. If murder in the strictly legal, as distinguished from a constructional sense, was committed, the incubus of that crime rests heavily on the women as on the men. The recommendation to mercy was illogical, and evidently the fruit of a sentimental view of the consequences entailed by the verdict with which we can have no sympathy. Our contention is simply and expressly that the conviction is bad in fact, and therefore, we presume, bad in law. The judge left the case to the jury on the allegation of murder by starvation. We have no hesitation in affirming that the fundamental proposition of this count, namely, that the deceased died of starvation, is not only unproved, but entirely unsupported by the evidence. The inference drawn by the medical witnesses for the prosecution was obviously not warranted by the post-mortem appearances as described by themselves, and it must be apparent to the profession that the report to which we allude is not of a nature to supply material for a satisfactory judgment. It is remarkable chiefly for the omission to state necessary and, as may have been supposed, self-evident particulars. The independent statement furnished by a correspondent, and printed in another column to-day, does not help to clear up the difficulty. On the contrary it introduces a fresh element of confusion by denying the existence of at least one important pathological condition previously described.

The position we are compelled to take in regard to this case is that the ground upon which the prosecution relied has no existence. It must obviously be impossible to prove *murder* by starvation without first showing *death* by starvation. The attempt to affirm the primary proposition has failed. Upon this point we claim a right to form a judgment. With the legal inference we have nothing to do, but it

323

Staunton Trial.

seems reasonable to assume that if the fundamental premise of a charge is negatived, the allegation raised upon it must fail. In a word, medical opinion upon the facts submitted cannot be developed to the extent of defining the disease which caused the death to which neglect may have contributed, but it is clear there was disease, and the life of Harriet Staunton was not therefore sacrificed by want of food alone. This much is apparent from the post-mortem appearances, although we are unable to proceed beyond the conclusion indicated. Our presumption—it is no more—inclines to the belief that the deceased was generally paralytic. The reasons which suggested this conjecture were given last week, and communications we have since received strengthen the belief. The opinion is, however, unimportant. The plea we urge as a final bar to the execution of the culprits is that they certainly did not compass the death by starvation; and whatever may be the legal interpretation placed by Mr. Justice Hawkins on the law, he insisted, and the jury returned their verdict, on the assumption that the deceased came to her death by wilful deprivation of food and necessaries. The post-mortem appearances were not consistent with the hypothesis of death from the cause assigned; they afford irresistible evidence of other causes at work, although it is not, owing to the defective manner in which the body was examined, possible to say which of several morbid conditions proved fatal to life.

In another place we publish a communication from Dr. Greenfield, the medical witness excluded from the case in consequence of a technical objection raised by the judge, and whose testimony would have supported the view propounded by Dr. Payne and Dr. Bristowe. It is needless to remind medical readers that Dr. Greenfield writes with great authority on the subject in hand. The studious moderation with which his opinions are expressed will be apparent. He does not attempt a final diagnosis, but he demonstrates, we think conclusively, the existence of more than sufficient evidence to dispose of the assumption on which the prosecution relied. The case may have been one of tubercular meningitis, or, as we have conjectured, general paralysis—tubercular deposits in the course of the disease known as "general paralysis of the insane" are not uncommon. It is not necessary, nor would any scientific witness undertake, to raise a specific theory upon the basis of such a report as that made by the original observers in this, happily, unusual case. The utmost justice required was that the allegation of death by starvation would be opposed by a well-considered and reasonable presumption that death, although perhaps hastened by neglect, was, in fact, due to disease. The testimony which Dr. Greenfield was prepared to give at the trial, and which, on public grounds alone, he now lays before the profession, would obviously have placed a construction upon the case entirely different from that presented by the medical evidence offered by the prosecution, and incompatible with the inferences drawn from it by the judge in his charge to the jury, and the verdict.

The issue raised is so serious that we venture to think the medical profession should mark its sense of the emergency by a combined expression of opinion. Again we protest that this view of the situation is not in the least degree suggested by sympathy with the prisoners or a low estimate of their crime—that of gross neglect. We offer no opinion of the relative culpability of the convicts under sentence of death. Still less should we desire to extenuate their offence as conscious, if not wilful, participators in the cruel treatment of Harriet Staunton. What we desire to place on record is a strong belief that the indications offered by a dead body imperfectly examined have been misinterpreted, and an inference drawn which the facts do not warrant, but which, on the contrary, they controvert. The interests of science

Appendix XI.

no less than justice call for an assertion which shall make this apparent. We have therefore to ask those members of our profession who share this conviction to send us their names, to be affixed to a memorial printed in another column, and which we will undertake to place before the Secretary of State for Home Affairs. The letters of authority to be appended to the memorial should be returned to this office without delay.

APPENDIX XI.

CHRONOLOGICAL ORDER OF LETTERS.

1876.

June 28.—From Louis Staunton to Patrick Staunton.

> " Gipsy Hill.
> " My dear Bay,—Many many thanks for your kind letter.
> . . . I shall be at the hospital about three o'clock."

Aug. 1.—From Alice Rhodes to Louis Staunton.

> " The Woodlands.
> " I was very sorry to see it rain so soon. . . . I am not bad yet."

Some date
between
  Aug. 1
  and 19,
probably
August 17.—" The lost letter." From Louis Staunton to Alice Rhodes.

> " There will be a time when Harriet will be out of the way."

Aug. 19.—From Alice Rhodes to Louis Staunton.
> " I have searched high and low for the lost letter."

Aug. 28.—From Louis Staunton to Patrick Staunton.

> " Gipsy Hill.
> " Dear Bay,—. . . I want you to send Harriet up to-morrow."

Aug. 31.—From Louis Staunton to Patrick Staunton.

> " Gipsy Hill.
> " My dear Bay,—. . . I feel sorry to think Harriet should have given you so much trouble."

Staunton Trial.

Sept. 1.—From Louis Staunton to Patrick Staunton.

> "Gipsy Hill.
>
> "My dear Bay,—. . . I received your letter and am sorry I said anything."

Some date
in Sept.
about the
middle of
the month.—From Harriet Staunton to Louis Staunton.

> "Friday.
>
> "My own Darling,—. . . I have been here a month on Saturday."

1877.

Jan. 20.—From Louis Staunton to Mrs. Butterfield.

> "Brighton.
>
> "I hear from my sister you called. . . . I will let every one know your character."

March 5.—From Mrs. Patrick Staunton to Mrs. Butterfield.

> "Cudham.
>
> "I hear from Alice . . . such a vile woman as you have proved yourself."

April 4.—From Louis Staunton to Mr. Butterfield.

> "Little Grays Farm.
>
> "I have received a communication from Mr. Hincksman. . . . It would be equally an easy matter to communicate with your bishop."

April 10.—From Louis Staunton to Mr. Butterfield.

> "Little Grays Farm.
>
> "Unless I receive an apology will instruct my solicitor to commence an action."

Draft of letter found at the Woodlands by the police, undated, but subsequent to March 5—in handwriting of Louis Staunton, but intended to be sent in name of Harriet Staunton.

> "Mrs. Butterfield,—I really am astonished at your audacity."

Appendix XII.

APPENDIX XII.

PUBLICATIONS ON THE SUBJECT OF THE STAUNTON CASE.

There is in existence a reprint of a newspaper report of the trial of the Stauntons, but I have not been able to meet with a copy. The British Museum Library contains a small pamphlet [Press mark, 6495, c. 40 (5)] taken from the *Police News*, entitled, " Harriet Staunton, The Life and Portraits of the four prisoners connected with the Penge Case." The " portraits " are atrocious wood-cuts, and the letterpress of no value.

Of the newspaper reports of the trial, those contained in the *Times* and the *Daily Telegraph* are the best; the latter is a good deal the fuller of the two. The correspondence columns of the *Daily Telegraph* and the *Echo* for the interval between the close of the trial and the remission of sentence contain a good deal of matter bearing on the case. Extracts from these, together with some valuable medical notes from the *Lancet*, are given above. *The Penny Illustrated Paper* for 2nd June, and 6th, 13th, 20th October, contains some rough portraits and illustrations, including views of 34 Forbes Road, Penge, and of the Woodlands.

The Central Criminal Court Session Papers, vol. lxxxvi., contain the minutes of evidence, taken in shorthand by James Drover Barnett and Alexander Buckler, shorthand writers to the Court; they are full and reliable (with occasional slips), but are not in form of question and answer. The Session Papers do not print the speeches of counsel nor the summing up of the judge.

In his " Selected Speeches," republished in 1908, Sir Edward Clarke, K.C., gives the corrected report of his speech on behalf of Patrick Staunton, together with an introduction to the case.

In " Leaves of a Life " (ii. p. 97), the late Mr. Montagu Williams, Q.C., devotes a chapter to the Penge case. It is very superficial, and is conspicuous for omissions and for mistakes which one would hardly expect from a counsel who had figured in the case only thirteen years before writing his reminiscences.

The late Major Arthur Griffiths gives a short account of the case in " Mysteries of Police and Crime " (iii. 108); the text is illustrated by reduced photographs of the prisoners and Harriet Staunton.

There are, of course, allusions to the case in the Reminiscences of Baron Brampton (Sir Henry Hawkins), but they are of a very perfunctory character.

A careful summary of the medical evidence will be found in Taylor's " Principles and Practice of Medical Jurisprudence " (i. 640).